## COMPUTERS AND EDUCATION SERIES
Keith A. Hall, Editor

# CRITICAL PERSPECTIVES ON COMPUTERS AND COMPOSITION INSTRUCTION

Edited by
**Gail E. Hawisher**
and
**Cynthia L. Selfe**

Teachers College, Columbia University
New York and London

Published by Teachers College Press, 1234 Amsterdam Avenue,
New York, NY 10027

*Library of Congress Cataloging-in-Publication Data*

Critical perspectives on computers and composition
instruction.

    (Computers and education series)
    Bibliography: p.
    Includes index.
    1. English language—Composition and exercises—
Study and teaching (Secondary)—United States.
2. English language—Study and teaching (Secondary)—
United States.  3. Computer-assisted instruction—
United States.  I. Hawisher, Gail E.  II. Selfe,
Cynthia L., 1951–     III. Series.
LB1631.C74  1989      428′.007′12      88-29593


ISBN 0-8077-2948-5


Manufactured in the United States of America
94  93  92  91  90  89    1  2  3  4  5  6

To Our Families

# Contents

# Preface

In the decade since the advent of the first fully assembled microcomputer, we have seen the proliferation of computers as educational tools at all academic levels. Along with instructors in other disciplines, English teachers in increasing numbers have come to regard computers as allies in their teaching, research, and professional efforts. Many in our profession now see computers as integral to composition instruction across elementary, secondary, and college curricula.

In recent years, however, English teachers have recognized the limitations of computer use in composition classrooms. We are now aware that both effective and ineffective uses of computer technology coexist within our profession and that there is a need to clarify the emerging role of technology in our work. As professionals, we have come to realize that technology cannot simply be incorporated into curricula without discrimination, without careful thought as to how the integration of technology will affect students and pedagogical approaches. In other words, we have passed the initial stage of uncritical acceptance and now see the necessity of constructing a more mature and balanced vision of technology's role in our teaching.

The evolution of this new, critical perspective on computers is reflected historically in the records of our professional meetings. Until the mid-1980s, computer sessions at the annual meetings of the National Council of Teachers of English (NCTE) and the Conference on College Composition and Communication (CCCC) mainly involved enthusiastic English professionals sharing observational and anecdotal evidence that computers could serve us well as writing and teaching tools. Today members of the profession are more skeptical. Although many who are new to technology still give glowing reports about computers and their effects on students and their writing, others are more cautious. They seek answers to the pedagogical and political problems that computers present for teachers of writing.

Evidence of this more cautious approach in assessing the advantages of computers in composition first became obvious to us at the 1986 Conference on Computers and Writing, sponsored by the Uni-

versity of Pittsburgh and attended by over three hundred teachers of
English from across the nation. At this conference, few participants
needed to be convinced that computers could be profitably employed
in English classrooms. Instead, well-attended sessions at the gathering
provided critical and careful evaluations of computers and their role
in the teaching of composition. Representative sessions from this conference cited the failures of computer-assisted writing software (e.g.,
Thiesmeyer, 1986), the limitations of current research in computers
and composition (e.g., Hawisher, 1986; Haring-Smith, 1986), and the
difficulties writers encounter in adapting their composing processes
to electronic media (e.g., Haas, 1986; Selfe, 1986; Van Pelt, 1986).
Also sponsored at this meeting was an open forum that invited participants to probe political issues that often arise when technology is
introduced into classes.

Since the Pittsburgh gathering, other meetings have continued to
examine critically the use of technology in English curricula. During
the 1987 Penn State Conference on Rhetoric and Composition, pre-
senters questioned pedagogical approaches with computers (e.g.,
Kaplan, 1987) and speculated on how particular kinds of software
may reinforce old, ineffective methods for teaching writing (e.g.,
Kemp, 1987). Reflecting this same questioning attitude, papers at the
1988 annual meeting of the Conference on College Composition and
Communication talked of issues related to desktop publishing (e.g.,
Kalmbach, 1988; Wahlstrom, 1988), examined the failed promise of
word processing for basic writers (e.g., Hawisher, 1988), and looked
at inequities that can arise in a composition classroom equipped with
computers (e.g., Collier, 1988; Selfe, 1988).

These sessions attempted to articulate and to address the kinds of
questions that we as a profession continue to ask. Teachers from all
levels want to know what they can expect from students when computers are introduced into writing classes. We want courseware reviews that evaluate the potential benefits for students while at the
same time identifying possible shortcomings. Furthermore, as a profession we suspect that certain groups of writers might profit more
from computers than others, but our assessment is incomplete. New
developments in technology and the ways in which these developments may interact with students' learning also give us pause. Advances in word processing, easy-to-learn graphics software, electronic
computer conferences, and features of desktop publishing might contribute to students' learning in predictable ways if we understood
more precisely how computers enhance the development of writing
abilities. These issues, which increasingly demand the attention of

English practitioners, researchers, and theorists, are presented and discussed in this volume.

Several of the chapters in this collection grew out of professional meetings and deal with the questions that electronic technology poses for writers and teachers of writing. In addressing the current problems in computers and composition, the contributing authors attempt to identify possible solutions for today's problems. Yet they also look to the future, with discussions of new developments that hold promise for writing teachers, despite the inevitable and attendant difficulties that accompany innovations.

The purpose of this book, then, is to help English teachers at all levels evaluate the role of computers in their work by presenting essays that are both thoughtful and provocative, that challenge the profession to use computers in ways that build upon sound composition pedagogy while simultaneously extending the current knowledge base in computers and writing. To this end, the essays are organized in three parts that reflect the concerns of the profession. Part I, An Emerging Knowledge-Base, includes chapters that discuss what we have learned about writers and computers over the past decade. The second part, Current Problems, presents discussions that try to assess where we are today and how current conditions—political and practical concerns—work against possible success for students and for English departments. Part III, Promising Developments, explores how new perspectives on teaching with computers provide fresh insights into how we might use the latest developments in electronic media to help our students learn. Thus the organization of the collection encourages readers to consider with the authors important issues in computers and composition and to examine thoughtfully the role of technology in our writing classrooms and in our professional lives.

The collection is aimed at English teachers at all levels of our profession but most particularly at writing teachers in secondary schools and universities. We also see the collection as a valuable text for professional educators who prepare prospective teachers, for school administrators who are integrating computers into English curricula, and for graduate students interested in pursuing research in the field. The ideas in these 12 chapters are intended to provoke response to a technological presence that has only begun to be felt in English curricula. Until we synthesize what we have learned during this last decade and consider how we might best build on what we have learned, we lack the informed perspective necessary for establishing the field of computers and composition within the wider arena of the study of discourse and the teaching of written communication.

# REFERENCES

Collier, R. (1988, March). *Technoproletarians and their tools: How the word processor is reshaping the politics of the English classroom.* Paper presented at the annual convention of the Conference on College Composition and Communication, Saint Louis, MO.

Haas, C. (1986, May). *Computers and the writing process: A comparative protocol study.* Paper presented at the Conference on Computers and Writing, Pittsburgh, PA.

Hawisher, G. E. (1986, May). *Research in word processing: Facts and fictions.* Paper presented at the Conference on Computers and Writing, Pittsburgh, PA.

Hawisher, G. E. (1988, March). *Basic writers, computers, and the activity of writing.* Paper presented at the annual convention of the Conference on College Composition and Communication, Saint Louis, MO.

Haring-Smith, T. (1986, May). *Research on word processing and composing: A critical survey.* Paper presented at the Conference on Computers and Writing, Pittsburgh, PA.

Kalmbach, J. (1988, March). *Making the transition from word processing to desktop publishing.* Paper presented at the annual convention of the Conference on College Composition and Communication, Saint Louis, MO.

Kaplan, N. (1987, July). *The technologies of teaching.* Paper presented at the Penn State Conference on Rhetoric and Composition, University Park, PA.

Kemp, F. (1987, July). *Freeing the student voice: Establishing discourse communities by means of networked computers.* Paper presented at the Penn State Conference on Rhetoric and Composition, University Park, PA.

Selfe, C. (1986, May). *Casting a broader net with theory and research.* Paper presented at the Conference on Computers and Writing, Pittsburgh, PA.

Selfe, C. (1988, March). *Computers and politics: A feminist "reading" of techno/power in English departments.* Paper presented at the annual meeting of the Conference on College Composition and Communication, Saint Louis, MO.

Thiesmeyer, J. (1986, May). *Should we do what we can?* Paper presented at the Conference on Computers and Writing, Pittsburgh, PA.

Van Pelt, W. (1986, May). *Word processing and student writing strategies: Responding to the advantages and limitations of the technology.* Paper presented at the Conference on Computers and Writing, Pittsburgh, PA.

Wahlstrom, B. (1988). *Transforming the word/print relationship: The potentials and problems of desktop publishing.* Paper presented at the annual meeting of the Conference on College Composition and Communication, Saint Louis, MO.

# CRITICAL PERSPECTIVES ON COMPUTERS AND COMPOSITION INSTRUCTION

# Part I

# AN EMERGING KNOWLEDGE BASE: THEORY AND RESEARCH

As a profession, we have begun to sort out how writers react to computers as tools and how written communication is shaped by electronic technology and by those writers who use this technology. From composition theory and research of the last 25 years, we know that the choices writers make are influenced by the immediate rhetorical situation to which they respond and by the larger cultural context within which they write. From our research in computers and composition of the last several years, we suspect that electronic technology interacts with writers and their choices in ways that result in profound changes as to how text is produced and conceived. Yet our work is still in its infancy. Until we define how computers alter our traditional notions of composition, we lack the means to develop a pedagogy specifically suited to the particular advantages afforded by computers. This first part is our attempt to summarize emerging theory and research in computers and composition so that readers may participate in the progress made to date.

In the first chapter, Cynthia Selfe theorizes that computers change our concepts of text and that successful writing software bridges the differences between the grammar of a screen and the conventions of a page. She argues that because our definition of a new literacy shaped by computers is just forming, our vision remains sketchy. But, she maintains, by examining the spatial concepts of text associated with print technology and by comparing them with the visual display of text on a screen, we can identify problems students might encounter in reading and writing computer-mediated text. To acquire what Selfe terms "multilayered literacy" skills, students must be able to move easily between the page and the screen, and teachers must be able to guide their efforts. Nonetheless, she argues, it may well be our students who show us how to meet the challenge of these changing literacy demands. Selfe envisions the computer-supported writing laboratory as providing fertile ground for careful study of this new dimension of literacy.

In the second chapter, building on this same notion of changing literacy demands, Christina Haas focuses specifically on reading in its relation to writing. Writers, she argues, may experience problems in getting a clear sense of their text on computers. Using her research at Carnegie-Mellon University as support for her observations, she contends that computer screens cause reading difficulties and describes different ways in which writers use hard copy to minimize these difficulties. Haas demonstrates a systematic approach to research that is sorely needed in the developing field of computers and composition.

James Collins, in the third chapter, shifts the research perspective from writers and composing to text-analysis programs and the confusion such instructional software is apt to cause for students. Collins presents results from his research on three computerized text-analysis programs and identifies discrepancies that exist among the programs. These discrepancies become more pronounced when compared to teachers' analyses of the same texts assessed by the software programs. If such programs are indeed to help students revise their writing, Collins argues, they must be tailored to students and students' writing problems rather than be modeled on earlier software aimed specifically at technical writers. Collins then describes two programs in development that exhibit the kinds of features instructional software packages must offer if they are to illuminate rather than obscure for students the kinds of problems they encounter in revising.

In an attempt to establish what we have learned from research in word processing of the past several years, Gail Hawisher presents in Chapter 4 an overview of more than 40 studies in computers and composition. Although results from these studies are still contradictory, she identifies several patterns and behaviors teachers can expect when they introduce computers into their writing classes. She recommends a broad agenda for research in computers and composition, arguing that we must approach our research systematically if we are to establish the field within the wider professional context of communication studies.

Thus the chapters in this first part begin to answer questions teachers ask as students encounter computers as tools for writing and as tools for learning to write. In addressing these questions, the authors also examine how computers may interact with writers and the activity of writing, presenting throughout the four chapters ideas for additional research and exploration.

# 1

# Redefining Literacy: The Multilayered Grammars of Computers

Cynthia L. Selfe

It is old news by now to note that computers have revolutionized the nature of written communication and, thus, the nature of literacy. We take for granted the fact that increasing numbers of writers and readers are using computers to generate, manipulate, share, and store written text and graphics.

But it may be news to contend that the real work of developing computers as aids to literacy has just begun. If the most reluctant among us now accept that computers have had an impact on literacy, not even the most enthusiastic claim to know just what that impact has been or how we should deal with it in our teaching. In fact, we are just beginning to get an idea of how radically our definition of literacy changes when communication activities are mediated by computers. Until we better envision this computer-mediated literacy—and our vision must accommodate reading, writing, and technology—our profession can hardly expect to provide students with the skills they need to function as literate members of our technologically supported society.

Nowhere is there greater potential for achieving a degree of success in this exceedingly complex venture than there is in the numerous computer-supported writing centers that have been set up in schools and institutions across this country. These nontraditional communication environments are valuable to us because they are sites in which language production and learning occur consistently within a technologically dependent context. Thus they can serve as laboratories in which we inform and update our notion of literacy as it is practiced in computer-supported communication environments. In these centers, we begin to gather the data that will eventually allow us to construct a new vision of literacy as it has been, and continues to be, affected by computers.

To date, I should add, we have only begun this data gathering and have had time only to identify the barest outlines of this new vision. Nor is rapid progress probable. Teachers and researchers trying to define the changing nature of literacy engage in a complex version of the old connect-the-dots game—one in which the players never see the entire picture they are trying to construct because it is still in the process of being formed. Often in this game our perspective is limited; each one of us sees only one or two of the dots and must experiment with different methods of connecting them. But even the sketchy and incomplete representations we have been able to put together are exciting enough to warrant our continued and increased attention.

We can progress more rapidly and effectively than we now do in our attempts to define literacy as it relates to computer-supported communication. To do so, we need to share information about the dots each one of us has already connected, to exchange educated guesses about the final form that the picture is taking. In this chapter, I work toward that end, sharing some preliminary observations about the changing nature of literacy and offering a rough sketch of what literacy may now involve within the context of computer-supported literacy communication environments.

## TRADITIONAL LITERACY

To understand how computers have altered the nature of literacy in the past decade, we need to begin with a broad baseline definition of that concept. And, if we agree for the purpose of this discussion to focus on print literacy rather than, for example, visual literacy or cinematic literacy, this definition need not be overly complex. Most of us would agree that literacy involves both reading and writing, and concerns the ways in which human beings make meaning from printed texts by interpreting content in light of their own purposes and needs.

We might also add to this definition that the responsibility for this process of constructing meaning cuts both ways in a literate culture, that it involves both readers and writers of text. Indeed, we know that literate individuals collaborate, in a sense, to make meaning, engaging in a unique kind of asynchronous, two-sided interpretation of personal experience, even when one party never meets the other. Finally, we might add that literacy training involves teaching individuals the shared system of conventions associated with reading and writing.

I will focus on this last point about conventions because it pinpoints the crucial reason why computers affect literacy so immediately. By conventions I mean those standard rules, variously referred to as "grammars" by Gumpert and Cathcart (1985) or as "formats" by Altheide (1985), which govern such things as arrangement, structure, form, and appearance of text. Armed with these rules, individuals can predict some things about the basic nature of texts that they read and write.

Let's consider the grammar of a page, for instance. In Western cultures, a page is read by starting in the upper left-hand corner and proceeding to the lower right-hand corner in a line-by-line fashion. It is composed of a predictable set of structural components, consisting of letters that combine to form words, words that combine to form sentences, and sentences that add up to paragraphs, pages, sections, and chapters.

Pages have a number of formal conventions as well: running heads, numbers, standard margins on the sides and at the top and bottom, footnotes, titles, subtitles, or headings. Finally, pages have physical conventions: they are made primarily of paper and bound so that they can be quickly flipped through; their aspect ratio (ratio of width to height) is approximately 2 to 3. Within individual books, pages are a fixed size, arranged in a fixed order, and thus represent static structural units of a text that do not change from reading to reading. No matter how many times we read a copy of a book, a given piece of material will be on the same page in the same location; the page will be in the same order in the book. Pages, in this sense, are immutable. In fact, we use this particular characteristic of pages to locate information within the spatial context of a text. If we want to find a piece of information again in the future, we note its spatial location, referring to a particular page by number. In sum, these grammatical conventions that we learn during our literacy training allow us to "cope" (Strassmann, 1983) with the world of print, to anticipate the characteristics that printed texts share, and thus to use these texts efficiently.

The significance of these conventions has been explored by scholars like Gumpert and Cathcart (1985), McLuhan (1967), and Ong (1982) who claim that the conventions associated with specific media determine not only how we see text but how we view the world as a whole and how we construct our reality. As evidence, Ong (1982) cites, among other examples, Goody's (1977) research on indexes to support his argument that until humans used print to represent their thinking in an essentially linear format on a collection of pages, they had no conception of retrieving a piece of information by identifying its spatial location. Thus, Ong suggests, when we invented indexes to help us find written information efficiently within such a context, we also discovered the essential concept of "indexing," the notion of cataloguing and retrieving information by recording its location in space. Because indexes have no equivalent in the natural world, until we created the print medium and the convention of "index," we had no way of envisioning, or even thinking of, systematic information storage and retrieval based on spatial location.

For another example of this important concept, we can look to film and television. Recent work with these media suggests that humans observe media conventions, for example, slow-motion, split-screens, and objects revolving in space; that they internalize them; and that they later apply these conventions as "tools of thought" to problems unconnected with the medium itself. For instance, in a study that concentrated on the "zoom shot" as it has been defined by the film and television industry, Salomon (1972) found that viewers who watched the technique of "zooming-in" on film could internalize the convention and then apply it as a problem-solving strategy in other situations. The medium (television/video) and a convention of the medium (the zoom shot), in other words, provided subjects with a new way of constructing reality and meaning that they could not have acquired through observation of the natural world.

## LITERACY AND COMPUTERS

If we accept that the conventions of specific media determine how we construct reality, we can begin to see how the use of computers as communication aids might affect literacy in two important ways. First, computers add several new grammars to the lists of things that individuals must learn before they become successfully literate in a computer-supported communication environment. We can posit grammars associated with computer keyboards and with computer screens, grammars connected with computer systems or with word-processing packages, and grammars related to the use of computer networks or printers. These new kinds of literacy are layered over and have a substantial impact on the tasks of reading and writing. Second, computers change the way we "see" text and construct meaning from written texts. Like the concepts of "indexing" and "zooming-in," some of the conventions associated with computers do not exist in the natural world, and these conventions change the way in which we think about communication problems.

To explore both of these claims, we can look for a moment at the grammar of the computer screen. Although some conventions of the printed page carry over into, and indeed, are mimicked by the conventions of a computer screen, the principal conventions of the two media are quite different. We have noted that pages are static structural units of a longer, spatially represented text; the text on a page does not change with time. Screens do not represent structural units of a text; rather, they are temporal windows on a virtual text. Virtual texts, unless they are translated into the print medium, exist only in the memories of the computer, the reader, or the writer.

Because text on a screen is a temporal rather than a structural unit, a reader of screen text lacks some of the spatial-contextual cues to which a reader of page text has access. A reader of a book can gauge its length in one glance and get an idea of format, organization, and arrangement by flipping through pages. In contrast, the reader of a virtual text on a collection of screens can see the whole text only in his or her mind, and must keep track of individual screens in the same way. Given this lack of spatial-contextual cues, movement through a virtual text is often considered more difficult than movement through a printed text, either slower (when scrolling is done line by line), or more erratic (when one screen dissolves instantly into another at the touch of a key).

Screens also have different formal conventions than do pages. They are not numbered; their margins are fluid and easily modified by writers or readers; the aspect ratio of screens, at 4 to 3, mimics that of a television rather than of most books. And screens have cursors, windows, and menu lines—characteristics not shared by pages.

Physical conventions also vary between the two media: unlike pages, screens are made of glass or plastic; unlike pages, screens must be activated by electric power sources. The text on a screen consists of phosphorescent pixels that are dynamic in their formation and in their display; text on a page, printed in ink, is static. On a screen, writers and readers can add and delete text, change margins and spacing, construct and reconstruct text physically; the text exists only in a fluid form. On a page, text is immutable.

## THE EFFECTS OF LAYERED LITERACY

At this point, we have identified two very different sets of conventions that individuals must learn if they hope to function literately within computer-supported communication environments: conventions of the page and conventions of the screen. This information suggests two concerns: How much of an impact do these different grammatical conventions have on individuals? Can people who have acquired literacy in the print medium acquire comparable computer-based literacy skills? This process of layering literacy, stacking in effect one grammar on top of another, has a profound impact in that individuals making the transition from page text to screen text must change the ways they read, write, and make meaning from written text.

There are, of course, highly charged political problems that accompany our culture's transition from traditional print literacy to a multilayered, computer-based literacy, and at the heart of these problems lies the issue of equal opportunity and education. Not everyone is equally capable of acquiring facility with computer-based grammars. Given the relatively recent advent of computers, and our continuing reliance on hard-copy texts, individuals over the age of seven learn the literacy conventions of the page much earlier than they do those connected with the screen; they practice these grammars more frequently, and they are more comfortable with them. As one of my students put it the other day, most people speak computers as a second language. If we carry this analogy even further, we can predict that some level of interference will be present for these people as they supplement their print literacy with the literacy conventions associated with computers.

This situation becomes more disturbing when we realize how closely individuals' economic security, career success, and academic progress are tied to an ability to master computer-based grammars. Increasingly, employees, students, and teachers are required to learn computer systems quickly and under highly stressful situations. Students in many colleges, for example, are now expected to acquire computer-based literacy skills on their own in order to compete in their English composition classes. The teachers of these classes, who seldom feel responsible for matters of computer-based training, often neglect to provide their students with adequate training; frequently the instructors do not understand the complex nature of the literacy task that they are assigning. The same situation is true of executives in business or industry who see computers as quick fixes to office or production problems and require employees to read and write on sophisticated computer systems without adequate training.

In some ways, our culture has already begun to cope with this multilayered literacy problem, with the fact that people must be, or become, literate consumers and producers of both page and screen text. For example, many commercial word-processing packages come equipped with translation aids that help readers and writers move back and forth easily between the grammar of the screen and that of the page. At the bottom of every screen in these packages is a ruler line or a status line that gives information both about the screen text and the translation of that text into hard copy. Typically, this line identifies the name of the virtual text being displayed on the screen and indicates how this text would appear if displayed on a traditional page, noting the spacing, page breaks, margins, and page numbers as they would appear in a print medium.

Similar translation devices exist in the full-page, what-you-see-is-what-you-get (WYSIWYG) editors such as the Radius Full Page Display for the Macintosh computer. These devices, because they mimic the aspect ratio of a printed page, can display a portion of virtual text just as it would appear in the print medium. The purpose of the Radius Display, and similar machines, is to make work with a virtual text easier by electronically simulating some of the structural and formal conventions associated with a printed page.

However much translation aids moderate the effects of multilayered literacy, though, they do not eliminate them. Individuals still must learn to cope with the conventions of the screen and the page, modifying reading and writing processes accordingly. I speculated earlier that some people may never achieve equal fluency for reading and writing with both grammars. This premise, based on compelling preliminary evidence, deserves further investigation.

We examine the case for reading first. We know from recent investigations, for example, that individuals read screen text more slowly (Hansen, Doring, & Whitlock, 1978), less accurately (Wright & Lickorish, 1983), and less effectively (Haas & Hayes, 1986) than they do text printed on a page. In these investigations, researchers noted that readers had more difficulty getting an overview of a text and found it harder to locate specific information (Haas & Hayes, 1986) on most computer screens than they did on a page. In addition, individuals proved less accurate in proofreading text on computer screens than they did on paper (Wright & Lickorish, 1983).

Although researchers have yet to determine why text on a computer screen is more difficult to read than text on a page, they suspect differences in variables such as resolution, font size, reading angle, and color may be responsible (see Haas, Chapter 2 of this volume). Another explanation, however, may be equally as credible. Given the fact that the computer screen is a relatively new medium, we might posit that these studies show the effects of a ''media generation gap'' in Gumpert and Cathcart's (1985) terms: individuals trained originally to deal with the grammatical conventions of a printed page have not achieved a similar fluency in coping with the grammar of a computer screen. I point out, in addition, how this generation gap might become especially political in nature, when individuals trained for much of their lives to rely on hard copy must learn, in a matter of days or weeks, to cope with screen copy and must do so under highly trying and demanding circumstances.

Writing, in a similar way, provides evidence of the various layers of literacy required in computer-supported writing environments and the problems involved in acquiring literacy skills during a period of transition. We can, for instance, examine the comments of this writer who continued to compose her drafts with paper and pencil, even after she had become basically competent in writing on a computer screen:

> I feel I can express myself better [with paper and pencil] . . . like I'm in control of the situation. Maybe I'm too far away with the computer. I mean the screen is *there,* and I am *here* [gestures]. With paper and a pencil, I'm touching the words. Also they [the words] look like you wrote them, not like the machine wrote them. (Selfe, 1985, p. 57)

Another writer, trying to articulate why she had to translate her screen copy into hard-copy form so frequently, identified related difficulties:

> My words are in there [points to the computer], but not in the same way or in the same form as they are here [points to hard copy]. . . . To me, writing changes magically somewhere between the screen and the printer. There is a transformation that occurs. I can write on the computer, and I can write on paper—but I need both to survive. (Selfe, 1984)

The comments of these two writers indicate their own conscious awareness of the multilayered literacy they have to master in order to work effectively in a computer-supported communication environment. They face two challenges: first, they must learn the conventions of the computer screen, and, second, they must become facile in moving back and forth between the conventions of screen and page.

## THE IMPLICATIONS OF MULTILAYERED LITERACY

In order to assess accurately the implications of these observations for teachers of English, we consider again the speculative model of grammars that may be functioning within a computer-supported communication environment. Each one of these grammars represents new layers of complex conventions that individuals must learn if they hope to function successfully and literately within such an environment. As our use of computers and networks becomes more sophisticated, we will undoubtedly add additional layers of literacy in English composition classes. Some teachers of technical writing, for example, are already requiring that students acquire expertise in databases, graphics programs, and spreadsheets for use within classes.

For English teachers, this notion of multilayered literacy suggests a wide range of implications for our definition of literacy; for the ways in which we deal with reading and writing, or readers and writers; for the manner in which we integrate computers into our English classes; and for the ways in which we set up and operate computer-supported communication environments in support of English composition programs.

It seems reasonable to assume that we will have to deal with layers of literacy instruction, just as our students deal with layers of literacy demands. For some of these layers, I suspect, the task will be relatively easy. We will probably, for instance, continue to teach reading and writing skills much as we now do—emphasizing multiple drafts, successive refinement of ideas, peer critiques and editing, and conferences—regardless of whether writing is completed and shared on screen or in hard copy.

However, to address the succeeding layers of literacy described in this paper, we will also have to begin identifying strategies for coping with the grammars that computers add to communication tasks. On the level of the screen grammar, for example, we may have to teach students new or different methods for reading texts on screen to supplement the instruction they have received in reading hard-copy texts. We may have to show them, for instance, how to move about in a virtual text: how to use search-and-replace commands to jump from section to section, how to reformat text for easier screen reading, or how to incorporate different kinds of intratextual organizational markers for readers who view texts only on a screen.

Similarly, we shall have to identify reading and writing strategies for helping students deal effectively with the conventions of word-processing packages, computer systems, and networks. The problem involves identifying and mastering these strategies ourselves, and this can be accomplished only by collective effort. Until teachers and writers begin cataloguing and sharing the literacy strategies that they have used in computer-supported writing environments and testing them on different populations, our efforts will remain scattered and unsystematic.

We are not limited to our own resources in this effort to identify and teach effective literacy strategies. In fact, the more I work with students in computer-supported communication environments, the less adequate I feel to undertake this task alone. I suspect that our generation, raised as we have been on the print medium, may not be capable of generating some of the more creative strategies for coping with the conventions of computer screens, computer systems, or computer networks. Our conceptual vision in these areas may be limited by the media generation to which we belong and its pencil-and-paper strategies (Selfe & Wahlstrom, 1988). We may have to turn to our own students for help, observing the literacy strategies they develop on their own for coping within computer-supported communication environments.

In support of this premise, I can describe the experience of teaching computer-supported writing courses at Michigan Tech. As part of these classes, which are frequently taught in the Center for Computer-Assisted Language Instruction (CCLI), students are frequently required to write their journals or papers on our local area computer network, exchange drafts with their peers by posting them on a computerized bulletin board, confer with a teacher through an electronic mailbox, or participate in an electronic conference.

In this computer-supported writing facility, some faculty members in our Humanities Department prefer to run "paperless" class-rooms—storing handouts and lecture notes on the computer and asking students to hand in their writing assignments on-line. In these classes, most reading and writing is done via the medium of the computer screen rather than the printed page. Soon after we began this practice, faculty within our program began to notice that the writing assignments students did for viewing on the computer screen were different in both form and content from the writing assignments they produced for viewing in the print medium. One of the first characteristics that became evident, for instance, was that students had learned on their own initiative to write text to be read on a screen rather than on a page, thus handicapping those students who printed such text out in a print medium. In screen-based papers, for example, students incorporated flashing notes and headings, boldfaced type, and high-lighted segments of text (light background color and dark characters rather than the usual dark background and light characters)—all conventions that do not print legibly in hard copy. In addition, students used formatting conventions that were screen-based rather than page-based, often using shorter paragraphs that could be viewed on a single screen, breaking the text into screen-sized chunks so that readers could more efficiently use the "page-up" and "page-down" keys as they read, and centering text within the window of the page.

A second, and perhaps more unusual, characteristic of screen-based texts involved the use of color as a visual cue to underlying logical content and structure. Students, for example, used three different colors to signify primary, secondary, and tertiary headings; used two different colors to "paint" contrasting arguments contained within a single paragraph; and used color-coding to identify thesis or topic statements and the evidence that supported these central ideas. These "painting" strategies are important because they go beyond mere decoration of a text to represent a visual revelation of logical structures. As Bernhardt (1986) notes, such visual cues heighten readers' "awareness of categories and divisions, changing the ways people conceive classificatory divisions" (p. 66). Bernhardt (1986) also maintains that teachers of writing should encourage students to "experiment with visual features of written texts" so that they can "increase their ability to understand and use hierarchical and classificatory arguments."

What has become obvious to the teachers within our program is that the writers in our classes who compose their texts for reading on computer screens have invented and exploited a new set of literacy skills that their teachers never imagined. Using different fonts, font sizes, symbols, highlighting, and graphic elements, they have not only adjusted their writing to the conventions of the screen and the computer, but have also reconceptualized the content of their assignments in terms of these conventions. It seems possible that the grammar of the computer, the word-processing package, or the computer itself changed the way in which writers think and express thought.

These insights raise the issue that there may be other computer conventions that similarly affect our world view. Whether, for example, the convention of the virtual text as it exists in a computer and on screen will encourage us to develop new ways of handling large texts in our mind's eye, leading us to a new conceptual ground that exists somewhere between the print literacy we know now and a literacy of the virtual text that we have yet to define; whether students who learn the concept of windowing in a word-processing package will then apply this literacy convention in new and creative ways to other communication situations; and whether writers who learn to reformat screen text will somehow see printed text in a different way.

In other words, our work is cut out for us. Our profession will have to work diligently in the next few years to identify and explore the changing nature of literacy within a computer-supported writing environment, and to consider the implications of these changes for our teaching. We are going to have to do this job even as the computer industry continues its explosive growth. I maintain that computer-supported writing labs and classrooms may be the best site for this work because they offer us opportunities for both research and teaching. In these facilities, we can observe the changing literacy demands on our students, gather evidence of the impact of these demands, develop teaching strategies that help our students cope with these demands, and then test these teaching strategies on a variety of populations. That job will be exciting and creative for us all.

## Acknowledgments

I want to acknowledge here those intellectual debts I owe to colleagues at Michigan Technological University. First, I have to thank Billie Wahlstrom for so graciously sharing with me the electronic journal entries from her Mass Communication class and for helping me make some sense of these "new" texts. I used these journal entries to corroborate the observations I made of journal and electronic conference entries in my own computer-supported writing classes. Second, I thank Marilyn Cooper. Over a memorable dinner, she helped me to understand many important differences between grammars of the page and of the screen. (I was so excited that I couldn't eat.) The three of us are navigating by triangulation as we attempt to connect the dots of computer literacy.

## REFERENCES

Altheide, D. L. (1985). *Media power.* Beverly Hills, CA: Sage Publications.

Bernhardt, S. A. (1986). Seeing the text. *College Composition and Communication, 37* (1), 66–78.

Goody, J. (1977). *The domestication of the savage mind.* Cambridge, England: Cambridge University Press.

Gumpert, G., & Cathcart, R. (1985). Media grammars, generations, and media gaps. *Critical Studies in Mass Communication, 2,* 23–35.

Haas, C., & Hayes, J. (1986). What did I just say? Reading problems in writing with the machine. *Research in the Teaching of English, 20* (1), 22–35.

Hansen, W. J., Doring, R., & Whitlock, L. R. (1978). Doing the same work with hard copy and with CRT terminals. *International Journal of Verbal Learning and Verbal Behavior, 10,* 608–613.

McLuhan, M. (1967). *The medium is the message: An inventory of effects.* New York: Random House.

Ong, W. (1982). *Orality and literacy: The technologizing of the word.* London: Methuen.

Salomon, G. (1972). Can we affect cognitive skills through visual media? An hypothesis and initial findings. *AV Communication Review, 20* (4), 401–422.

Selfe, C. (1984). Computers and the composing processes of students. Unpublished raw data.

Selfe, C. (1985). The electronic pen: Computers and the composing process. In J. Collins & E. Sommers (Eds.), *Writing on-line: Using computers in the teaching of writing* (pp. 55–66). Upper Montclair, NJ: Boynton-Cook.

Selfe, C., & Wahlstrom, B. (1988). Computers and writing: Casting a broader net with theory and research. *Computers and the Humanities, 22,* 57–66.

Strassmann, P. (1983). Information systems and literacy. In R. W. Bailey & R. M. Fosheim (Eds.), *Literacy for life: The demand for reading and writing* (pp. 115–121). New York: Modern Language Association.

Wright, P., & Lickorish, A. (1983). Proof-reading texts on screen and paper. *Behavior and Information Technology, 2* (3), 227–235.

# 2

# "Seeing It on the Screen Isn't Really Seeing It": Computer Writers' Reading Problems

Christina Haas

The computer has completely changed the way I write. . . . I rely on the machine completely. . . . I couldn't go back to using paper. . . . I usually jot down a few notes and then begin typing. . . . Then I get a printout to read through after the first draft. . . . I get several printouts as I revise—to read and to mark with changes and notes. . . . I always proofread on a hard copy.

These excerpts from an interview with Donna, a published technical writer and graduate student with several years' computer experience, are intriguing. Donna calls herself an "adamant computer writer" and believes she relies on the machine "completely." Like many writers who use word processors or computers, Donna likes the ease of making changes to her text, and she believes she makes more of them. She likes her computer's neatness, its speed, and—because she doesn't have to worry about typing or formatting concerns—she says she spends more time "really working on the piece."

Yet when prompted to describe how she typically writes on the machine, Donna does not tell a tale of complete reliance on the computer. Rather, while writing on the machine, she uses paper at almost every juncture in her writing process. Donna's interview is representative of many computer writers' responses. Her enthusiasm for the computer is clear; what is also clear—to us if not to her—is that she doesn't rely "completely" on the machine, but supplements her computer use with pen and paper.

Most of us who use computers in writing appreciate the machine, but we also, to varying degrees, draw on the medium of pen and paper. It may not be surprising at first glance that writers use hard copy; after all, we all learned to write with pen and paper and few of us have computers available all the time. What is intriguing about computer writers' use of hard copy are the patterns that emerge—patterns both in the ways paper is used during writing and in the reported problems that hard copy helps writers overcome.

The most common complaints of computer writers are difficulties they experience in reading their texts on-line. These problems can take a variety of forms. Some writers mention a difficulty in knowing how the finished product is going to look, while others have difficulty detecting errors on the screen. Writers seem to like the portability of paper: "I just have to take it away [from the workspace] to get a perspective on it."

Other on-line reading problems are less well defined. Writers also say they find it difficult to look at large sections of their writing on-line or move quickly to a specific place in the computer text. Others say they don't trust their own ability to read critically from the screen, reporting a problem "getting a sense" of their on-line texts. Most of the computer writers I have interviewed do what Donna reported doing when faced with these reading problems: they print out their texts and read from hard copy. One writer put it this way: "I use hard copy because seeing it on the screen isn't really seeing it."

Determining why writers who use computers often rely heavily on paper and how they use the hard copy can inform our theories of the relationship between reading and writing, telling us more about how writers read their own texts. In addition, studying writers' use of hard copy can furnish information to teachers and other educators about how computers can be put to best use for writers. I begin with a discussion of related research in human factors followed by a thorough description, based on interviews, of four kinds of reading problems encountered by writers using word processing. Throughout this description, results are presented from an observational study of computer writers' use of hard copy for reading.

## READING ON THE SCREEN: RESEARCH IN HUMAN FACTORS

That computers cause problems for readers is not news: several researchers have suggested that reading on a computer screen may be problematic. Taking tests on computers is slower than taking the same tests on paper, according to Hansen, Doring, and Whitlock (1978), who explained their results as a function of slower on-line reading time. Gould and Grischkowsky (1984) conducted a study in which 22 of 24 subjects read more slowly from a cathode-ray tube (CRT) display than from paper. In a series of follow-up studies, Gould and his colleagues (Gould et al., 1987) systematically explored variables that may explain the results of the 1984 study, including reading angle, resolution, font size, and experience. Gould and his colleagues were able to identify conditions under which people could read as efficiently from CRT displays as from paper, although the results seem to be cumulative, with a number of display factors (e.g., display orientation, character size, font, or polarity) contributing to differences in reading speed.

Not only is reading on a computer screen slower; it may be less accurate. Wright and Lickorish (1983) found subjects' proofreading on hard copy to be more accurate than that on computer screens, and Heppner, Anderson, Farstrup, and Weiderman (1985) discovered Nelson-Denny reading performance scores to be significantly better with paper than with computer. In addition, the subjects in the study by Heppner et al. (1985) reported that they could read faster and understand printed material better when working with hard copy.

John R. Hayes and I examined subjects' performance in writing-related reading tasks in a series of three comparison studies (Haas & Hayes, 1986). We found that students were less accurate in recalling spatial location of items (i.e., describing where in a text a particular piece of information occurred) when they read from a screen than when they read from paper. A second study compared students' retrieval of information from a standard green-on-black CRT display, from a bit-mapped, high-resolution black-on-white display, and from paper. Scores for the standard CRT condition were significantly slower. Results from a third study showed that reading-to-reorganize was significantly slower on a small screen display than on paper or on a large screen display. For these writing-related reading tasks, spatial factors seem to play an important role in how well readers perform.

Given the constraints on reading outlined above, it is not surprising that several researchers on writing with computers have mentioned the unwillingness of writers to do without hard copy. Researchers have pointed out that both experienced writers (Bridwell, Nancarrow, & Ross, 1984) and student writers (Harris, 1985) report a continued and extensive use of pen and paper.

## READING ONE'S WRITING ON-LINE: FOUR AREAS OF IMPACT

A series of ongoing observational studies of computer writers provided information about how writers view word processing, the changes in their writing that they perceive, and the problems they have encountered with word processing. Various procedures have been employed to collect data: interviews with more than 30 experienced computer writers, monitoring of 14 writers' use of hard copy through process logs which they kept for several months, and observations of individual computer writers and classes of students writing with computers. The writers who were observed exhibited a wide range in age and computer experience, from a beginning graduate student who used word processing mainly as a "fast typewriter" to a computer scientist with 18 years' experience with computers. Some of the writers were interviewed or observed once; others met with me several times, were observed regularly, and allowed me to examine some of their texts. One subject, a novelist, shared his experiences learning to use word processing after more than 30 years' composing at the typewriter. Interviews with this writer were conducted periodically over the course of several months. An earlier description and analysis of some of these interviews is presented in Haas and Hayes (1986).

The hardware and software used by the writers also varied. Some writers used mainframe, time-sharing computers and terminals and the text-editor EMACS (Stallman, 1981); others used personal computers, like the Apple Macintosh or the IBM-PC, running software packages such as *Wordstar.* A number of the writers used an advanced system under development at Carnegie-Mellon, the Andrew system, a UNIX-based system that runs primarily on an IBM PC-RT (Morris, Satyarayanan, Conner, Howard, Rosenthal, & Smith, 1986). A few of the writers were fluent in more than one system. In spite of these machine differences, the uses to which writers put hard copy were remarkably consistent and—predictably—hard copy was often used for reading during writing. I postulate that writers used hard copy for reading because, as is suggested above, reading on a computer can be problematic in a variety of ways.

The interaction of reading and writing is complex. There are several ways in which reading is crucial to the writing process, and there were in fact several distinct reading problems for computer writers. In the following sections I outline four areas in which the computer had a negative influence on writing by causing reading difficulties for the writers I interviewed. These problems seemed to be caused by different computer features, and they were overcome with computer or with paper in various ways and to varying degrees of success. The four areas of impact are formatting, proofreading, reorganizing, and critical reading or "getting a sense of the text."

### Formatting

Since many texts that writers produce are intended to reach readers on paper, it is not surprising that writers were concerned with final hard-copy format. Formatting concerns took a variety of forms; one writer used paper printouts because he knew readers would read it from paper: "I like to see it the way they will see it." Sometimes writers needed to check the finished text for page breaks or placement of figures and tables.

The source of this problem for writers is fairly easy to identify. Because very few editors are WYSIWYG or "what-you-see-is-what-you-get," the differences between what is on the screen and what will be on the printed page can differ from machine to machine and may include different font size and type, differences in leading and resolution, no page breaks, differences in line-length, no integrated graphics, and abbreviated margins. Some advanced systems (e.g., the Andrew system under development at Carnegie-Mellon) have a special program that writers can run to see a "picture" of their finished texts. However, many computer writers must generate a printout in order to see the finished format of their computer text.

The hard-copy solution to the problem of formatting is fairly straightforward, if time- and paper-consuming. Writers seemed to make a best-guess, on-line approximation of the format they wanted and then generated a hard copy to skim, looking for specific problems. If necessary, they may have gone back into the editor to make changes. Writers often repeated this process several times.

### Proofreading

A second area in which computers affected writers negatively was during close reading or proofreading. Many computer writers reported not "trusting" their ability to proofread on the screen, and they often used hard copy to read for local errors. Interestingly, several writers noted that computer-based spelling and grammar checkers tend to compound the problem; writers learned to depend on the computer tools for low-level problem detection and so either did not proofread at all, or did so haphazardly. This problem was exacerbated by the fact that many problems are not detected by computer-based tools for instance, missing pluralization or the mistyping of one word for another, for example, "test" for "text."

While computers may greatly facilitate a writer's ability to *make* low-level changes, the skill and speed with which writers *detect* the need for changes may be decreased when using a computer screen. Gould and Grischkowsky (1984), Gould et al. (1987), and Wright and Lickorish (1983) have concluded that readers are slower and less accurate when proofreading on-line. Given these conclusive findings, writers who proofread their texts on hard copy printouts are apparently doing the right thing.

## Reorganizing

A third way in which using computers created difficulties for writers was in planning and testing large text reorganization moves. While word- and sentence-level revisions and reorganizations are easy on a computer, writers reported that computers constrain large text reorganizations, for example, those involving a move of several paragraphs of text, or a move over a large amount of text space.

Planning the reorganization move, or deciding what needs to be moved where, is difficult because one generally has only one view (screen) on the document at once, although split-screen options or multiple windows of text may alleviate this problem. Planning a reorganization is also difficult because writers often "get lost" in computer texts, which provide many fewer cues for spatial recall than do paper texts. As one writer put it, "That's when you just have to get your pen and spread the thing [the text] out all over the floor." Haas and Hayes (1986) found that students reading to detect needed reorganizations worked more slowly on a PC screen than they did on a larger screen or on paper (Haas & Hayes, 1986). Many writers also made extensive use of graphical markings such as arrows, stars, or brackets; these markings are quick and easy to make on paper but difficult to make on-line.

Testing the reorganization move on a computer is problematic because one has to make the move to test it; that is, in order to see how the text would read with a large text reorganization, one actually has to reorder the text. With paper, on the other hand, a writer can place the sections in question next to one another by reshuffling pages, or he/she can quickly flip through the text, reading and "trying out" the reorganization move. In addition, because the word processor may reformat the text once a major change is made, it is often hard to remember exactly how the change was accomplished.

An extended example illustrates these difficulties. While Donna is producing an article (or other lengthy document), she may realize that her introduction is too long and either needs to be cut, or parts of it should be moved. If Donna were in fact "completely reliant" on the computer, her reorganization might proceed like this: she would read through the introduction and then try to "keep it in mind" as she skimmed the rest of the document to see if part of the introduction could be used elsewhere. Or, if she had an advanced editor, she might use a split-screen option and have two views of the document: a window with the introduction and a window where she read the rest of the text. Of course, the whole introduction may not fit in a window, so she would need to scroll or key forward and back in both windows and, since there are limited page and other spatial location markers (e.g., the top right corner of page five, or the middle of page twelve), she could easily become "lost," or confused about which part of the text she is viewing and where it is in relation to the rest of the document.

After reading through the text, Donna may decide she wants to try moving three paragraphs of the introduction into the discussion of a major point about halfway through the text. Using the computer alone, she could "cut" the three paragraphs, then scroll through the document until she finds the place where it should be inserted. Once she "pastes" the text in, she reads the section to test her new reorganization. Given the limited space on the screen, and the difficulty in quickly skimming through the text, the reorganization cannot be tested until it is actually executed. If Donna decides that she does not in fact want her text reorganized in this way, she must "cut" the text again and scroll back to insert it in the original spot, which she may or may not have remembered to mark with an asterisk.

But since Donna is an experienced and smart computer writer, in actuality she would probably get a printout of the text and plan and test her reorganization on the hard copy. She could pull out the page, or pages, that contain the introduction and lay them out in front of her and then read through the paper, referring frequently to the introductory pages spread out before her.

The interval between looking at the body of the article and the introduction is very short—a few seconds, at most—and the space available to spread the text out is as big as Donna's desk, or the floor of her living room. Once she identifies a potential reorganization, she can bracket the three paragraphs she wants to move (also using the spatial cue that the paragraphs are on the bottom of page two and the top of three), turn to page eleven where she plans to insert them, place the two parts together, and read through to "test" the reorganization.

If she doesn't like it, she simply doesn't execute the move. Only after planning and testing several reorganizations in this way, does Donna move back to her computer to reorder her text on-line.

Most of the experienced computer writers that I have interviewed and observed reorganize their texts the way Donna did, that is, by using hard copy. There are, however, software features that could help in planning and testing these large reorganizations. Large screens, which make more text available at once, can be helpful (Haas and Hayes, 1986), as can "search" features, which allow writers to move quickly to other places in their texts. However, it may be an inherent shortcoming in the computer as a writing tool that *planning* a text change is difficult without *executing* that change. Many computers reformat completely after text changes: thus, undoing a revision and recovering the original may be difficult. Some programs support an "undo" feature, but it is usually limited to the last command the writer issued. With some word-processing systems, writers can exit without saving changes, then call up the file again to retrieve the original, unchanged text. However, this option is not possible if the text has been "saved"; the changes remain incorporated and recovery of the original text may be too time-consuming, requiring too high a level of expertise.

The speed and efficiency with which the computer reformats after changes was a problem in other ways. One student writer told me, "I like to make my changes on hard copy so that I can see they're really changes—then I feel like I'm really accomplishing something." A published novelist spoke of the fact that with his computer he felt a loss of the "history of the text—those lines you discard and then want to pull back later—with the computer they're just gone."

## Critical Reading and the "Text-Sense Problem"

A fourth area of computer negative impact occurred during critical reading or assessment. Successful writing requires self-assessment, or reading to evaluate. Hayes, Flower, Schriver, Stratman, and Carey (1986) describe three phases of revision: detection of the problem through reading, diagnosis or determining its nature, and adopting strategies to solve the problem. While local revision may involve reading to detect a mismatch between the written text and conventional rules or maxims, whole text revision often requires reading for and detecting a mismatch between the written text and the author's intentions or the audience's needs.

Using a computer to write seemed to constrain writers' ability to read and assess how well the text met their own intentions, what Witte (1985) calls matching of the projected text, or "pre-text," to the written text. Writers that I interviewed mentioned this problem with amazing regularity, and often used the words "sense of the text" when describing this problem: "With the computer, I have no sense of the whole text." Some writers used metaphors to describe the problem: "My text is hard to pin down on-line"; "There is a problem getting a feel for the piece"; "It's hard to get your center of gravity in the writing."

"Getting a sense of the text" is the kind of self-critical reading that is crucial for successful writing and revising. Reading for a sense of text includes testing the text by matching it to the writer's goals to determine if text reorganization or other revisions are needed. In addition, when reading for a sense of text, writers try to "construct" the text as a reader would, thereby noting problems that readers might have with the text. We can learn more about the text-sense problem by placing it in context and examining several factors.

Localization of the text-sense problem.   As was suggested earlier, the text-sense problem occurs during assessing and reviewing junctures in the writing process: when moving from one text section to another, when moving from first draft to initial assessment and revision, or prior to a final reading and review. The text-sense problem seems to occur in this way: writers produce some amount of text, stop to check progress, assess results, or match text to goals, and discover that they cannot adequately assess the text when it is on-line. So writers generate hard copy, read the printout, make changes (on-line or on paper), or, satisfied that the text is all right, resume computer writing. Although writers may interrupt themselves to print hard copy, then wait for several minutes (or hours) for the printout, they often do little more than read it. In fact, the text-sense problem seems to be a complex constructive reading problem—a problem of reading to construct, or reconstruct, the macrostructure of meaning in one's own text.

When writers speak of the text-sense problem, they may be describing a difficulty in representing their text, that is, its meaning and structure, to themselves. To detect a mismatch between intended text and actual text, a writer must have a representation not only of his or her intended or "projected" text but also a representation of the actual text. If reading to "get a sense of text" is important for representing a text to oneself, it is much more closely tied to the compositional or "meaning-making" aspect of writing than are proofreading or check-

ing format and therefore may be a more important problem for computer writers.

Type of writing.   The text-sense problem does not seem to be constant across writing tasks but occurs most frequently and acutely in those Bereiter and Scardamalia (1982) labeled "compositional tasks," that is, tasks in which the structure of information in the writer's memory does not easily map onto the finished text and tasks that require the forging of new connections and links in the writer's knowledge. For instance, one writer told me, "It was easy to do my [doctoral] exams on the computer because I really knew that stuff and I had a good idea from [my adviser] what the questions would be." However, in texts where writers are forming and developing new ideas, getting a sense of the text—i.e., adequately representing the text to oneself—may be more difficult. If the text-sense problem is a problem in representing one's text to oneself, it is not surprising that it is more acute in cognitively difficult writing tasks where the structure of knowledge, newly formed, exists tenuously in the writer's memory. In this situation, the external memory furnished by the written text is particularly important.

In addition, the text-sense problem occurs most frequently in long writing tasks, rarely occurring in a product only one or two screens long. This phenomenon makes sense from a cognitive point of view: the size of the text makes it difficult to hold an adequate representation in memory. The difficulty of the writing task may negatively affect "getting a sense of the text" as well. One writer said that writing letters of recommendation for students, a task he does frequently, was easy to do on-line without hard copy. However, he found that writing a letter of application for a summer scholars' program—a task of about the same length but one which was much less well rehearsed and possibly more important to him—was impossible to do without frequent hard-copy reading and editing.

The writer's relationship to on-line texts.   Some writers report that they needed to read their texts from hard copy to "get some objectivity." This may be related to the display problems that contribute to proofreading and other reading problems (for instance, poor resolution makes reading for fine features like letters difficult), but it may also be related to the fact that the computer is stationary: one can't take it on a walk or even into the next room. Many of the writers I spoke with mentioned their need to get away from their workspace—whether writing with computer or with pen and paper—to establish some distance or objectivity with their writing. Paradoxically, other writers complained that they felt *too much* distance from their computer texts: "I just don't feel that I know my text as well when it's on the screen." They mentioned "immediacy" and "intimacy" as qualities that were missing when they read their own texts on a computer screen.

The word processor's effect on the spatial sense of text.   In an earlier study (reported in Haas & Hayes, 1986) it was discovered that the reader's ability to recall spatial location within texts was constrained by the machine. Rothkopf (1971) has described the phenomenon of spatial recall: in reading a novel, we may not remember the maid's name, but we can remember that she was introduced in a lower paragraph, on the right-hand side, about one-third of the way through the book.

Spatial location is not constant on a computer screen; it is not controlled horizontally on most machines; computers with variable-width windows do not even have constant vertical markers. Writers tend to use cues like top and bottom of page, or left and right side, to mentally mark important points or specific parts of their writing. Recent work on how people learn from texts has pointed to the importance of "spatial learning strategies" in understanding and remembering texts (e.g., Holley & Dansereau, 1984). Kotovsky, Hayes, and Simon (1985) hypothesize that one factor contributing to differences in difficulty of isomorphs of the same problem is increased spatial memory load in some of the versions of the problem. Certainly the fact that scrolling text does not have a constant physical configuration contributes to computer writers' problems representing their texts to themselves and suggests that physical and spatial aspects of the text may provide cues to writers, helping them represent structure, meaning, and intent.

Computerized reformatting and the text-sense problem.   Because, for many writers, text production is faster on-line and because there is no need to recopy after changes, writers may not spend so much time producing and reproducing their texts as before. Consequently, they may not devote so much time to fixing it in spatial and episodic memory. The writing and recopying done by hand may serve a rehearsal function, helping writers to "know" their own texts better.

In sum, with difficult or lengthy texts, writers often had difficulty assessing their writing on-line and so used hard-copy printouts to help them "get a sense of the text." Generally, writers were vague—and somewhat puzzled—about the problem. It clearly was not a problem they had expected or for which they had an explanation. The presence of this problem is intriguing, however, for it suggests that a writer's reading of his or her own text, the representation of that text, and the assessment of its value are complex activities, involving not only conscious attention to intention and audience but also a representation of the text as a spatial and a physical object.

## IMPLICATIONS

What does the problem of "getting a sense of the text" mean for students who use computers for writing and for those of us who teach computer writing courses? Most of the writers I interviewed possessed a keen sense of their own writing processes, their strengths and weaknesses as writers, and how using a computer helped or hindered them during various writing tasks. They also had a metacognitive awareness of the problems that the computer caused them and had strategies for dealing with these problems. In particular, they seemed to know when and how to use paper to supplement their computer writing. These writers were able to combine their knowledge of their own reading and writing processes with their knowledge of the computer and draw upon the strengths of both pen-and-paper and the machine. It may not be realistic, however, to expect students to bring this level of self-awareness to bear on computer writing tasks. Based on research in metacognition (Scardamalia and Bereiter, 1985; Flavell, 1979; Brown, 1978), we might expect that student writers (1) would not recognize that writing on-line has drawbacks which might affect their reading of their own texts, and (2) would not use hard copy to supplement their computer writing the way experts do. Problems in reading on-line, then, may pose significant difficulties for students learning to write with word processors, difficulties that should be given careful attention as the use of computers in education becomes more widespread.

What do these findings mean for our theories of writing? Far from being the idiosyncratic musings of computer skeptics, the reports of computer writers suggest that there are important limitations to using computers for writing and that reliance on pen and paper can help circumvent those limitations. The computer-writing problems outlined here are not ones we could easily predict from our current theories of writing: while we believe that reading and writing are closely tied, the role of reading in the process of writing has not been fully articulated or explored. The advent of the computer in classrooms and offices of writers offers us a unique opportunity—and need—to examine how writers read their own texts, how they represent their texts to themselves, and how various physical, temporal, and spatial factors influence how they "see" their texts.

## Acknowledgments

Some of the research discussed here was supported by a grant to the author, Christine Neuwirth, and John R. Hayes from The Fund for the Improvement of Post-Secondary Education (FIPSE), grant number G008642161; by a grant to the author and John R. Hayes from the Carnegie-Mellon University Program in Technology and Society, Division of Social and Decision Sciences; and by the Information Technology Center at Carnegie-Mellon.

## REFERENCES

Bereiter, C., & Scardamalia, M. (1982). From conversation to composition: The role of instruction in a developmental process. In R. Glaser (Ed.), *Advances in instructional psychology* (Vol. 2, pp. 1–64). Hillsdale, NJ: Lawrence Erlbaum Associates.

Bridwell, L., Nancarrow, P. R., & Ross, D. (1984). The writing process and the writing machine: Current research on word processors relevant to the teaching of composition. In L. Bridwell & R. Beach (Eds.), *New directions in composition research* (pp. 381–398). New York: Guilford Press.

Brown, A. L. (1978). Knowing when, where, and how to remember: A problem of metacognition. In R. Glaser (Ed.), *Advances in instructional psychology* (pp. 77–165). Hillsdale, NJ: Lawrence Erlbaum Associates.

Flavell, J. H. (1979). Metacognition and cognitive monitoring. *American Psychologist, 34,* 906–911.

Gould, J. D., Alfaro, L., Finn, R., Haupt, B., Minuto, A., & Salaum, J. (1987, April). Why reading was slower from CRT displays than from paper. In *Proceedings of computer human interaction, 1987.* Association of Computing Machinery (ACM), 7–12.

Gould, J. D., & Grischkowsky, N. (1984). Doing the same work with hard copy and with cathode-ray tube computer terminals. *Human Factors, 26,* 323–337.

Haas, C., & Hayes, J. R. (1986). What did I just say? Reading problems in writing with the machine. *Research in the Teaching of English, 20,* 22–35.

Hansen, W. J., Doring, R., & Whitlock, L. R. (1978). Why an examination was slower on-line than on paper. *International Journal of Man-Machine Studies, 10,* 507–519.

Harris, J. (1985). Student writers and word processing: A preliminary evaluation. *College Composition and Communication, 36,* 323–330.

Hayes, J. R., Flower, L., Schriver, K., Stratman, J., & Carey, L. (1986). Cognitive processes in revision. In S. Rosenberg (Ed.), *Advances in applied psycholinguistics: Vol. 2. Reading, writing, and language processing* (pp. 176–240). Cambridge, England: Cambridge University Press.

Heppner, F. H., Anderson, J. C. T., Farstrup, A. E., & Weiderman, N. H. (1985, January). Reading performance on a standardized test is better from print than from computer display. *Journal of Reading,* 321–325.

Holley, C. D., & Dansereau, D. F. (1984). *Spatial learning strategies: Techniques, applications, and related issues.* New York: Academic Press.

Kotovsky, K., Hayes, J. R., & Simon, H. A. (1985). Why are some problems hard? Evidence from Tower of Hanoi. *Cognitive Psychology, 17,* 248–294.

Morris, J., Satyarayanan, M., Conner, M., Howard, J. H., Rosenthal, D., & Smith, F. D. (1986). Andrew: A distributed personal computing environment. *Communications of the ACM, 29,* 184–201.

Rothkopf, E. Z. (1971). Incidental memory for location of information in text. *Journal of Verbal Learning and Verbal Behavior, 10,* 608–613.

Scardamalia, M., & Bereiter, C. (1985). Fostering the development of self-regulation in children's knowledge processing. In S. Chipman, J. Segal, & R. Glaser (Eds.), *Learning and thinking skills: Research and open questions* (pp. 563–577). Hillsdale, NJ: Lawrence Erlbaum Associates.

Stallman, R. M. (1981). EMACS: The extensible, customizable, self-documenting display editor. *SIGPLAN NOTICES, 16,* 147–156.

Witte, S. P. (1985). Revising, composing theory, and research design. In S. Freedman (Ed.), *The acquisition of written language: Revision and response* (pp. 250–284). Norwood, NJ: Ablex.

Wright, P., & Lickorish, A. (1983). Proof-reading texts on screen and paper. *Behavior and Information Technology, 2,* 227–235.

# 3

# Computerized Text Analysis and the Teaching of Writing

James L. Collins

Computer programs that analyze writing for certain features are becoming popular in the teaching of writing, so popular in fact that computerized text analysis is probably a close second to word processing in the list of ways teachers and students use computers in composition classrooms. Teachers of writing can choose among programs to check spelling, style, usage, and mechanics, or they can choose programs that offer combinations of these checkers. With such a variety of software available to us, it seems all we need do to assure students' success is to choose the most powerful program, the spelling checker with the largest dictionary, or the style checker with the longest list of items to be examined.

Since text analysis programs appear to make the teaching of writing easier, we might be tempted to purchase and use the software without evaluating its accuracy. It is advisable first to review current uses of computerized text analysis in the teaching of writing and explore new methods for developing and using text analysis software. In general, I recommend a shift from computer programs intended for writers working in isolation to computer programs for writers and teachers working in collaboration.

Text analysis software currently is designed to examine completed or nearly completed pieces of writing for certain easily identifiable or quantifiable aspects of the discourse, including diction, style, spelling, some common errors, and statistics (number of words, number of sentences, words per sentence, and characters per word). The software treats text as strings of characters; it decides if a word is misspelled, for example, by comparing a string of characters, a word in the text, to a list of strings of characters, a dictionary stored in memory or on disk. Text analysis software concentrates on surface aspects of writing, on matters of linguistic etiquette and style, and often does not help with the errors student writers make. Since the computer must treat words as strings of characters, it has no access to contexts of meaning, to symbol-referent relations, to the content and logic of the writing. This is where the human text analyst—a teacher or peer in the various roles of reader, listener, respondent, editor, and collaborator—is necessary. Text analysis software should be improved for use in instructional contexts. The software would then provide tools to clarify and illuminate the discussion when writers confer with their readers, especially their teachers.

I hold firmly to the principle that a writing teacher is to teach writing, not word processing or computerized text analysis. Programs can gauge the maturity of syntax or word choice, find certain kinds of mistakes and stylistic elements, and generate statistics about the texts, but these features do little to improve the ways writers generate text or the ways teachers work with writers. At SUNY-Buffalo we are working on text analysis software designed primarily for the composition classroom and for interaction between writers and respondents. Before describing this software, however, I shall discuss uses of current text analysis software by examining how several programs operate and what they say about samples of student writing.

## THREE POPULAR TEXT ANALYSIS PROGRAMS

The programs included in my analysis are the *Milliken Writing Workshop* postwriting program, Conduit's *Writer's Helper,* and Sensible Software's *Sensible Speller* and *Sensible Grammar.* I selected these because they are commercially available and are becoming popular with writing teachers, probably because they are inexpensive and rather widely advertised.

### Description

The three programs show similarities with *Writer's Workbench,* probably the best known text analyzer. During its development from about 1975 to 1980, *Writer's Workbench* was designed for business settings, not academic ones. Its 15 text analysis programs were developed at AT&T Bell Laboratories for their own writers and only later, beginning in 1981, adapted in modest ways for writing courses at Colorado State University. The *Writer's Workbench* programs analyze text for such things as forms of the verb *to be,* diction (any of about 500 wordy, overused, or sexist words and phrases), vague words, typographical and spelling errors, homophones, punctuation (missing parentheses and certain patterns such as periods followed by capitals), split infinitives, passive constructions, nominalizations, abstract words, readability, and sentence statistics. The programs included in this study are similar, as Table 3.1 indicates.

The Conduit *Writer's Helper* package includes 11 prewriting programs in addition to the 11 postwriting programs in Table 3.1. Milliken's package includes the listed postwriting programs and also prewriting programs and a word processor (paradoxically, a source of restriction and inflexibility, since their postwriting programs will only work with files created by their own word processor). Conduit's *Writer's Helper* works with standard text files and *AppleWorks,* while *Sensible Grammar* accepts standard text files and files created by eight popular word processors. Sensible's software package is the most flexible of the three for other reasons as well. Any of its lists of words and phrases can be edited by users, any of the lists can be toggled on or off, and two of them, contractions and legal terms, can be set to "remove" or "use" settings. The program also offers six options for handling possible grammar errors it finds, and *Sensible Grammar* uses a Macintosh-like environment with pull-down menus, windows, and the option of using a mouse.

Table 3.1  Programs in Three Text Analysis Software Packages

| Milliken | Sensible | Conduit |
|---|---|---|
| Spelling Checker | Sensible Speller | -- |
| Mechanics Checker: | Sensible Grammar: | Evaluation: |
|   Tired words |   Cliche expressions |   Homonyms |
|   Homonyms |   Contractions |   Gender related |
|   Pronoun problems |   Faulty phrases |     language |
|   Typing errors |   Informal phrases |   "To be" verbs |
| Proofreader: |   Legal terms |   Teacher's words |
|   Style |   Personal phrases |   Usage errors |
|   Final check |   Pompous phrases |   Outline of first |
|   Length of sentences |   Redundant phrases |     sentences |
|     and Paragraphs |   Sexist phrases |   List of sentences |
| |   Vague phrases |     one at a time |
| |   Wordy phrases |   Readability |
| |   Punctuation |   Sentence length |
| | |   Paragraph length |
| | |   Word frequency |

## Evaluation

In evaluating the three programs, I was especially interested in how accurately they identify errors in student writing. I measured accuracy by comparing the output of the programs to error analyses performed by two carefully trained, experienced writing teachers on student writing produced in response to the same topic at grade levels 8 and 13. The teachers scored all the sentence- and word-level errors in the student essays using National Assessment of Educational Progress (1980) mechanics scoring guidelines. Both teachers scored all of the essays, and I included only errors on which they were in complete agreement with the computer programs.

From the 55 essays in the study, I randomly selected five at each grade level to illustrate the serious problem with accuracy emerging from my analysis. The results are shown in Table 3.2.

Expressed as the percentage of times each program found the same errors identified by the teachers for all ten essays (B/T), the accuracy measure yields 32% for Milliken, 29% for Sensible, and 2% for Conduit. Milliken turns in the best performance of the three programs on these ten essays by finding slightly less than one-third of the errors teachers find. Sensible is a close second and Conduit a distant third. The poorer performance of Conduit's *Writer's Helper* in comparison to the other programs on this accuracy test is due to the absence of a spelling checker among the Conduit programs. Milliken gets 82% of its agreement with teachers from finding the same spelling errors the teachers find, and Sensible gets 85% from the same source. Take away their spelling checkers, and Milliken and Sensible

Table 3.2   Items Flagged in Individual Essays by Programs (P), by Teachers (T), and by Both (B)

| Essay | Grade | Total Words | Milliken | | Sensible | | Conduit | | Teachers |
|---|---|---|---|---|---|---|---|---|---|
| | | | P | B | P | B | P | B | T |
| 1 | 13 | 606 | 70 | 1 | 17 | 2 | 67 | 0 | 9 |
| 2 | 13 | 439 | 49 | 5 | 18 | 9 | 47 | 1 | 16 |
| 3 | 13 | 188 | 37 | 15 | 16 | 10 | 28 | 0 | 33 |
| 4 | 13 | 338 | 24 | 4 | 11 | 4 | 15 | 0 | 7 |
| 5 | 13 | 625 | 81 | 2 | 28 | 1 | 66 | 0 | 4 |
| 6 | 8 | 114 | 9 | 1 | 8 | 1 | 11 | 0 | 10 |
| 7 | 8 | 142 | 17 | 4 | 9 | 2 | 9 | 2 | 19 |
| 8 | 8 | 123 | 20 | 1 | 4 | 2 | 21 | 0 | 8 |
| 9 | 8 | 179 | 21 | 3 | 11 | 3 | 31 | 0 | 14 |
| 10 | 8 | 375 | 44 | 8 | 16 | 7 | 32 | 0 | 19 |

perform almost as dismally as Conduit on these ten essays; the accuracy rates for finding the same errors as teachers would be 6% for Milliken, 5% for Sensible, and 2% for Conduit.

Another measure of accuracy is available by including the numbers of items the programs found that the teachers didn't count as errors. These "non-errors" are as follows: Milliken, 328; Conduit, 324; and Sensible, 97. The high number of non-errors for Milliken and Conduit is caused by their flagging all occurrences of certain strings of characters. For Milliken, the strings are homonyms and usage items such as "good" and "seem" which it finds with its program to locate "Tired and Tricky" words. For Conduit, the strings are homonyms and forms of the verb *to be*.

My justification for including the non-errors in my accuracy measures is that the programs are inaccurate nearly every time non-errors are flagged. This sentence from the sample in my study is an example: "It is very important for adolescents to, develope, a scent of purpose." The errors and non-errors found by teachers and programs in this sentence are as follows:

> *Teachers:* 2 comma errors and misspelling of "develop" and "sense"
> *Milliken:* Use of "very" and "to" and misspelling of "develop"
> *Sensible:* Use of "very important" and misspelling of "develop"
> *Conduit:* Use of "is," "very," and "to" and a possible homonym problem with "scent"

The programs miss what teachers, and student writers, would look for in this sentence, with the exception of the misspelling of "develop." Even the obvious problem with "scent" is overlooked (Conduit flags the word but does so for the wrong reason). By flagging "very" and "to" and "is," the programs are inaccurate because they are distracting the writer from the real errors in the sentence. Sensible fares better than Milliken and Conduit in the non-error category because Sensible avoids flagging words and phrases commonly used in student writing. And Sensible is right; the words and phrases are grammatically correct and only occasionally stylistically annoying. Expressed as a percentage derived by dividing the number of times each program flagged the same errors teachers found by the sum of those errors and non-errors for all ten essays, the accuracy rates are 13% for Milliken, 42% for Sensible, and less than 1% for Conduit.

The degree of inaccuracy—both bypassing of errors teachers find and flagging of non-errors—is considerable. The programs clearly do not show a comfortable fit with the realities of student writing in this sample. Agreement with teachers (errors identified by both programs and teachers in the ten essays) is rare for Milliken and Sensible and disappears for Conduit. Of course, we would have to do additional testing to determine if these poor performances would be repeated in other samples of student writing. For now, though, it looks as if the programs won't do students much good and might even be misleading, owing to the high numbers of non-errors the programs find. If, indeed, these programs are descended from the same roots as AT&T's *Writer's Workbench,* as I suggested earlier, they might be better suited to flagging the stylistic infelicities of writing done for business purposes than for finding the errors of student writers. Certainly, the programs' use as instructional tools, as courseware, is questionable.

## ANOTHER KIND OF PROGRAM: *MINA*

I move now from the commercially available programs to a discussion of MINA, a text analysis program being developed and tested at the University of Pittsburgh. This program is a good example of how software for writing classrooms should be developed. It is grounded in current composition theory and research, it focuses on whole texts rather than on individual sentences, and its analysis of text is based on the kinds of errors inexperienced writers actually make.

The designers of MINA examined 2000 student essays to identify and catalog errors; the result is a taxonomy of errors students produce. The designers also had a pedagogy for editing writing in mind and mapped their ideas onto computer technology. The pedagogy holds that students make errors in writing, beyond accidents of transcription, for certain reasons. Errors are not randomly generated; rather, they are produced in accordance with fixed and usually idiosyncratic rules. Inexperienced writers must learn to detect errors in writing, since their inadequate rules suggest the errors aren't really there. These errors are "systematic misconceptions, errors caused by rules which are themselves faulty" (Hull and Smith, 1985, p. 90). It's not just a matter of correcting errors the computer finds; inexperienced writers must learn to locate errors themselves and then to adjust their misunderstanding of the rules to avoid producing the error again. The designers of MINA, after Shaughnessy (1977) and Bartholomae (1980), believe it is best to work on *patterns* of error, one pattern at a time. This means the software will work on one type of error, asking the student to find and correct all occurrences of that type, before moving to another type. Unlike the software discussed above, MINA does not work on all types of errors in sequence from the beginning to the end of the text, or even on all errors in a single sentence. Instead, it presents one pattern of error at a time, throughout the whole text.

Currently, MINA can search for *60* different error patterns. MINA begins with a message like this:

> I've scanned your essay and noted 11 errors. You have what I think are 5 SOUND ALIKE WORD ERRORS. The first is in the line in boldface.

The highlighted lines in this case would contain an error in confusion among *to, too,* and *two.* A help file is available to give information about the error, using *there, their,* and *they're* as an example. If the student can't find the error, a smaller area is highlighted. When all five occurrences of errors in the sound-alike category have been dealt with, the program moves to another category, such as linking-word comma errors, where the comma comes after *and* or *but* instead of before.

## GUIDELINES FOR DEVELOPING TEXT ANALYSIS SOFTWARE

Hull and Smith (1985) clarify the theoretical assumptions that guided the development of MINA and offer maxims for teachers interested in using or devising computer software to help with writing. I have summarized their points here as the first three items in the following list and then added one of my own to prepare for remarks on new directions for text analysis software:

1. Any program that promises to teach a skill must give students opportunities to practice that skill.
2. A program that teaches students to make improvements in their writing is better than one that makes improvements for them.
3. Programs for teaching writing and revising should be created in accordance with an understanding of what good teachers actually do.
4. The most useful programs for writers should help with matters of content and form, as well as with style and mechanics.

The most common writing problems (and the most serious, since they diminish communicative effectiveness) involve content or form, or both. The problems range from the underdeveloped meaning characteristic of inexperienced writers' "writer-based prose" (Flower, 1979) to the inexplicit logic found in much of the writing of high school and college students. These are not problems with mechanics, style, or diction, but rather with the underlying representation of ideas in written language. The real work of writing involves transforming inchoate ideas and private presentational frames and images into discursive language (Collins and Miller, 1986), a process in which content and form assume great importance. Writers must, quite literally, spell ideas out completely for communication to be successful. If text analysis software is to help writers, then it should help them turn ideas that are underrepresented or ill-formed in their writing into explicit discourse.

The following illustrates what I mean by problems with content and form. The essay was written by a tenth grader in response to an assignment asking for a description of a school event.

> There are many school events, one of wich are Pep Rallys. Pep rallys are supposed to Build up School Spirit to get the energy flowing through the blood and your Body. You get siked for the sport events for the foot Ball teem Basket Ball, swiming, etc. You must be mentally and phisicly prepaired for a sport event.
>
> The thing you see done are one teem come out and every Body cheers for them one at a time: foot Ball, soccer, track, etc. They come out and we cheer for them then they have a cheering contest the gym is divided up into four parts freshmen, Sophomores, juniors, Seniors. one class at a time cheers and whoevers the loudest gets a class prize. Then the cheerleaders come out and do a whole mess of cheers and nobody can understand what they are saying. Then every Body runs of the bleacher and runs around and yells alot. "Were the Best'! etc. then every Body goes home and then the sport events start and Nobody else cares but the jocks.

The writing shows many surface errors, and I'll return to them in a moment. First, though, I want to point out that the writer's logic isn't clear; we can't tell whether he likes or dislikes pep rallies, whether he wants to describe them, satirize them, or perhaps both. The essay tends to portray pep rallies as a harmless waste of time, but if that's the writer's position, it's not made explicit enough. Software capable of asking questions about purpose as well as highlighting and rearranging portions of the text might help the writer work his or her way out of what appears to be a confusion of purpose in the essay.

Once we have settled problems of content and form, we can turn our attention to problems at the sentence and word level. Here I believe software can be most useful if it allows the writer to work on one pattern of error at a time, as in the MINA program discussed above, beginning with the most frequently occurring patterns of error. In the "pep rally" example, the software would begin with capitalization problems, say, by highlighting all the upper case B's and S's, and then would group together all the sound-based misspellings, such as *siked* and *prepaired*.

### THE WRITING TEACHER'S TOOLBOX

By now it is clear that writers need help most with correcting underdeveloped content, incomplete patterns of logic, missing verb inflections or punctuation, and so on. In other words, except for spelling errors, most of what's wrong with student writing is wrong because something's missing from the writing. This raises an interesting question: How can computers be programmed to find what is missing in student writing? An obvious answer is to write the programs for teachers working with writers, and to let the teachers and writers find what's missing. Computerized text analysis by itself must be limited to what actually appears in the text, but teachers conferring with writers have access to the writers' intended meanings. Aiming text analysis programs at teachers and writers working together opens up a text-context connection that is not available when software is written only for writers working in isolation. The *Sensible Grammar* program, for example, responded to the sentence "Through my four years I tried to communicate." It said that a comma is missing following the "through" clause, and that "communicate" is pompous and "tell" should be substituted. A teacher, of course, would not make such errors in analysis but would instead talk with the writer about clarifying the meaning of the sentence.

At SUNY-Buffalo we are designing and testing a text analysis program we call *Writing Teacher's Toolbox*. As the name suggests, the software is intended for teachers to use while working with student writers. Because the software uses input from teachers and writers, it can do more than non-interactive software. In providing text statistics, for example, the program counts total words, total sentences, words per sentence, and repeated words; then, once T-units and clauses are marked by the writer or teacher, the program figures words per clause and words per T-unit. In its graphics mode, the program allows teachers and writers to draw lines between features of the text and to draw boxes around portions of text ranging from single words to whole paragraphs. The program also has a search-and-highlight feature that finds and marks, all at once or one at a time, certain features of the text that the teacher or the writer asks for, such as repeated words or phrases; one or more words, such as certain nouns or pronouns; verbs ending in *-ed*; words beginning with upper-case letters; high-frequency, low-meaning words such as *things* or *nice*; jargon terms and clichés; and so on.

## Tutorials Built in by Teachers

Making the program interactive also lets teachers build in tutorials to supplement teacher-writer conferences. After a teacher has worked with a writer on one or two examples of a pattern of error, the teacher can use the program to mark additional examples and then have the program present these additional examples from the text one at a time to the writer in the form of a tutorial. An example: A college student writes an essay that includes the sentence, "You have to understand your parents and communicate with them, talking things over and learning to understand the reasons for doing things they do." After conferring with the teacher using our software, the writer continues working on pronoun and empty word problems alone at a computer. The program presents the items the teacher has marked, one item at a time. It first highlights *you* and *your,* explains that these always refer outside of the text to the reader, and asks the writer to type in the purpose and audience. The program then asks the writer to decide if the "you" and "your" references are appropriate for the purpose and audience. Once that matter is settled, the program highlights *them* and *they* and asks the writer to type in the referent for these pronouns. The program highlights the whole pattern of reference and asks if it's clear enough for the audience. Here an "N" would lead into a branch on pronoun reference, but since the answer is "Y," the program goes on, this time highlighting *things* and asking the writer to identify these things. Finally, the program asks the writer to revise the sentence in the directions suggested by the analysis.

## Graphics to Use with Form and Content Problems

By far the most exciting aspect of the *Writing Teacher's Toolbox* is its ability to combine text and graphics. This part of the software promises to provide help with problems of form and content, as illustrated in the following two examples.

Patterns of reference.  The first example consists of the second paragraph of a tenth grader's essay describing fights he has witnessed:

> I saw another fight before at the playground over some candy one kid have a bag of candy and this boy took the bag a eatin a piece of his candy he hit him in the arm the boy who took the candy kicked him in the face and he got a black eye so the boy who was punching him stop and walk out of the playground, with his friend talking about how hard he hit him in the face.

This paragraph shows many errors in spelling and punctuation. Even if these errors were corrected, though, the paragraph wouldn't communicate clearly. The main problem is the paragraph underrepresents the writer's meaning by using personal pronouns and demonstratives exophorically, that is, in a way that refers outside of the text, to the context of situation, the actual fight at the playground. The result is difficulty in telling who did what to whom. Our software, which allows us to draw on the writer's text on the computer screen, is capable of highlighting patterns of reference and would be useful in calling the writer's attention to the problem of exophoric reference, as indicated in Figure 3.1.

The software could help make a point about unclear reference in the paragraph by showing how referents for pronouns and demonstratives are located outside of the text; these are the two fighters and are represented by the shaded and blackened circles. The shaded boxes highlight pronouns that are even less clear because readers can't tell to

Figure 3.1    Patterns of Reference in Student Paragraph

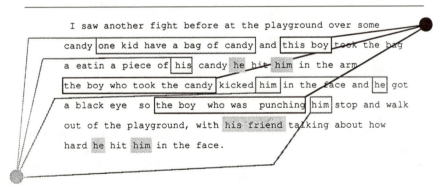

which fighter they refer. Once the reference problems are cleared up, our software could be used to call the writer's attention to missing end punctuation, and then perhaps to the missing *ed* to form the past tense of regular verbs.

Analysis of content and logic. My second example of the use of the graphics mode in the *Writing Teacher's Toolbox* shows how it can be used as a content and logic analyzer. The program allows the construction of a graphic representation of the blocks of ideas in the text and also of the relatedness between blocks. Our model for this process of block-structuring written texts is the computer programmer's use of algorithms. An algorithm is an English-language solution to the programming problem; it's what gets coded in the programming language. In a block-structured language, such as Pascal, algorithms are represented as connected blocks, some contained within others, and some existing at higher and lower levels. This method breaks a large problem into component problems, and each block, or subproblem, is made as specific as it needs to be to solve the component problem. This block-structuring of computer programs is analogous to the writing process. Writers have a major goal, or problem to solve, for each piece of writing, and they identify component goals, one at a time, and solve the problems inherent in achieving those goals. This portion of the *Writing Teacher's Toolbox* allows the teacher or writer to construct a block diagram over the text of a piece of writing, to insert additional text within the blocks, to move the blocks around, and to label the ideas within blocks and then shrink the blocks to show the organization of the whole piece of writing at once.

A sample of this process is shown in Figure 3.2, where an evolving block diagram for a student's essay is presented.

The diagrams help the writer to check patterns of organization and relatedness, and they also, since writing processes are recursive, help the writer generate additional content. The left half of Figure 3.2 presents the naturally occurring blocks in the writer's text; the teacher and the writer create these blocks as they discuss the writing. While discussing these blocks of text, the teacher and the writer notice that three of the blocks contain the same idea in slightly different words; these three are then grouped as the top block in the right half of Figure 3.2, where the blocks are also labeled to guide the further development of ideas within the blocks. The block-diagramming can also use arrows, lines of different sizes and shadings, positions of blocks, and highlighting of transitional words and phrases, all of which can be used to show relationships between and among ideas. The end result

Figure 3.2 Block Diagrams of Student Essay

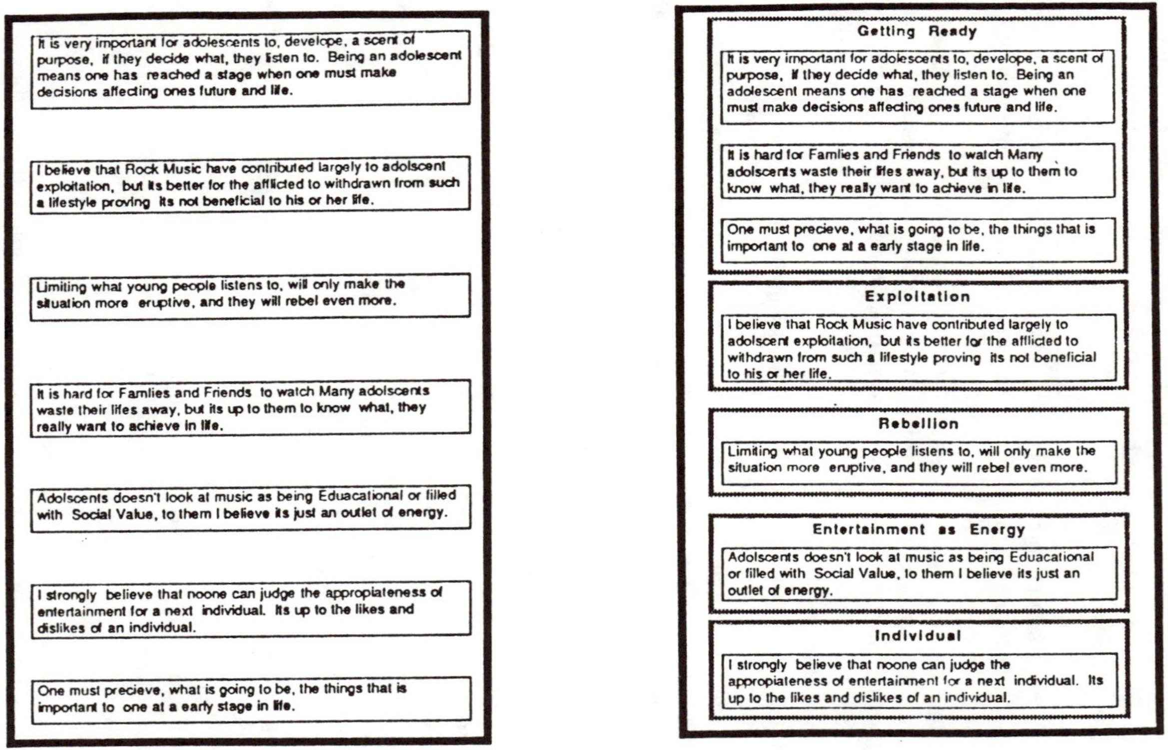

**First diagram (with headings):**

**Getting Ready**

It is very important for adolescents to, develope, a scent of purpose, if they decide what, they listen to. Being an adolescent means one has reached a stage when one must make decisions affecting ones future and life.

It is hard for Families and Friends to watch Many adolscents waste their lifes away, but its up to them to know what, they really want to achieve in life.

One must precieve, what is going to be, the things that is important to one at a early stage in life.

**Exploitation**

I believe that Rock Music have contributed largely to adolescent exploitation, but its better for the afflicted to withdrawn from such a lifestyle proving its not beneficial to his or her life.

**Rebellion**

Limiting what young people listens to, will only make the situation more eruptive, and they will rebel even more.

**Entertainment as Energy**

Adolscents doesn't look at music as being Eduacational or filled with Social Value, to them I believe its just an outlet of energy.

**Individual**

I strongly believe that noone can judge the appropiateness of entertainment for a next individual. Its up to the likes and dislikes of an individual.

**Second diagram (without headings):**

It is very important for adolscents to, develope, a scent of purpose, if they decide what, they listen to. Being an adolescent means one has reached a stage when one must make decisions affecting ones future and life.

I believe that Rock Music have contributed largely to adolscent exploitation, but its better for the afflicted to withdrawn from such a lifestyle proving its not beneficial to his or her life.

Limiting what young people listens to, will only make the situation more eruptive, and they will rebel even more.

It is hard for Families and Friends to watch Many adolscents waste their lifes away, but its up to them to know what, they really want to achieve in life.

Adolscents doesn't look at music as being Eduacational or filled with Social Value, to them I believe is just an outlet of energy.

I strongly believe that noone can judge the appropiateness of entertainment for a next individual. Its up to the likes and dislikes of an individual.

One must precieve, what is going to be, the things that is important to one at a early stage in life.

is a flowchart or network to help writers conceive of the whole piece of writing and of the location of parts within the whole.

## CONCLUSION

Although *Writing Teacher's Toolbox* is still in the development stage, it shows great promise. In comparison to software currently available to writers and their teachers, programs such as MINA and *Writing Teacher's Toolbox* indeed offer welcome changes for the writing classroom.

The three commercial programs I reviewed suggest that the technology of computerized text analysis has a long way to go. The problem, though, is not with technology, but rather with the uses composition classes make of technology. When the basic premise of how writers work separates text analysis from problems of content and logic, and when it separates writers from reader response, any software is limited in how much help it can offer. Nonetheless, existing technology already offers many ways to help writers. We don't have to wait for breakthroughs in artificial intelligence or for further advances in computer hardware. We can take what we know about writing and the teaching of writing and look for ways to use computers intelligently in those processes.

## REFERENCES

Bartholomae, D. (1980). The study of error. *College Composition and Communication, 31,* 253–269.

Collins, J. L., & Miller, B. E. (1986). Presentational symbolism and the production of text. *Written Communication, 3,* 91–104.

Flower, L. S. (1979). Writer-based prose: A cognitive basis for problems in writing. *College English, 41,* 19–37.

Hull, G. A., & Smith, W. L. (1985). Error correction and computing. In J. L. Collins & E. A. Sommers (Eds.), *Writing on-line: Using computers in the teaching of writing* (pp. 89–101). Upper Montclair, NJ: Boynton/Cook.

National Assessment of Educational Progress. (1980). *Writing achievement, 1969–1979: Results from the third national writing assessment.* Denver: Education Commission of the States.

Shaughnessy, M. P. (1977). *Errors and expectations: A guide for the teacher of basic writing.* New York: Oxford University Press.

# 4

# Research and Recommendations for Computers and Composition

Gail E. Hawisher

In extolling the educational worth of computers in general, Papert (1981) stated, "[Computers] will change work and play, but the most important change will not come through what the computers can do for us, but through their effect on how people learn" (p. 99). In the same article, he noted that the "computer presence . . . will perhaps even reverse the order [of learning language skills] in that mastery of writing may develop faster once it starts, than mastery of speech" (p. 100). Papert's predictions are noteworthy, not because we, as writing teachers and researchers, necessarily believe them, but rather because of the optimism they reflected in 1981 for the promise of this strange new tool in fostering learning and literacy.

This enthusiasm was not restricted to mathematicians or to others whom we commonly associate with technology. In his 1984 foreword to *Computers and Composing,* Corbett argued that English teachers must rise to the challenges of electronic communication and that "after only a week of hands-on experience with this wondrous machine, [he] acquired a keen sense of its potency and its potential" (p. xii). Our students, too, told us of the wonders of word processing, and our own writing on the machine suggested the credibility of their opinions. Thus, those of us who taught with computers and studied the influence of computers on writers and their products approached our research with high expectations. It is no surprise, then, that in our ebullience, we sometimes expected so much of computers and word processing that our research became "technocentric," a term Papert used in a 1987 article in the *Educational Researcher.*

According to Papert (1987), technocentrism is analogous to Piaget's notion of egocentrism; that is, just as a child has difficulty in moving beyond the self in comprehending phenomena, so those of us caught up in technocentrism have difficulty in "decentering" the computer in our research. Furthermore, he maintains that technocentrism manifests itself in such research questions as "What is *the* effect of *the* computer on cognitive development?" (p. 23). Humanists, he goes on to assert, are especially susceptible to technocentrism because of the awe and misunderstanding with which we often approach technology. Thus misconceptions are likely to lead us to ask such questions as "What is *the* effect of the computer on *the* writing process?"

I shall return to Papert's notion of technocentrism and its application to our field of research, but first I shall review the kinds of inquiry into computers and composition with which we, as a profession, have been engaged for the past several years. I do not wish to criticize early studies but rather to sort out what we have learned so that new research can add to an accumulating knowledge-base in assessing the value of word processing for writing and for teaching writing. After presenting an overview of 42 studies conducted since 1981, I discuss some directions that researchers might profitably pursue in the future.

## OVERVIEW

Research into computers and composition over the past several years has concentrated on the effects of word processing on students and other writers, on the processes in which writers engage as they write, and on the products writers create with the aid of computers. Few studies have examined how computers affect and interact with the cultural context or learning environment in which they are used—either for writing or for instruction. Many of the investigations dealing with the school setting, however, both acknowledge and emphasize that change or lack of change in writers' behavior or products cannot be attributed to computers alone; the writing instruction students receive is also important in shaping the influence of computers. Several investigations are concerned not with instruction but rather with how computers facilitate experienced and professional writers' work.

### Selection Criteria

Several criteria were applied in choosing the 42 studies reported here. First, the studies are either published pieces, national conference papers from 1981 onwards, or dissertations listed in *Dissertation Abstracts International* for the same period of time. In the case of dissertations, abstracts were used to identify studies before the full text was subsequently examined. Second, each of the studies regards computers as tools for writing rather than as intact instructional delivery systems. Although heuristic and invention software, text analysis programs, and drill and practice courseware might well influence writers and their products, they were not the focus of this overview. Third, the research reported here includes more than surveys of students' or other writers' attitudes toward working with computers. Although surveys can provide significant information on writers' reported use of word processing and its perceived influence on writing habits and processes, these 42 studies all relied on additional methods of inquiry. When surveys were included, the researchers' aim was to corroborate findings from other methods of study and observation. Fourth, research that was basically an informal inquiry or that did not specify a particular methodology was not selected for this review. (For a review of this earlier, exploratory research, see Hawisher, 1986b).

## Research Design

Studies in word processing over the past several years can be classified into two categories: those that employ primarily quantitative methods of inquiry and those that rely largely on qualitative techniques. The qualitative studies can be divided further into case studies and ethnographies. When we look at the research design of the studies reviewed here, 26 can be termed comparative (or quantitative) and 16 naturalistic (or qualitative). Twelve of the qualitative investigations were classified as case studies and four as ethnographies. (See Tables 4.1 and 4.2.)

When we examine the quantitative and qualitative research with regard to the characteristics of the sample, the context or setting for the study, and the results of the study, some interesting patterns emerge. I shall first review the comparative investigations and then discuss the case studies and ethnographies.

## EXAMINATION OF RESEARCH

### Comparative Studies

By far the most common population of interest for the quantitative studies was students of some sort. Of the 26 comparative studies (refer to Table 4.1), seven examined samples of undergraduate college students, eight focused on secondary school students, and eight on elementary students. Only three of the comparative studies reviewed here looked at writers outside the school context—two studies conducted by Haas and Hayes with the same sample of 15 faculty and staff and Gould's investigation of 10 IBM researchers. In terms of setting, then, we can say that the majority of the quantitative studies focused on the effects of word processing used in school to teach writing rather than to facilitate writing outside the academic context.

Almost all of these quantitative studies conducted in the school setting described the instruction as *process-oriented.* That is, writing is viewed as an *activity* in which writers engage in prewriting, composing, and revising of multiple drafts. The activity also includes "conferencing," that is, teacher and student conferring between drafts and/or peer evaluation. Although two of the quantitative studies excluded peer evaluation from the research design for fear that it would make judging the influence of word processing more difficult (e.g., Cirello, 1986; Hawisher, 1986a, 1987), the majority regarded peer interaction as integral to a process-based environment. It would seem, then, that most of these studies were not only sensitive to the role instruction plays in combination with word processing but also created a setting in which the pedagogy was grounded in theory and research.

Most of the comparative studies also tried to control for the potentially biasing effects of teacher differences. These attempts usually took the form of having the same instructor, often the researcher, teach all treatment groups. If the instructor were biased toward one of the treatments, however, this method would exert little control. Hillocks (1986) stipulated for the studies in his meta-analysis of empirical research in writing from 1963 to 1982 that there be twice as many instructors as treatments. To control for teacher bias, in other words, the studies that focused on students writing with and without computers needed four instructors, with the two treatments then counterbalanced over four classes. Only a few of the studies conformed to this criterion (e.g., Coulter, 1986; Hawisher & Fortune, 1988; Sommers, 1986; Wetzel, 1985). Many researchers contented themselves with using one instructor for both treatment groups, and some neglected to report the number of instructors.

For the most part, then, these comparative studies explored how word processing in combination with a process-oriented teaching methodology influenced writers' processes and products. Two of the studies (i.e., Duling, 1985; Miller, 1984) looked at the word processor only as a revision tool; that is, the students produced all first drafts by

*(text continues on p. 52)*

## Table 4.1  Comparative Studies

| | Sample | Number | Duration: Weeks | Word-Processing Package | Computer | Description of Instruction | # Instructors | Composed at Computers | Attitudes | Errors |
|---|---|---|---|---|---|---|---|---|---|---|
| | | DESIGN | | | TOOLS | | CONTEXT | | | |
| Beesley (1986) | 6th graders | 23 | 18 | BSW 1982 | Apple | process oriented | 1 | Y | X | X |
| Burnett (1984) | Gr. 1–5 low achievers | 10 | 8 | BSW 1982 | Apple | process oriented | • | Y | X | – |
| Cirello (1986) | Gr. 10 basic writers | 30 | 20 | BSW 1982 | Apple | process w/o peer review | 1 | Y | – | – |
| Coulter (1986) | 1st year college | 62 | 16 | • | • | • | 6 | Y | – | – |
| Daiute (1986) | 7th & 9th graders | 57 | 36 | CATCH | Apple | process-centered workshop | 1 | Y/N | – | X |
| Dalton & Hannafin (1987) | Gr. 7 low achievers | 80 | 36 | FreeWriter | Apple | process oriented | • | N | X | – |
| Deming (1987) | college basic writers | 24 | 10 | BSW | Apple | process oriented | 1 | Y | – | – |
| Duling (1985) | 9th graders | 20 | 36 | Scripsit StoryWriter | TRS 80 PET | Engl. curr. of lit. & writing | 1 | N | – | X |
| Gould (1981) | IBM research-ers | 10 | – | EDIT REDIT | IBM main-frame | – | – | Y | – | – |
| Haas (1986) | experienced academics | 8 | – | EMACS* MINCE | Andrew mainframe | – | – | Y | – | – |
| Haas & Hayes (1986) | experienced academics | 15 | – | EMACS* MINCE | Andrew mainframe | – | – | Y | – | – |
| Hawisher (1986, 1987) | 1st year college | 20 | 16 | Volkswriter | IBM | process w/o peer review | 1 | Y/N | X | – |
| Hawisher & Fortune (1988) | college basic writers | 40 | 16 | WordStar | Zenith | process oriented | 4 | Y | – | – |
| Juettner (1987) | 11th & 12th graders | 19 | 16 | Magic Window | Apple | comb. trad. & process oriented | 2 | Y | X | – |
| Kaplan (1986) | 5th graders | 56 | 5 | SELECT | DRC Rainbow | conference process approach | 2 | Y | – | – |
| King, Birnbaum & Wageman (1984) | college basic writers | 10 | 16 | BSW 1982 | Apple | remedial tutoring | 1 | Y/N | X | – |
| Kurth (1987) | 10th & 11th graders | 28 | 12 | Word-Perfect | Apple IBM | process oriented | 1 | Y | X | X |
| Levin, Riel, Rowe, & Boruta (1985) | 6th graders | 10 | 36 | Writer's Assistant | Apple | process oriented | 1 | • | X | X |
| Miller (1984) | 6th graders | 28 | 5 | BSW 1982 | Apple | • | 2 | N | X | – |
| Moore (1987) | 4th & 5th graders | 204 | 16 | BSW | Apple | process oriented | 12 | Y | X | – |
| Pivarnik (1985) | Gr. 11 basic writers | 76 | 36 | WordStar | TRS 80 | process oriented | 1 | Y | – | – |
| Posey (1986) | college basic writers | 13 | 14 | BSW | Apple | process-centered workshop | 1 | Y | X | – |
| Sommers (1986) | college students | 79 | 16 | BSW Homework AppleWriter | Apple | process oriented | 6 | Y/N | X | – |
| Wetzel (1985) | 3rd–5th graders | 36 | 10 | BSW 1984 | Apple | tchrs. used rsrchr's scripts | 8 | Y | – | – |
| Woodruff, Lindsay, Bryson, & Joram (1986) | Gr. 8, avg. & enriched | 16 | 1 | icon-driven word proc. | ICON | – | • | Y | X | X |
| Woolley (1985) | 5th graders | 120 | 2 | BSW | Apple | process oriented | 2 | Y | – | – |

Y=yes  N=no  N/Y=yes & no  •=information not given  X=examined  –=not a concern of study  *with mouse

Table 4.1, *Continued*

| | | | | VARIABLES | | | ANALYSIS | | | | | RESULTS | | | | | | NOTEWORTHY |
|---|---|---|---|---|---|---|---|---|---|---|---|---|---|---|---|---|---|---|
| Quality | Syntax | Processes | Revision | # Words | Cognitive Skills | Assessment | Revision | Interview | Surveys | Protocols | Journals | Positive Attitudes | Fewer Errors | Improved Quality | Increased Revision | Increased Fluency | Increased Length | |
| X | – | – | X | X | – | H | Observation | X | X | – | – | Y | Y | N | Y | – | N | Revision analysis focused on writing of 6 students |
| X | X | – | – | – | – | H&A | – | X | – | – | – | Y | – | Y | – | Y | – | Experiment replicated 9 times with different students |
| X | X | – | – | X | – | H | researcher's criteria | – | X | – | X | – | – | N/Y | Y | Y | Y | Significant improvement on 2 of 3 writing tasks |
| X | – | – | X | – | X | H | Bridwell (1980) | – | – | – | – | – | – | N | N | – | – | No significant correlation between time spent in writing and quality, revision frequency, or cognitive gain |
| X | – | – | X | X | – | H | Faigley & Witte (1981) | – | – | – | – | – | Y | N/Y | – | – | – | Also looked at effect of computer prompt for revision |
| X | – | – | X | – | – | A | observation | X | – | – | – | Y | – | Y | Y | – | – | All post-tests handwritten |
| X | – | – | X | – | – | H | Faigley & Witte (1981) | – | X | – | – | – | – | N | Y | – | – | WP group made significantly more micro-structure revisions |
| X | X | – | X | X | – | H | Bridwell (1980) | – | – | – | – | – | Y | N | N | – | N | All 1st drafts handwritten |
| X | – | X | X | X | – | H | videotapes | – | – | – | – | – | – | N | Y | – | Y | Word processor was line editor, not screen editor |
| – | – | X | X | – | – | – | protocols | X | – | X | – | – | – | – | – | – | – | Looked at planning and rereading; less planning in computer condition |
| X | – | – | – | X | – | A | – | – | – | – | – | – | – | N/Y | – | – | Y | Highest quality writing produced at workstation with larger screen |
| X | – | X | X | – | – | A | Faigley & Witte (1981) | – | – | – | X | Y | – | N | N | – | – | Same students wrote 4 essays with and without computers |
| X | – | – | – | X | X | H&A | – | – | – | – | – | – | – | N | – | – | Y | Few differences between the 2 groups in kinds of thinking prized in college |
| – | X | – | – | X | X | – | – | X | X | – | – | Y | – | – | – | N | Y | Researcher tracked schemata students developed for using WP |
| X | – | – | X | X | – | H | Faigley & Witte (1981) | – | – | – | – | – | – | Y | N | – | Y | Experimental group wrote longer & better pieces in a revision-centered instructional environment with WP |
| X | – | – | X | – | – | A | checklist | X | X | – | X | Y | – | Y | – | – | Y | All female students |
| – | – | – | X | X | – | – | researcher's criteria | – | X | – | – | Y | Y | – | N | – | N | Use of spelling checker probably accounted for fewer errors of WP group |
| – | – | – | X | X | – | – | – | X | X | – | – | Y | Y | – | – | – | N | Students made and corrected more surface errors with WP |
| X | – | – | – | – | – | H | – | – | X | – | – | – | – | N | – | – | N | All first drafts handwritten |
| X | – | – | X | X | – | H | Faigley & Witte (1981) | X | X | – | – | Y | – | Y | Y | – | Y | Revision analysis focused on writing of 8 students |
| X | – | – | – | – | – | H | – | – | – | – | – | – | – | Y | – | – | – | A second writing sample supported initial results |
| X | – | X | X | – | – | H | • | X | X | – | X | Y | – | N | Y | – | – | Writing posttests were handwritten |
| X | – | X | X | – | – | H | Faigley & Witte (1981) | – | – | – | – | Y | – | Y | Y | – | – | Revision analysis focused on writing of 4 students |
| X | – | – | – | – | – | H | – | – | – | – | – | – | – | N | – | – | – | Significant positive correlation between typing speed and quality of writing |
| X | X | X | X | X | X | H | • | X | X | X | – | N/Y | Y | N | – | – | Y | Study focused on how students' cognitive ability affected use of WP |
| X | – | – | – | – | – | H&A | – | – | Y | – | – | – | – | N | – | – | – | Students in experimental group wrote at computer for 16 45–min. periods |

H=holistic   A=analytic

## Table 4.2 Case Studies and Ethnographies

| | Sample | Number | Duration: # Weeks | Word-Processing Package | Computer | Setting | Number of Instructors | Description of Instruction |
|---|---|---|---|---|---|---|---|---|
| | | DESIGN | | | TOOLS | | CONTEXT | |
| **CASE STUDIES** | | | | | | | | |
| Bessera (1986) | college basic writers | 6 | • | DEC type | mainframe | private room and computer lab | 1 | process oriented |
| Bridwell, Johnson & Brehe (1986) | published graduate students | 8 | 10 | WordStar | IBM | working at computers/lab | – | – |
| Bridwell, Sirc & Brooke (1985) | college students | 5 | 10 | WordStar | IBM | working at computers/lab | 1 | business writing class |
| Catano (1985) | novelists | 2 | 52 | Brown Univ. system | mainframe IBM | working at computers/lab | – | – |
| Collier (1982, 1983) | nursing students | 4 | 6 | AES | AES-C20 | classroom; also computer lab | 1 | • |
| Daiute (1984, 1985) | 12-year-olds | 8 | 5 | CATCH | Apple | • | • | • |
| Flinn (1985) | 6th graders | 8 | 36 | Milliken word processor | Apple | classroom with computers | 4 | National Writing Project classes |
| Harris (1985) | college students | 6 | • | • | • | writing center or microcomputer lab | • | • |
| Lutz (1983, 1987) | professional or experienced writers | 7 | – | MTS | mainframe | • | – | – |
| Nichols (1986) | college basic writers | 5 | 7–10 days | BSW 1982 | Apple | private room in library and computer lab | 1 | no composition instruction during study |
| Schipke (1986) | professional writers | 2 | 12 hrs over many months | Scripsit OASYS 64 | TRS 80 NB1 | home office | – | – |
| Selfe (1985) | college students | 8 | 16 | • | • | computer lab | – | – |
| **ETHNOGRAPHIES** | | | | | | | | |
| Curtiss (1984) | high school seniors | 53 | 18 | BSW 1982 AppleWriter | Apple | computer lab classroom | 1 | process oriented |
| Dickinson (1986) | 1st & 2nd graders | 21 | 32 | • | Apple | classroom with one computer | 1 | process oriented |
| Herrmann (1985, 1987) | high school students | 8 | 36 | BSW 1982 | Apple | classroom with computers | 1 | process oriented |
| Reid (1985) | 4th graders | a class | 28 | Milliken's Writing Workshop | Apple | classroom, hall, and lab | 1 | 2 days of writing per week |

Y=yes  N=no  N/Y=yes & no  •=information not given  X=examined  –=not a concern of study

Table 4.2, *Continued*

| | | | | | ANALYSIS | | | | | THEMES |
|---|---|---|---|---|---|---|---|---|---|---|
| Composed with Computers | Interview | Keystroke | Assessment | Survey | Revision | Protocols | Journals | Observation | Video/Audio Tapes | |
| Y | X | X | H | X | X | Retrospective | X | X | X | Students did not demonstrate increased prewriting with computers |
| Y/N | X | X | – | – | – | – | X | – | X | Researchers identified 3 kinds of writers whose adaptation to computer composing varied with their style. Writers produced longer texts for final draft |
| Y | X | X | – | X | Bridwell (1980) | X | – | – | X | Writer, computer, and task all interrelated in determining how WP will be used by individuals |
| Y | X | – | – | – | – | – | – | X | – | Writers reported that WP seemed to facilitate their collection of information and to stimulate creativity |
| N | X | – | X | – | Collier (1982) | X | – | – | X | Although students seemed to revise more frequently, they did not revise more successfully |
| Y | X | – | H | – | Faigley & Witte (1981) | – | – | X | – | After using CATCH, a WP program with revision prompts, most students revised more and corrected more errors, but few produced texts that were rated higher |
| Y | X | X | – | – | Bridwell (1980) | X | X | X | X | Children revised larger chunks of text at computers; pen and paper writers focused instead on surface features |
| N | X | – | – | – | Faigley & Witte (1981) | – | X | X | – | Fewer macrostructure changes were made with computers. It should be noted that 1st drafts not necessarily written on computer |
| Y | X | X | – | – | Faigley & Witte (1981) | – | – | X | X | Both professionals and experienced writers made many more revisions at computers |
| Y | X | – | – | – | X | X | – | – | – | Writers used the system to do more of the same of what they were doing without WP; longer texts with WP |
| Y | X | – | – | – | X | X | X | X | – | WP helped professional writers carry out their established practices and routines with greater efficiency |
| Y/N | – | – | – | X | – | X | – | X | X | Individuals' attitudes toward WP and the ease with which they could adapt their writing habits to computers determined how they used WP |
| Y/N | X | – | X | X | X | – | X | X | – | 51 of the 53 students came to value WP as a tool for creating quality writing |
| Y | X | – | – | – | – | – | X | X | X | Talk between students at computer more likely to focus on style and content than on production of acceptable handwritten text, a common concern for these students without computers |
| Y/N | X | – | – | – | X | – | X | X | X | Computers seemed to reinforce differences in both socioeconomic and academic standing that already existed among students |
| Y | X | – | – | X | – | – | – | X | X | Computer seemed to act as catalyst in transforming writing from a private to public activity |

hand and only revised at a computer. Harris's (1985) case study of college students is similar in that students could produce their first drafts in any fashion they pleased; they were required only to revise with word processing. Increasingly, however, studies in word processing seem to be moving away from exclusive emphasis on revision and instead examine how writers *compose* with computers, how they plan, generate, and evaluate text either on-screen or in some combination with hard copy.

This new emphasis on the interaction of computers with composing processes other than revision is especially true of an investigation (e.g., Haas, 1986) outside the instructional context, with writers who are experienced at word processing rather than novices who are learning a system. In fact, if we look at the earliest study among the 26—Gould's (1981) pioneering investigation of IBM researchers—and Haas's (1986) study of Carnegie-Mellon faculty and staff, we can trace the direction in which research in computers and writing seems to be moving and follow the rapid advancements which have been made in technology. The first part of Haas's study, which she conducted with Hayes (see Haas & Hayes, 1986b), is actually a replication of Gould's early study. The second part, however, departs from Gould's methods: whereas Gould in 1981 used videotapes to look at writers composing, planning, and rereading with a line editor and examined the variables of time, length, quality, and frequency of revision, Haas in 1986 used think-aloud protocols to examine how the processes of planning and rereading interact with composing at an advanced workstation with a large-screen monitor and mouse, as well as their interaction with a standard personal computer. Thus, as research in composition has refined methods borrowed from cognitive psychology, we see more and more of this same sort of analysis in studies of computers and composition.

The results from these quantitative studies are many and varied (refer to Table 4.1). Students seem to have positive attitudes toward writing and word processing after working with computers; students exhibit finished products that have fewer mechanical errors than those written with traditional tools; and many students write longer pieces with word processing than with traditional methods. We find conflicting results when we examine two variables: revision and quality. Slightly more studies found an increase in revision as found no increase in revision, and fewer studies found improvement in quality as found no improvement. These findings suggest that writers' predispositions as revisers or nonrevisers are more significant in predicting behavior than the influence of the machine and the ease with which writers revise with word processing. Quality of writing, similarly, does not seem to be tied to computer usage.

There is some indication that basic writers may profit more from a word-processing environment than other students. Of the 24 comparative studies that examined quality, 10 found improvement. (All these studies employed trained raters and presented inter-rater reliability coefficients or percentages of agreement.) Yet, of the eight dealing with basic or developmental writers, five reported improved writing with word processing in samples ranging from elementary (e.g., Burnett, 1984) to secondary school (e.g, Cirello, 1986; Dalton & Hannafin, 1987; Pivarnik, 1985) to college (e.g., King, Birnbaum, & Wageman, 1984). When I examined research directed at this group of writers in a 1986 review (Hawisher, 1986b), I found that all three studies of basic writers reported improvement in students' writing. At that time I suggested that further investigation was warranted with regard to the possible benefits a computers-and-writing curriculum might provide to students deficient in writing skills. By freeing basic writers from the laborious task of writing by hand, computers might be especially promising tools for low-achieving students.

To test this hypothesis, a colleague and I (see Hawisher & Fortune, 1988) conducted a study in which trained raters assessed essays produced with and without word processing by first-year college basic writers. Results from this study indicated that regardless of whether students wrote at computers or with pen-and-paper and regardless of whether they were male or female, improvement both in quality and in the kinds of thinking prized in the college setting was minimal. Although we continue to believe that the medium might well make a difference for some groups of writers, our investigation failed to advance this conclusion for first-year basic writers. Another study appearing since the review (e.g., Deming, 1987) also found no significant differences in the writing of this student population. Contradictory results are beginning to emerge with basic writers as they have earlier with other student populations.

Why some studies and not others found that unskilled writers made greater progress in writing with word processing than with conventional tools is perplexing. Two studies, one finding improvement in students' writing (i.e., Dalton & Hannafin, 1987) and another citing no improvement (i.e., Posey, 1986), required students in the experimental group to complete post-tests by hand rather than with word processing. These procedures seem especially demanding for students who have difficulty composing in the first place. To teach basic writers how to write with a new tool and then to deprive them of this tool when testing their writing is also likely to confuse results from the research. If we eliminate these studies from consideration and examine the three remaining that were directed at older students (i.e., King, Birnbaum & Wageman, 1984; Pivarnik, 1985; Cirello, 1986), we find that Pivarnik's and Cirello's investigations extended beyond one semester and that both reported writing improvement with word processing.

It may be that one semester is simply not long enough to encourage discernible growth in writing with computers, especially when dealing with word-processing novices. This last explanation, however, fails to account for the success of the ten female students in the semester study by King et al. (1984). It also doesn't seem to apply to those studies of competent students that reported increased success with word processing (e.g., Kaplan, 1986; Moore, 1987; Sommers, 1986), although one study citing improvement (i.e., Daiute, 1986) was conducted over an academic year. Investigations into computers and their influence on the quality of students' writing continue to yield conflicting results regardless of the population of interest.

## Case Studies

When we turn to the kinds of subjects examined in the case studies, differences appear in the targeted samples as well as in the focus of the research. Although some studies looked at elementary pupils, secondary school students, and college undergraduates, we find an additional emphasis on professional writers. In fact, four of the twelve investigations relying on case study methodology dealt with published writers. In these, as in those case studies examining the educational setting, the major research questions were the following:

How do writers adapt their strategies to computer writing?
Do writers' habits change with the technology?
How do writers regard writing with computers after working with
    them over a given period of time?

A general theme of these studies is similar to one drawn from the comparative studies; that is, a writer's or student's particular habits and strategies for composing seem to take precedence over the influence of the machinery. While most writers adapt easily to a computer and find word processing an asset to their writing, they bring their routines and patterns of writing with them. If they weren't extensive revisers before word processing, they probably will not become extensive revisers as a result of learning word processing even when revision strategies are part of the instruction. As Nichols (1986) pointed out in his case study of basic writers, "writers [use] the system mostly to do more of the same" of what they were doing with conventional methods (p. 90). Some don't even do more of the same. Although Bridwell, Sirc, and Brooke (1985) suggest that one of their subjects was interested in reformatting as a pen-and-paper composer and expanded this interest as a computer composer, two of the undergraduates they studied seemed to use the system to avoid revising; that is, they interacted with their first drafts less intensely, printing out clean copy with few changes as final drafts.

One of the more intriguing hypotheses generated by the case study research is Catano's (1985) suggestion that the two novelists he studied used the computer to collect information and create meaning in such a way that word processing seemed to foster synthesis of their ideas. If, indeed, word processing can be used to help *students* interact with their texts in ways that encourage higher order thinking skills, we need to find out how. Seldom, however, are we able to study students intensely for a full year, the length of time Catano observed the two novelists.

Several of the case studies reported here also analyzed writing products quantitatively (e.g., Bridwell, Johnson & Brehe, 1986; Bridwell, Sirc & Brooke, 1985; Collier, 1983; Daiute, 1984, 1985; Flinn, 1985; Harris, 1985; Lutz, 1983, 1987; Nichols, 1986; Schipke, 1986). In general, their findings are congruent with the results of the comparative studies; that is, texts tend to be longer with word processing and students' final products exhibit fewer mechanical errors. Again, when revision and quality are examined, the results are mixed. It should be noted, however, that far fewer of the qualitative studies tried to assess writing quality (e.g., Collier, 1983; Daiute, 1984, 1985; and Curtiss, 1984) and that, excepting Daiute's studies, the judging of the writing was informal, with no checks for reliability or rater agreement.

## Ethnographic Studies

If case studies can be considered careful, naturalistic examinations of individuals, then ethnographies are their counterpart for examining a culture. Context, which includes the social situation in which the activity of writing takes place and by which it is shaped, is integral to an ethnographic perspective. The ethnographies presented here all deal with the culture of the school and classroom. Two of the studies looked at how elementary school students interact with a computer in a classroom context, and the other two examined students and computers in a high school setting. Some of Dickinson's (1986) findings from a first- and second-grade combined class are provocative. While students did their paper-and-pencil writing silently and privately at their desks, writing at a computer seemed to create a collaborative social organization in which considerable talk related to the writing took place. Moreover, the conversation among students seemed to focus on content and style, whereas collaborate efforts with pencil and paper often became bogged down in talk over handwriting. These studies of young children who have not yet developed writing strategies with pencil and paper offer us a fresh perspective on how writers may use word processing when they are not trying to adapt old strategies to a new technology. Reid's (1985) ethnographic study of fourth graders also notes that computers seemed to transform writing from a private to public activity. This theme corresponds to Selfe and Wahlstrom's (1986) observations of the kinds of interactions that occurred among writers in a college computer writing lab. Herrmann's (1985) ethnographic study of high school students, on the other hand, indicated that the presence of computers exacerbated differences among the eight students she studied in both their socioeconomic standing and their academic standing. Can we find ways to reverse this potentially harmful influence by regarding it as a challenge rather than as a verdict? These ethnographies, then, in elucidating the subtle influences of computers in social interactions among students and teachers, suggest the importance of the cultural context in shaping writers' work with word processing. The success or failure of students' encounters with word processing and writing might well depend on the context into which computers are introduced.

## Some General Observations

Observations concerning both the quantitative and qualitative research reported here seem appropriate. When we look to the description of the context in which the research was conducted, there is often a decided lack of detail. Ironically, the quantitative studies seem to present a more complete description in this area, perhaps because the instructional context was often regarded as part of the treatment and, therefore, in keeping with the conventions of empirical research, discussed in detail. The qualitative studies present rich detail in researchers' descriptions of their naturalistic observations and interviews but often fail to describe adequately the full environment and social milieu by which the activity of writing might well have been shaped.

Another flaw of several of the studies is their failure to include and describe the word-processing package. Only three of the studies omitted the specific computer and word-processing software, but the majority did not report the capabilities and idiosyncratic workings of the software. For example, the early *Bank Street Writer* (1982) forces writers to leave an insert mode in order to edit, certainly a maneuver which is antithetical to a recursive writing process. *Wordstar* uses an abundance of control characters to perform operations, decidedly differing from other programs with their greater reliance on function keys. Some programs facilitate the moving of text by allowing writers to highlight the targeted segment and reinsert it somewhere else very quickly; other programs make this block movement of text tedious and cumbersome. My point is that different programs might well facilitate some writing strategies to the exclusion of others, but we can't infer this without a description of the features of the word-processing package.

A final general comment has to do with whether writers are composing at a computer or entering prewritten text. A great many more of the studies in this review seem to be focusing on writers' composing at computers than in the past. Most would agree that to use a word processor as merely a transcription tool limits its capacity to influence composing processes. Moreover, composing at computers has come to mean a combination of hard-copy and screen-related activities. Bridwell, Sirc, and Brooke (1985), for example, in their case studies of undergraduates define computer composing as "whatever [the writers] did while they were working with the word-processing systems, even though several of them continued to use paper for planning and some drafting" (p. 179). Some researchers (e.g., Lutz, 1983, 1987)—mistakenly, I think—took pains to limit or prevent writers from printing out drafts during composing sessions, thinking that hard copy was the province of pen-and-paper composing rather than computer composing. The longer we as writers and researchers work with computers, however, the more we realize that the screen often leads to reading difficulties and that intermittent printings of a draft allow us to compensate for having "screens-full" rather than "pages-full" of text (see Chapters 1 and 2 of this volume; Haas & Hayes, 1986a).

## RECOMMENDATIONS

The foregoing review and discussion leads to a consideration of future directions of research to add to our accumulative knowledge in computers and composition. I would like to make several recommendations as to how we might approach research projects and whom we might study, and speculate on different contexts for this research. I then discuss the computer as a research tool.

### Research Approaches

Build upon previous research. Qualitative studies often provide rich description, revealing patterns and themes that can then be studied through quantitative methods. This is normally the way in which some perceive qualitative and quantitative research as intersecting. Seldom, however, do we see this relationship in research practice with computers and composition. For example, in their case studies of experienced writers, Bridwell, Johnson, and Brehe (1986) observed writers devoting more time to pausing and planning than had been reported in other studies for writing in general. This prewriting or planning often took the form of writers pausing or jotting notes to themselves while they were writing at computers. These notes were sometimes metacomments, suggesting directions for organization and bearing scant resemblance to the final written products. Certainly, the way writers adapt this planning and note-jotting to computer writing bears further investigation. One wonders, for example, if these organizational promptings differ when writers compose at computers compared with conventional methods.

As mentioned earlier, Christina Haas (1986) has begun to examine this phenomenon of planning on computers with the experienced writers she studied. Although Haas's experiment is small in scale and more of an attempt to replicate Gould's (1981) study than to experiment with some of the insights gleaned from an earlier qualitative study, it illustrates, I think, a pattern that could be followed as we establish our field of research. Studies should build upon one another. As we conduct our research, we must be aware of what has gone before us and how new research can confirm or contradict but, nevertheless, extend our emerging knowledge base.

Let us consider how to extend our investigations. In the two studies discussed above, Bridwell and her colleagues (1986) looked at planning as it manifests itself in written notes and pauses at the machine, whereas Haas (1986) concentrated on how this planning manifests itself in verbal protocols. Another investigation might examine how experienced word-processing writers use the bottom of their screens, or splitscreens that contain two or more files, or the special note options of some word processors—or, for that matter, hard copy for their interspersed planning. (See Chapter 2 of this volume for a discussion of how some writers use hard copy.) If experienced writers can indeed use these features effectively, then perhaps we want to introduce these methods to students in instructional settings to examine how they integrate note-taking with computer composing. Some note-taking strategies might help students move back and forth between the conventions of standard printed text and the virtual text of a computer (see Chapter 1 of this volume).

Design a series of studies.   In writing of composition research in general, Hillocks (1986) discusses the need for a series of studies to examine a range of variables. Citing the work of Carl Bereiter, Marlene Scardamalia, and their colleagues at the Ontario Institute for Studies in Education (OISE) and Linda Flower, John Hayes, and their colleagues at Carnegie-Mellon University (CMU), Hillocks suggests that these researchers are noteworthy for their systematic research agendas. Both OISE and CMU have contributed important studies for computers and composition as well. (Refer to Haas, 1986; Haas & Hayes, 1986a; Woodruff et al., 1986, in Table 4.1.) Lillian Bridwell, Donald Ross, and their colleagues at the University of Minnesota have also been active in carrying out such research with word processing. (Refer to Bridwell, Johnson, & Brehe, 1986; Bridwell, Sirc, & Brooke, 1985, in Table 4.2.) More recently at CMU, Christine Neuwirth, Christina Haas, and John Hayes have mapped out a series of seven studies with computers, as part of a funded grant from the Fund for the Improvement of Postsecondary Education (FIPSE). The proposed studies (Neuwirth, Haas, & Hayes, 1986) systematically explore three elements of the writing process: planning, revising, and reviewing. They are noteworthy in that each is prefaced with such statements as "If Study 1.1 obtains the expected results . . . we will then conduct Study 1.2" (p. 10). In this way, each of the studies builds upon the previous ones and, when completed, should prove valuable to the field of computers and composition. As Hillocks (1986) suggests, more researchers need to engage in a systematic series of studies designed to add to an emerging knowledge base.

Use a longitudinal approach.   A definite need also exists for longitudinal studies with writers and word processing. When one scans the research presented in Tables 4.1 and 4.2, it becomes apparent that the majority of studies took place over a relatively short duration of time. The longest study lasted for one full year (i.e., Catano, 1985), and several were conducted over an academic year (e.g., Daiute, 1986; Dickinson, 1986; Duling, 1985; Flinn, 1985; Herrmann, 1985; Levin et al., 1985; Pivarnik, 1985). But some were carried out over exceedingly short periods of time (e.g., Collier, 1983; Daiute, 1984, 1985; Miller, 1984; Nichols, 1986; Woodruff et al., 1986; Woolley, 1985) ranging from one to six weeks. One (i.e., Harris, 1985) didn't report the duration of the study. Since most of these investigations were also concerned with how the computer interacted with the writing processes of inexperienced computer-users, one wonders how much of the influence of word processing was captured over these short periods. New research might be directed, instead, to examining inexperienced users of word processors over their four-year period in college. This sort of longitudinal approach might suggest emerging patterns of composing that we have as yet not observed.

## Research Population

Focus on experienced student-users of word processors.  Up to now most of our research with students has focused on inexperienced users of word processors out of necessity; few students worked extensively with word processing prior to their experience in our classes. This situation is changing. At Illinois State University, for example, where all first-year students are taught their required writing course at computers, advanced writing classes are often comprised of students who have composed with computers for three years or more. This new group of student computer composers bears investigation.

Focus on experienced writers who are proficient at word processing.  Another recommendation is to do more studies of experienced writers who use word processing all the time for their composing. Several years ago few writers could perhaps be so categorized, but today we have burgeoning numbers of computer composers. Schipke (1986), in her research of a free-lance science writer and a speech writer, adds considerably to Catano's (1985) study of experienced writers who are unskilled in word processing. Schipke notes that the ways these experienced writers used word processing varied considerably with the knowledge they possessed over their topic. Additional studies might shed light on whether word processing does indeed contribute to stimulating creative thought, as the professional writers in Catano's (1985) study suggest.

## Research Contexts

Interaction of computers and classroom activities.  For the instructional context, we need to examine how computers interact with the activities of the classroom. Preliminary evidence (Selfe & Wahlstrom, 1986; Dickinson, 1986) suggests that computers foster collaboration among writers, transforming the process of writing from a private to a public act (Reid, 1985) for both young students and adults. These initial studies have been surveys or qualitative investigations. Another way of approaching this question might be to compare classroom activities that occur in process-centered, computer-equipped classrooms with activities in process-centered, conventional classrooms. During classroom observations, researchers would code activities, using similar categories as those outlined by Applebee (1981) in his description of writing in secondary schools. Applebee (1981) lists writing without composing, and informational, personal, and imaginative uses of writing as types of writing activities that might occur in a classroom. Added to this list might be other precisely defined categories to describe the amount of time each class period devotes to teacher presentation, student presentation, group work (with and without computers), and writing (with and without computers). These data would then be analyzed to determine similarities and differences in several composition classes taught with and without computers. The types of work assigned outside of class would also be examined. Such an approach would allow us to assess the kinds of collaboration that occur among students and teachers, as well as to determine the types of learning activities that instructors tend to rely on in computer-assisted and conventional writing classes.

Introduction of computers into English curricula.  Little research has been completed that examines how computers interact with the departmental English program or the larger school curriculum as a whole. In other words, one might hypothesize that when computers are introduced into writing classes, the entire school is affected, regardless of whether the change is at the elementary, secondary, or college level. During writing-across-the-curriculum workshops at Illinois State for faculty from throughout the university, one question arises frequently: "Now that all students prepare in their composition classes on computers, can we expect them to write and revise their work for us with word processing?'' Thus teachers in other classes not only begin to request students to complete class work with computers but also expect them to revise assignments readily. Teachers believe they can set higher standards than previously and have them met by students. Although these particular attitudinal changes are all to the good, no systematic research of which I am aware has investigated such phenomena.

Other changes occur as well. With the introduction of computers comes the need to prepare teachers to work with new technology through workshops and in-service opportunities. Social structures within schools begin to change, with those teachers who ''know'' technology receiving perhaps more admiration or, sometimes, a heavier workload. In addition, teachers themselves can prepare materials faster with computers and modify them easily from year to year. In other words, the introduction of computers into English curricula is a contextual change that encourages and brings about alterations in the political, social, and educational structures of an entire system. Research that attempts to identify the influences of computers on an English department or an entire school is sorely needed.

## The Computer as a Research Tool

The advantages of using the computer as a research tool have been noted elsewhere (Bridwell, Johnson, & Brehe, 1986). For the first time we have a tool with an enormous memory for recording writers' generating and revising of text. Using public-domain macro software at Illinois State University, we have developed a keystroke-monitoring program that captures all keystrokes writers make in a given session, thus providing a record of their composing and revising. Lutz (1983, 1987) and Flinn (1985) also report using keystroke-capturing programs for their research. A sophisticated program developed by the University of Minnesota team seems especially promising. In addition to capturing keystrokes, it offers a built-in record of the time writers spend in composing as well as in pausing. It also allows for a playback of text that researchers can then use for retrospective protocols; that is, writers describe what they were thinking as their text scrolls before them at the same rate of speed with which they produced it. (See Bridwell, Nancarrow, & Ross, 1984, for a more complete description of the program.) Given the advantages of such records, it is surprising that we don't see more research conducted with these programs.

One of the problems, I believe, is that while keystroke programs enable computers to collect enormous amounts of data, these data must still be analyzed by human beings. One paragraph with all its revisions often yields a full page or more of data, and these data increase exponentially with several drafts of a paper. Thus a three-page, double-spaced draft might well yield ten pages of data, which then must be compared with the writer's actual text to understand what was generated and revised. The keystroke printout alone is unde-cipherable in terms of seeing change in relation to the writer's text. Thus, although we now have the technology to help with in-process revision data collection, we still lack an expedient tool to aid in analysis.

More time and energy should be spent in developing programs that are easily decipherable by trained text analysts. We envision a program that prints the real text in one column with the changes in a second column, at least allowing a ready scanning and comparison of keystroke printout and text. The computer could also be programmed to record changes that involve larger segments of text along with appropriate function keys, rather than concentrating on individual keystrokes. We have learned through our research that although writ-ers seem to make more typographical errors initially (Bridwell, Sirc, & Brooke, 1985), they quickly correct them, and final texts tend to exhibit fewer surface errors with word processing (Daiute, 1986; Dul-ing, 1985; Levin et al., 1985; Woodruff et al., 1986). Therefore, we might concentrate on developing programs that focus on chunks of text, since in good writers' writing, larger revised segments often contain meaningful changes (Faigley & Witte, 1981).

Although the development of additional research programs re-quires careful planning between researchers and programmers, the time devoted to this endeavor would be well spent in facilitating re-search efforts. Ideally, of course, it would be helpful if technology could also be enlisted to analyze some of the changes, but this eventu-ality seems distant in terms of the computer's current capability to process natural language. In any event, we need to develop computers as research tools. We have only begun to tap the potential of technolo-gy and its possible contribution to research.

## CONCLUSION

What have we learned from our research of the past several years? Is it, as Papert (1987) suggests of computer research in general, tech-nocentric? Perhaps, but we are also slowly but surely building a re-search base that relies less on a technocentric perspective than on a view informed by the interaction of technology with the culture in which it exists. Even though a review of the titles of some of the more recent studies reveals a technocentric emphasis, the quantitative studies, as well as the qualitative, often consider context. Moreover, several of the studies, such as that by Woodruff et al. (1986), are asking complex questions such as how does cognitive development in students interact with and affect their use with computers. Notice the emphasis here is on *students* rather than on *computers.* It is worth remembering, I think, that most of the studies cited here were begun an average of three or more years ago. None of these studies, for example, looked at writers interacting with the Macintosh with its icon system and highly developed graphic capabilities.

When I reviewed 24 studies in computers and writing in 1986 (see Hawisher, 1986b), few of the patterns noted here were evident. Instead the results seemed to be confusing and contradictory—as they still are to a great extent today. But in the past couple of years there has been a coming together of findings that begin to form a research base; students appear to write longer texts that demonstrate fewer mechanical errors at computers, and they exhibit positive attitudes toward writing with computers. These positive attitudes toward computer composing, moreover, tend to contribute to a spirit of cooperation rather than competitiveness within a classroom. This resulting change in social interactions among students and instructors might be capable of creating an improved classroom culture, if we can act upon it.

Kuhn (1970), whom both Kinneavy (1980) and Hairston (1982) cited in describing the preparadigm stage of rhetoric and composition, also has something to say that applies to our research in computers and composition. Kuhn notes that when a field is establishing itself, its research is inconclusive and that the same ground is covered repeatedly. Studies in word processing and writing are only now emerging from this preparadigm stage of development. It will be interesting to see how we pursue our research in computers and composition during the next several years. As Papert (1987) has suggested for computer research and as Purves and Purves (1986) have argued in discussing the study of writing in general, we must give culture—along with technology—its due.

### Acknowledgment

I would like to thank James Raths, University of Vermont, for calling my attention to many of the studies reported here and for his invaluable assistance in reading drafts of this chapter.

# REFERENCES

Applebee, A. N. (1981). *Writing in the secondary school: English and the content areas.* Urbana, IL: National Council of Teachers of English.

Beesley, S. M. (1986). The effects of word processing on elementary students' written compositions: Processes, products, and attitudes. (Doctoral dissertation, Indiana University, 1986). *Dissertation Abstracts International, 47,* 4006A.

Beserra, W. C. (1986). Effects of word processing upon the writing processes of basic writers. (Doctoral dissertation, New Mexico State University, 1986). *Dissertation Abstracts International, 48,* 34A.

Bridwell, L. S. (1980). Revising strategies in twelfth grade students' transactional writing. *Research in the Teaching of English, 14,* 197–222.

Bridwell, L. S., Nancarrow, P. R., & Ross, D. (1984). The writing process and the writing machine: Current research on word processors relevant to the teaching of composition. In R. Beach & L. S. Bridwell (Eds.), *New directions in composition research* (pp. 381–398). New York: Guilford.

Bridwell, L. S., Johnson, P., & Brehe, S. (1986). Composing and computers: Case studies of experienced writers. In A. Matsuhashi (Ed.), *Writing in real time: Modelling production processes* (pp. 81–107). Norwood, NJ: Ablex.

Bridwell, L. S., Sirc, G., & Brooke, R. (1985). Revising and computing: Case studies of student writers. In S. Freedman (Ed.), *The acquisition of written language: Revision and response.* Norwood, NJ: Ablex.

Burnett, J. H. (1984). Word processing as a writing tool of an elementary school student (a single-case experiment with nine replications). (Doctoral dissertation, University of Maryland, 1984). *Dissertation Abstracts International, 47,* 1183A.

Catano, J. (1985). Computer-based writing: Navigating the fluid text. *College Composition and Communication, 36,* 309–316.

Cirello, V. J. (1986). The effect of word processing on the writing abilities of tenth grade remedial writing students. (Doctoral dissertation, New York University, 1986). *Dissertation Abstracts International, 47,* 2531A.

Collier, R. M. (1982). *The influence of computer-based text editors on the revision strategies of inexperienced writers.* (ERIC Document Reproduction Service No. ED 266 719)

Collier, R. M. (1983). The word processor and revision strategies. *College Composition and Communication, 35,* 149–155.

Corbett, E. P. J. (1984). Foreword. In J. W. Halpern & S. Liggett (Eds.), *Computers and composing: How the new technologies are changing writing.* Carbondale, IL: Southern Illinois University Press.

Coulter, C. A. (1986). Writing with word processors: Effects on cognitive development, revision and writing quality. (Doctoral dissertation, University of Oklahoma, 1986). *Dissertation Abstracts International, 47,* 2551A.

Curtiss, D. H. (1984). The experience of composition and word processing:

An ethnographic, phenomenological study of high school seniors. (Doctoral dissertation, Boston University, 1984). *Dissertation Abstracts International, 45,* 1021A.

Daiute, C. (1984). Can the computer stimulate writers' inner dialogues? In W. Wresch (Ed.), *The computer in composition instruction* (pp. 131–139). Urbana, IL: National Council of Teachers of English.

Daiute, C. (1985). Do writers talk to themselves? In S. Freedman (Ed.), *The acquisition of written language: Revision and response* (pp. 133–159). Norwood, NJ: Ablex.

Daiute, C. (1986). Physical and cognitive factors in revising: Insights from studies with computers. *Research in the Teaching of English, 20,* 141–159.

Dalton, D. W., & Hannafin, M. J. (1987). The effects of word processing on written composition. *Journal of Educational Research, 80,* 338–342.

Deming, M. P. (1987). The effects of word processing on basic college writers' revision strategies, writing apprehension, and writing quality while composing in the expository mode. (Doctoral dissertation, Georgia State University, 1987). *Dissertation Abstracts International, 48,* 2263A.

Dickinson, D. K. (1986). Cooperation, collaboration, and a computer: Integrating a computer into a first-second grade writing program. *Research in the Teaching of English, 20,* 141–159.

Duling, R. A. (1985). Word processors and student writing: A study of their impact on revision, fluency, and quality of writing. (Doctoral dissertation, Michigan State University, 1985). *Dissertation Abstracts International, 46,* 3535A.

Faigley, L., & Witte, S. (1981). Analyzing revision. *College Composition and Communication, 32,* 400–414.

Flinn, J. Z. (1985). Composing, computers, and contexts: Case studies of revision among sixth graders in national writing project classrooms. (Doctoral dissertation, University of Missouri-St. Louis, 1985). *Dissertation Abstracts International, 46,* 3636A.

Gould, J. D. (1981). Composing letters with computer-based text editors. *Human Factors, 23,* 593–606.

Haas, C. (1986, May). *Computers and the writing process: A comparative protocol study.* Paper presented at the 1986 Conference on Computers and Writing, Pittsburgh, PA.

Haas, C., & Hayes, J. R. (1986a). What did I just say? Reading problems in writing with the machine. *Research in the Teaching of English, 20* (1), 22–35.

Haas, C., & Hayes, J. R. (1986b). *Pen and paper vs. the machine: Writers composing in hard copy and computer conditions.* Pittsburgh, PA: Carnegie-Mellon Technical Report No. 16.

Hairston, M. (1982). The winds of change: Thomas Kuhn and the revolution in the teaching of writing. *College Composition and Communication, 33,* 76–88.

Harris, J. (1985). Student writers and word processing: A preliminary evaluation. *College Composition and Communication, 36,* 323–330.

Hawisher, G. E. (1986a). The effects of word processing on the revision strategies of college students. (Doctoral dissertation, University of Illinois, 1985). *Dissertation Abstracts International, 47,* 876A.

Hawisher, G. E. (1986b). Studies in word processing. *Computers and Composition, 4,* 6–31.

Hawisher, G. E. (1987). The effects of word processing on the revision strategies of college freshmen. *Research in the Teaching of English, 21,* 145–159.

Hawisher, G. E. (1988). Research update: Writing and word processing. *Computers and Composition, 5,* 7–23.

Hawisher, G. E., & Fortune, R. (1988, April). *Research into word processing and the basic writer.* Paper presented at the annual meeting of the American Educational Research Association, New Orleans, LA.

Herrmann, A. (1985). Using the computer as a writing tool: Ethnography of a high school writing class. (Doctoral dissertation, Teachers College, Columbia University, 1985). *Dissertation Abstracts International, 47,* 02A. (University Microfilms No. DA8602051)

Herrmann, A. (1987). An ethnographic study of a high school writing class using computers: Marginal, technically proficient, and productive learners. In L. Gerrard (Ed.), *Writing at century's end: Essays on computer-assisted composition* (pp. 79–91). New York: Random House.

Hillocks, G., Jr. (1986). *Research on written composition: New directions for teaching.* Urbana, IL: National Council of Teachers of English.

Juettner, V. W. (1987). The word processing environment and its impact on the writing of a group of high school students. (Doctoral dissertation, The University of Arizona, 1987). *Dissertation Abstracts International, 48,* 635A.

Kaplan, H. (1986). Computers and composition: Improving students' written performance. (Doctoral dissertation, University of Massachusetts, 1986). *Dissertation Abstracts International, 47,* 776A.

King, B., Birnbaum, J., & Wageman, J. (1984). Word processing and the basic college writer. In T. Martinez (Ed.), *The written word and the word processor* (pp. 251–266). Philadelphia, PA: Delaware Valley Writing Council.

Kinneavy, J. L. (1980). *A theory of discourse* (2nd ed.). Englewood Cliffs, NJ: Prentice-Hall.

Kuhn, T. (1970). *The structure of scientific revolutions* (2nd ed.). Chicago: University of Chicago Press.

Kurth, R. (1987). Using word processing to enhance revision strategies during student writing activities. *Educational Technology, 27,* 13–19.

Levin, J., Riel, M., Rowe, M., & Boruta, M. (1985). Muktuk meets jacuzzi: Computer networks and elementary school writers. In S. Freedman (Ed.), *The acquisition of written language: Response and revision* (pp. 160–171). Norwood, NJ: Ablex.

Lutz, J. A. (1983). A study of professional and experienced writers revising and editing at the computer and with pen and paper. (Doctoral dissertation, Rensselaer Polytechnic Institute, 1983). *Dissertation Abstracts International, 44,* 2755A.

Lutz, J. A. (1987). A study of professional and experienced writers revising and editing at the computer and with pen and paper. *Research in the Teaching of English, 21,* 398–421.

Miller, S. K. (1984). Plugging your pencil into the wall: An investigation of word processing and writing skills at the middle school level. (Doctoral dissertation, University of Oregon, 1984). *Dissertation Abstracts International, 45,* 3535A.

Moore, M. A. (1987). The effect of word processing technology in a developmental writing program on writing quality, attitude towards composing, and revision strategies of fourth and fifth grade students. (Doctoral dissertation, University of South Florida, 1987). *Dissertation Abstracts International, 48,* 635A.

Nichols, R. (1986). Word processing and basic writers. *Journal of Basic Writing, 5,* 81–97.

Neuwirth, C., Haas, C., & Hayes, J. R. (1986). *Does word processing improve students' writing? A critical appraisal and proposed assessment.* Unpublished manuscript. Carnegie-Mellon University, Pittsburgh, PA.

Papert, S. (1981). Society will balk, but the future may demand a computer for each child. In G. Hass (Ed.), *Curriculum planning: A new approach* (4th ed., pp. 99–101). Boston: Allyn and Bacon.

Papert, S. (1987). Computer criticism vs. technocentric thinking. *Educational Researcher, 16,* 22–30.

Pivarnik, B., (1985). The effect of training in word processing on the writing quality of eleventh grade students. (Doctoral dissertation, University of Connecticut, 1985). *Dissertation Abstracts International, 46,* 1827A.

Posey, E. J. (1986). The writer's tool: A study of microcomputer word processing to improve the writing of basic writers. (Doctoral dissertation, New Mexico State University, 1986). *Dissertation Abstracts International, 48,* 39A.

Purves, A. C., & Purves, W. C. (1986). Viewpoints: Cultures, text models, and the activity of writing. *Research in the Teaching of English, 20,* 174–197.

Reid, T. R. (1985). Writing with microcomputers in a fourth grade classroom: An ethnographic study. (Doctoral dissertation, Washington State University, 1985). *Dissertation Abstracts International, 47,* 817A.

Schipke, R. C. (1986). Writers and word processing technology: Case studies of professionals at work. (Doctoral dissertation, University of Pennsylvania, 1986). *Dissertation Abstracts International, 47,* 1226A.

Selfe, C. (1985). The electronic pen: Computers and the composing process. In J. Collins & E. Sommers (Eds.), *Writing on-line: Using computers in the teaching of writing* (pp. 55–66). Upper Montclair, NJ: Boynton/Cook.

Selfe, C. L., & Wahlstrom, B. J. (1986). An emerging rhetoric of collaboration: Computers, collaboration, and the composing process. *Collegiate Microcomputer, 4,* 289–296.

Sommers, E. (1986). The effects of word processing and writing instruction on the writing processes and products of college writers. (Doctoral dissertation, State University of New York at Buffalo). *Dissertation Abstracts International, 47,* 2064A.

Wetzel, K. A. (1985). The effect of using the computer in a process writing program on the writing quality of third, fourth, and fifth grade pupils. (Doctoral dissertation, University of Oregon). *Dissertation Abstracts International, 47,* 76A.

Woodruff, E., Lindsay, P., Bryson, M., & Joram, E. (1986, April). *Some cognitive effects of word processors on enriched and average 8th grade writers.* Paper presented at the annual meeting of the American Educational Research Association, San Francisco, CA.

Woolley, W. C. (1985). The effects of word processing on the writing of selected fifth-grade students. (Doctoral dissertation, The College of William and Mary, 1985). *Dissertation Abstracts International, 47,* 82A.

# Part II

# CURRENT PROBLEMS: PRACTICE AND POLITICS

During the past decade, as computers have become increasingly central to the teaching of English, we have identified a number of advantages to technological support. Computers have, for example, given us new ways to work effectively with nontraditional writers, to invite people in geographically isolated areas into our classrooms and academic conversations, and to foster productive collaboration among our students. Technology has, in these ways, encouraged new vigor and fresh perspectives in the teaching of writing.

Unfortunately, the rapid growth of the use of computers in our profession has had concomitant disadvantages. If the most reluctant among us now accept that technology has had an impact on those activities we traditionally associate with literacy, not even the most enthusiastic of us claim to know the entire scope or shape of that impact. Moreover, in our rush to buy equipment, establish computer-supported writing labs and classrooms, and teach computer-supported writing classes, we have had insufficient time as a profession for sharing problems related to computer hardware and software, for exchanging pedagogical experiences, and for considering the political impact computers have on English programs and the schools in which they exist.

In this second part we provide a forum for such exchanges and identify problems that currently characterize our efforts. The part begins with two practical examinations of the computer's use as a writing tool. In Chapter 5, John Thiesmeyer asks a crucial question: Given our experiences with computers, can we claim to have writing software that helps people become more efficient or effective writers? The answer, he argues, is no. Because programmers tend to create software that capitalizes on what computers do easily (e.g., pattern-matching, counting) and because this software often prods writers with prescriptive and sometimes ill-advised instructions (e.g., "replace *construct* with *build* in the phrase 'theoretical construct'"), text analyzers, along with other forms of computer-assisted writing aids, often confuse rather than help writers. Thiesmeyer's chapter provides a critical and comprehensive overview of the strengths and weaknesses of available computer-based writing tools for writers.

In Chapter 6, Lisa Gerrard is more optimistic in discussing the potential of computers and computer-based writing software in helping students—specifically, basic writers—develop their writing abilities. Gerrard argues that the structured environment of computer invention and revision programs can provide basic writers with a framework that frees them to express difficult and sometimes sophisticated ideas. Although she is aware of the inherent shortcomings in both invention and text analysis software, she points to the many positive behaviors that computers encourage in basic writers when combined with a good instructor's guidance. This guidance is the key for Gerrard: Just as Collins argued in Chapter 3 that instructional software should consist of tools to facilitate composition teaching, Gerrard calls for instructor intervention in basic writers' work with computers. Without a competent teacher, she warns, computers can result in unsatisfactory learning for unskilled writers.

The preparation of competent teachers to work with computers and writing in secondary schools is explored in Chapter 7. Turning to political issues, Andrea Herrmann discusses the problems of introducing computers into writing curricula, English programs, and the secondary school itself. Currently, she contends, the power structure of many schools prevents adequate preparation of teachers and the effective integration of word processing and other writing software into English programs. She argues that efforts to integrate computers and writing into school systems will succeed only when there is cooperation and collaboration among teachers and administrators, as well as among teachers and students.

Continuing with the topic of changing traditional political structures to cope with nontraditional technology, Deborah Holdstein, in Chapter 8, examines the college setting and the current state of instructor-training programs. Noting that the emphasis and time devoted to such programs is in keeping with English departments' historically reluctant involvement with first-year writing curricula, she outlines an approach that stresses ongoing faculty colloquia as a support system for instructors involved with computers. Adequate training for computers and composition instructors, Holdstein maintains, goes a long way in ensuring the effective assimilation of technology into English departments at the college level.

A common thread running through the chapters in this section is their focus on problems that exist today and that must be addressed if technology is to work for teachers and for students. In examining the inadequacies of current efforts in computers and composition, each author offers practical advice in overcoming obstacles to success.

# 5

# Should We Do What We Can?

John Thiesmeyer

A thoughtful look at recent articles, reviews, and advertisements, in both academic journals and popular computer periodicals, tells us that not much is happening these days in developing new ways to use computers in writing. (*College Composition and Communication, College English, Communications of the ACM, Computers and the Humanities, InfoWorld, Research in the Teaching of English, SCOPE,* and *T.H.E. Journal* are some of the journals I consult—a representative though not exhaustive list.) From word processors to spelling and usage checkers, from prewriters to statistical analyzers to crude sentence parsers, essentially all the computer-assisted writing aids we are currently using were invented a decade or more ago. Differing versions of these programs continue to appear, of course, but new wrinkles far outnumber new conceptions.

I am not complaining about this state of affairs; it seems normal and appropriate. When the ability to program computers became widespread, people thought about composition (among other things) and wrote software to carry out all the compositional and editorial tasks they could easily define in programming terms. Though some of the programs (like word processors) have become elaborate and powerful, and others (like spelling checkers) are of evident utility, the variety of tasks both immediately definable and programmable turned out not to be large. *Tant pis, tant mieux.* We entered a consolidation phase several years ago, of testing, using, cloning, and modifying the tools we have. And now, after the exciting years when these tools first emerged, and the subsequent period of their testing and refinement, can we confidently claim to have worthwhile computer aids to writing?

Despite the years of work, despite the many favorable reports on electronically aided composition, I believe it is premature to make such a claim. Computer-assisted writing has yet to face squarely some of its most serious problems: problems in composition theory, in software design, and in program evaluation. In this chapter, I show why the use of much software to aid writers remains problematic, its promise as yet unrealized. Though my tone may be critical, my intentions are constructive, and I offer in conclusion some reasons for continuing our computer-assisted-writing experiments. Even without harder evidence of their efficacy, there are ways that computers can be used responsibly to help writers think about and improve their work.

I will focus on software that attempts to improve writing directly, through intervention in the writing process at various stages. Programs whose primary purpose is instructional, like drill-and-practice exercises, are excluded. As an English teacher, however, I cannot resist occasionally questioning or remarking on a program's potential for improving not only the writing but the writer. If computer-assisted writing tools have no salutary effects, even indirectly, on their users, then in the long run they will contribute to the decline rather than the improvement of writing.

## THE PROGRAMMER'S JOYRIDE

There is a kind of Murphy's Law of Programming which says that if it can be coded, it should be. Programmers (I speak as a participant-observer) often feel an irresistible desire to add yet another whistle or bell to their software, creating new features because they are easy, or obvious, or merely possible to program.

Joyriding is an impulse of one's programming adolescence, regardless of chronological age. Its manifestations can be merely superficial or silly. One is tempted, for example, to make one's first applications not only interactive but effusive. "Great, Sally, you're really on a roll!" says the software. But this is not user-friendliness, it is merely personification of the computer, and the adolescent programmer has failed to realize that such repetitious effusions quickly cloy. To make computer programs linguistically responsive in a nontrivial way will require solutions to the most difficult problems in artificial-intelligence research (Thiesmeyer, 1987).

Typically, the joyriding impulse generates cluttered screens or unnecessary special effects. But the same impulse can have subtler, more pervasive and troubling consequences in programs aiming to be helpful to writers. As in the following cases, it may defy some of our theoretical intuitions and bypass what we know about writing and learning.

## Spelling Checkers

One kind of joyride is exemplified in the evolution of a type of writer's aid whose general usefulness can hardly be doubted: the spelling checker. Early spelling programs were content to mark each dubious orthography, leaving it to the writer to investigate and correct if necessary. The joyride began when programmers realized they could offer, out of the program's stored lexicon, a menu of alternative spellings phonetically or anagrammatically similar to the one in question; the user need only touch a key to choose a new version of the word. Possibly it would be the one intended. Some programs even record such choices so the writer can be told, based on past decisions, which alternative is most likely. Today there are not only programs that run concurrently with word processors, to blink or beep misspellings as soon as they are made (see, e.g., Mace, 1986), and phonetic "spelling corrector" software developed by Henry Kucera (see *English Spelling Corrector*, 1985, in the Guide to Programs) of Brown University in conjunction with linguists at Houghton Mifflin, but even a hardware device to intercept and decry misspellings as they are typed on a keyboard, before they reach the computer (Bermant, 1986). The logical next step, surely not far off, is to have the spelling program make corrections silently and automatically, using probabilities derived from individual habit, phonetics, and statistical analysis.

In such cases, programmers have not thought through the problem. Functions beyond bringing misspellings to the writer's attention may be supererogatory or counterproductive. Although poor typists may be helped by programs that allow one-keystroke correction of obvious mistakes, poor spellers can scarcely be expected to make consistently correct choices from lists of variants. Even when the correct alternative is obvious (*separate* for *seperate,* for example), one-key substitution plays to the writer's weakness—inhibiting both the slow growth of spelling competence and any benefits in precision to be gained from incidental exposure to dictionary definitions (for a contrasting view, see Holdstein, 1987, p. 23). Good spellers scarcely need the lists and often prefer to check questioned items for themselves. I suspect that few writers at any level will appreciate the distraction of checkers giving immediate, insistent feedback as they compose. The coming generation of silent electronic emenders not only will beg some important educational questions (should Joanie bother to learn spelling?) but may also contribute in subtle ways to the contin-

uing decline of Johnny's reading. (See Thiesmeyer, 1984, for additional remarks on the design of spelling checkers.)

## Usage Checkers

My second example is not properly a programmer's but rather an
editor's joyride. It is a ride usually taken, however, not out of editorial
conviction but because programming makes it easy. Usage-checking
programs (often miscalled "style" or "grammar" checkers) are a form
of writing aid, similar to spelling checkers, which examine a text for
words and phrases considered poor or problematic by the program
developer. Of the dozen or more academic and commercial usage
checkers I have investigated (some intensively, by trial and analysis;
others through their documentation), none is content simply to flag
the language in question and offer a brief identifying message like
"jargon" or "wordy." Instead, all the programs are prescriptive: for
each miscreant word or phrase identified they provide a preferred
alternative. Again we hear the tramp of an approaching regiment, the
standardized automated phrase-substitution programs (SAPS).

The far more elaborate software IBM has spent years developing
for the analysis of sentence structure as well as usage—a sentence-
parsing system earlier called *Epistle,* now *Critique*—is also highly
prescriptive in its experimental teaching version, according to the
latest descriptions I have seen (Richardson, 1985; Braden-Harder,
1986).

I have made the point elsewhere (1985) that the insistent prescrip-
tiveness of these programs is misguided and can only lead to a homog-
enized prose. It strips initiative from writers and variety from their
work, subverting the purposes the software is meant to serve. The
authors of these programs have neglected ends in favor of means;
whatever their level of programming skills, their programs too often
hinder rather than help the writer. In considering the design and use
of text-analysis software like spelling and usage checkers, we must not
lose sight of the difference between merely polishing the surface of
prose and promoting thoughtful revision. "Writing is rewriting," as a
colleague of mine says, but mindless substitution of one word or
phrase for another scarcely qualifies.

## Text Statistical Analyses

Another kind of joyride is taken by many programs that offer
numerical or statistical reports on texts. This fad began with Ellis Page
in 1968 (Wresch, 1984, p. 5), was incorporated during the mid-1970s

into the programs composing Bell Labs' seminal text-analysis software *Writer's Workbench* (UNIX Writer's Workbench Collegiate Edition Software, 1985), and is carried on to some degree in all subsequent text-analysis programs. Any definable repeating pattern in a text can be counted by a program, and the results manipulated in many ways: printed raw, graphed, averaged, compared, processed by formulas. These procedures are easy for even a novice programmer, and we should not be surprised to find them prominently featured in writing software. But of what use are they to the writer? Let us consider briefly three examples.

First: Several programs offer to print a histogram or other graphic representation of sentence lengths. The only rationale I have seen is that the graph may signal lack of variety in sentence structure (see, e.g., Cohen & Lanham, 1984). But a considerably more informative graph of sentence lengths can be made using any word processor to list the sentences themselves (make a copy of the text, put a paragraph marker at the end of each sentence, print the copy). Besides lack of variety, such a sentence list can help spot fragments, run-ons, and other internal sentence flaws. Any less informative graphing of sentences seems pointless, and commercial trumpeting of the graphic alternatives is meretricious.

Second: An easy number to calculate for a text is average sentence length, and most text-checking software provides it. Why? In order to be compared, evidently, with some norm. *Writer's Workbench* (UNIX Writer's Workbench Collegiate Edition Software, 1985) will even allow the derivation of "norms" by counting sentence lengths (or other parameters) in large quantities of text submitted to it (Ten years' worth of "A" papers? Ten novels of Faulkner, or of Hemingway? The *New York Times*'s complete output for 1910?). A teacher, editor, or the program itself can then advise users that their writing falls to one side or the other of whatever norm is being used and should be altered accordingly. The thoughtlessness of this procedure is too seldom noted. Not only does it obscure crucial differences (an identical "average sentence length" can be achieved, for example, by a lively text with widely varying sentences and a dull one with little variety) but, as Erwin Steinberg (1986) has argued, sentence-length prescriptions are so empty that they are seldom followed even by their perpetrators. Writers advised to change the average length of their sentences are victims of a meaningless standard.

Third: One of the more invidious calculations, foisted on writers by its air of scientific objectivity, is the so-called "readability formula," which purports to identify the education level required of a text's readers. Such calculations are usually based on quantities like average word and sentence length, number of polysyllabic words, and ratio of content- to function-words. Their weakness as indices is shown, in part, by their proliferation: over a hundred of these formulas have been devised. Many can be calculated by text-processing programs; *Writer's Workbench* offers four, perhaps tacitly admitting that none is especially reliable. But whatever their worth as measures of how well a text is suited to an audience—and I remain skeptical—Thomas Duffy (1985) and others have shown that they have no demonstrable value in helping writers improve their work.

The calculation-augmented composition analysis (CACA) illustrated above is not merely mindless number-crunching. The insidious danger of numerical joyrides like these, of working up information just because it is easy to do, is that the tail may wag the dog. A writing instructor, for example, offered the data, may invent reasons for using it. Innocent users may revise their prose unnecessarily, even to its detriment. Examples of such applications of dubious standards unfortunately abound in the literature of computers and composition.

A programmer's joyride, then, is not a program. It is the elaboration of a program beyond any sense of need or worth. Few programmers are immune to the impulse, whose effects are evident to some degree in all the writing software I know. (Compare the evolution of overbearing operating systems like UNIX and the elaboration of well-intentioned word processors like *Nota Bene* and *WordPerfect* to the daunting point.) The impulse is not restricted to programmers: during nearly a year's acquaintance with a team of academic software designers at a well-known research university, I observed academic members of the group happily inventing new wrinkles without questioning their educational worth, out of a seemingly boundless faith in the programmers' ingenuity and the power of the machine.

I hope the above examples are persuasive that, in devising software aids to writing, the joyriding impulse must be thoughtfully and repeatedly weighed in terms of editorial strategies and desired outcomes.

## ART BEFORE THE COURSE

If it is vexing to find educational programs undercutting their own best intentions by thoughtless excesses, it is worse to see software that "helps" its users by invoking complex cognitive skills they do not have.

## Outliners

That is the sad case with the outliners, the so-called "idea processors," which have been touted as an aid to academic writers for several years (see, e.g., Daiute, 1985, pp. 78–81) and are currently promoted heavily in the commercial market for business users as well. These programs make it easy to organize sets of words, phrases, headings, sentences, or larger units into subordinated structures and to reorder those structures at whim. The notion behind such a facility is, of course, that by constructing and revising an outline of a proposed composition, the writer will overcome many of the usual obstacles, not only to getting started but also to writing coherently and well.

In some abstract sense, and perhaps for some experienced writers, the notion may have worth. But the eager program designers have not questioned what abilities might be needed to formulate the contents of usable outlines. By the very fact that they are not simple lists, outlines presuppose high-level analytical skills. The writer of an outline must understand or create the subordinating relationships: they do not inhere in the items themselves and are not created by visual rearrangement.

I was recently a visiting instructor in a freshman-level composition course organized around Flower's (1985) *Problem-Solving Strategies for Writing*. A primary emphasis of the course and the text was on "problem analysis": the effort to determine in any writing assignment what the central issues are and how they are divided. In keeping with these aims, I found myself asking students, more frequently and forcefully than in the past, questions like, "What is the *problem* here? What are the *issues*? What is the *point* you wish to make?" Such questions applied at all levels of our discourse, from class discussions to conferences, from criticizing individual paragraphs to evaluating whole arguments, from rough drafts to final submissions.

There is nothing new about such questions, nor anything exclusive to composition courses. But what my experience in this course brought home, more starkly than had twenty-five years of previous teaching, is that, with almost no exceptions, first-year college students are baffled when the questions are asked. They do not arrive at college with the ability to analyze topics into significant parts, they do not understand when told it is needed, and there is no clear method for teaching it to them. What they have learned and can provide is what Flower (1985) calls the "brain dump" (not to be confused with brainstorming)—a kind of formless regurgitation of what they have read or think they know. Asked to analyze, they describe or narrate. Colleagues with longer experience of the course than mine commented that problem analysis is always the hardest thing to teach.

Rather than venture into the discussion of how people acquire high-level cognitive skills (see Hashimoto, 1985, pp. 73-78), I shall simply admit that I do not know how such abilities are come by. They appear to grow, in some, over the college years—perhaps through sheer repetitive practice, perhaps by emulating teachers or gifted peers, perhaps by maturing in the world.

It does seem clear, at any rate, that the problem-analyzing skill is sophisticated. It is an aspect of the ability described in William Perry's well-known essay (1963/1984) on "Examsmanship and the Liberal Arts," posing "understanding of form" as the foundation of intellectual progress. My point is that people who do not already have the skill are in no position to write useful outlines, software-mediated or otherwise, and that software cannot itself embody the skill and supply the deficiency.

I cannot say whether the business users for whom today's elaborate commercial outlining programs are intended suffer from the same cognitive deficiencies as college undergraduates. Perhaps many do not. It remains the case, however, that outliners do not create ideas; they have no use unless concepts and their relationships are already understood. Perhaps it is significant that in an enthusiastic report on such a program, calling it "marvelous . . . at its heart, an idea processor . . . currently the most advanced," the reviewer could find no other examples of its practical use than making organization and bullet charts (Thompson, 1986). In short, the organizing software may be useful—if one already has an organization.

Dobrin (1987) argues, however, that idea processors are of little use even to experienced writers. He suggests that idea processors confuse symbols representing ideas (texts and graphics on screens) with ideas themselves. Changing the relationships among such symbols is easy; but any change in the relationships among ideas necessarily alters them, and those alterations cannot be kept track of by software. Furthermore, he says, by encouraging many-levels-nested arrangements of symbolized ideas (i.e., elaborate subordinated outlines), these programs actually hide rather than reveal the contexts that determine ideas' meanings; they inhibit instead of encouraging thinking. Ultimately, Dobrin believes, idea processors are based on a mistaken model of cognition (see also Dobrin, 1986).

Variations of the outlining software that offer a list of the first sentences of all paragraphs of a draft, to be inspected for organizational weaknesses, are equally beside the point. Even if we could ratify the assumption that initial sentences are reliable indices of paragraph content, inexperienced writers are no more able to evaluate their structures after than before the fact. First-sentence-abstraction routines are another illustration of composition assistance driven by programming rather than conceptual considerations, of software designers doing something not for principle or known practical effect, but merely because they can.

## Inadequacy of Usage Checkers

Returning to the usage-checking programs discussed earlier, we can uncover a second weakness in design, one that not only limits their effectiveness but may grievously mislead the inexperienced writer.

Most of these checkers are fundamentally pattern-matchers. They compare the words and phrases of a text against a stored list of the locutions to be flagged as troublesome, and signal to the user the ones that are found. The usage checkers I have investigated (including all of the best known: *Electric Webster, Grammatik II, HBJ Writer, Mac-Proof, Punctuation & Style, Writer's Workbench, Writer's Helper*) employ lists ranging from a few hundred to about a thousand items. But no one knows how big a list is needed to catch most, or even a high proportion, of the relatively common usage mistakes and infelicities of style that plague inexperienced writers, or of the wordy and redundant phrases even able writers might appreciate having flagged in their work. My research indicates that a list comprising ten thousand items—more than an order of magnitude greater than the largest used by today's programs—would still be inadequate.

Furthermore, a large number of common usage problems cannot be specified by simple lists. A single example will demonstrate this point. A usage program might well point out the tired cliché *lay it on the line* when it occurs in a text. But *lays her life on the line* and *laid the success of his business on the line* are equally instances of this usage. Its paradigm is *[lay/lays/laid/laying]* xxx on the line, where xxx represents an indefinite set of possible words and phrases. Thus a list that would capture all cases of this one cliché must not only conjugate the verb (remarkably, that is a precaution not always followed by usage-program designers) but must also accommodate the indefinitely large number of nouns and noun phrases that might plausibly be encountered in the xxx position. If such a list could be drawn up in principle (and it is not clear that one can), it cannot in practice. The possible nouns are multiplied by their possible arrangements in phrases, then quadrupled by the possible conjugate forms, to a set larger than anyone would undertake to list.

And that is only one troublesome wording. That there are certainly many hundreds, probably thousands, of similar cases meriting inclusion in a dictionary of questionable usage indicates the scope of the problem facing developers and users of this form of assistance.

It is clear that a simple list of a thousand or so troublesome words and phrases can come nowhere near identifying all the usage problems in weak writing. It finds at best a small fraction, a token representation, of the problems in a typical undergraduate essay. To my knowledge, no designer or promoter of such software has acknowledged the extent of this inadequacy. My point is not just that usage checkers provide only minimal assistance. A writer who imagines that, after using such a program and making indicated changes, his or her text will be relatively free of problematic usages will be seriously misled. Most errors, in fact, will remain.

I should note here that *RightWriter*—the one prominent usage checker I did not mention above, because it claims to use "artificial-intelligence techniques" in the form of a large vocabulary manipulated by usage rules instead of simple pattern-matching—evidently shares the inadequacy of the others. In an informal test using student papers, *RightWriter* found about 15% of the obvious errors in usage and mechanics—approximately the same coverage achieved by *Writer's Workbench* using a combination of rule-based and pattern-matching techniques, both of which *Workbench* pioneered over a decade ago.

Thus in the case of usage checkers we see again, though less obviously, perhaps, that software intended to be helpful may subvert its own purposes. The writer lacking highly developed cognitive or linguistic abilities cannot easily generalize from a program's fractional coverage to an awareness of the various types of usage problems that coverage represents. One does not acquire from a token analysis the skills needed to find those questionable wordings that the programs fail to uncover, and the writer may be betrayed by unjustified confidence in the program's utility.

### Where's the Proof?

Should we do anything at all? Let me be provocative for argument's sake, and maintain that despite the dozens of published testimonies to the effectiveness of one or another computer-based writing aid, there has appeared no satisfactory demonstration that, as a result of its use, people become better writers. (Note that I do not claim that no one has improved his or her writing with computer assistance. Doubtless some have. It is only that we have no plausible evidence that the effect is consistent and reliable.)

## Word Processing

To show how broadly I intend my claim of inadequate evidence to apply, let me take as example the word processor itself. No doubt many would assume that at least this wonderful tool, without which few of the others would even exist, can be spared from questioning as a significant aid to writers and teachers. Schwartz (1985) has been especially ingenious in suggesting ways to use word processors as writing aids (see also Hult & Harris, 1987). We have all heard and read encomia from professional writers to their writing programs (we have also heard diatribes), and many of us have positive feelings about our own increased writing ease or productivity since we took the plunge. Moreover, since the earliest classroom trials we have been hearing about the enhanced motivation of students to write and their grateful appreciation of the ease of revision. In a survey of studies, Hawisher (1986) found that out of nineteen studies that assessed users' attitudes after word-processing experiences, fifteen reported unqualified positive responses and the rest were positive with qualifications.

The chorus of praise is not universal, however, even today. "We need to be cautious in accepting claims that word processing can improve our students' writing," said Harris (1985) after one investigation, calling such claims "largely unsubstantiated" (pp. 330, 323). Following a trial during which students responded enthusiastically, Rodrigues (1985) judged nevertheless that "the quality of their finished products was not significantly higher than that of previous years' students" (pp. 338–339). Hawisher's (1986) useful survey shows not only that results are mixed but also that we are far from achieving consistency in research methods or comparability of outcomes.

My own experience with word processors and student writing— working with many more students over a longer period, though less systematically, than Harris, Rodrigues, or any of the twenty-three other researchers cited by Hawisher—confirms that after an initially favorable response to the fun of playing with the technology, and the inevitable "Hawthorne effect" by which any innovation in a work situation initially raises productivity and morale, students are no more likely to start their papers before the eleventh hour, and most take minimal advantage of the machinery to promote revision of their work. Left to themselves, the hundreds of students I have observed do little more with a word processor than they would have done with a typewriter. In fact, many do less. Before computers, student writers might compose a rough draft by hand, mark it up for revision, then polish it while typing the final draft for submission. The word processor's ability to produce clean-looking copy allows today's student to submit what is in effect a rough draft, modified only by a few on-screen changes.

The question of whether word processors improve writing will not be settled by tallying opinions or recounting experiences. Much of what passes for "research" into the effects of word processing (and of writing aids generally) consists of tabulations and reports of student feelings, attitudes, and beliefs about what they have been doing. Students are given questionnaires; they are asked to keep journals; their casual remarks are recorded as evidence for or against the efficacy of the technology; and the information is compiled into anecdotal presentations by their teachers.

Let us set aside possible objections to the small population samples used in many studies and ignore for the moment the questionable propriety of "experimental" procedures that generalize from individual case studies or protocols. My feeling is that such techniques often succeed in discovering interesting questions but seldom provide convincing answers. But I wish to focus on the other epistemological problem I see embedded in most published accounts.

To adduce student opinions and feelings as primary evidence for the worth of word processors (or of anything else) is to fall victim to a prevailing pseudoscientific research model in which people's attitudes toward a thing are crystallized by observers into judgments about its intrinsic value, perceived as a fact. It is easy to see the fallacy. If 80% of the people agree that the President is doing a good job, does that prove we have a good president? No: posterity can judge differently, and so can expert political analysts, among others. If 68% of the students in a course check a box on an evaluation form indicating that Smith is a good teacher, does that prove he is? No, though it suggests they like him and maybe his teaching. But seeing the fallacy in this type of argument does not armor us against it. Perhaps for lack of anything else to use, we continue to evaluate public figures, ourselves, our courses, and computer assistance in writing by invoking it.

If the "descriptive research" I am here criticizing has a potential to help "formulate more specific and useful hypotheses for later empirical investigation," as Selfe has suggested (personal communication, March 15, 1987), that potential is little realized in the studies, and studies of studies, I have consulted. Subjective assessments of word processors cannot be taken as objective measures of worth. It is not a negligible matter, of course, that we feel more productive, or that some students express delight in composing on screen, or that teachers introducing word processing to their students may experience a sense of renewed commitment. There is little doubt that for many writers, computers have rendered the climate in which they compose more salubrious. But such feelings do not constitute them more competent than they would have been otherwise.

In any assessments we make of computer assistance in writing, we need to be especially alert for post hoc fallacies. If writers exhibit better attitudes toward writing after word processing and we wish to claim the new attitudes important, we should be very sure we know their sources. In many reports I have seen, it is entirely possible that the change is owing to increased energy and enthusiasm shown by writing instructors, or to a sense of being specially privileged by access to new technology, and not to any uses of word processors as such. Where the use of word processors is optional and not required by a course or institution, causality may be even more difficult to determine.

The only reports I have seen of plausibly objective attempts to gauge the effect of word processors on writing quality are by Haas and Hayes (1986) and Hawisher (1987). Haas and Hayes concluded that microcomputer-based writing was longer, but of lower quality in both content and mechanics, than pen-and-paper writing by the same subjects. They also found some indication that advanced high-resolution large-screen workstations can help improve writing. Haas and Hayes's sample population was not students, but academic and professional staff experienced with computers. It was also small (fifteen), not randomly chosen, and the writers were probably aware of the experimental goals. Although this study had the right impulses, it does not tell much about the machines' worth in more typical writing situations.

Hawisher's (1987) study partly remedies the last defect. The study was of twenty college freshmen, writing alternately with pen and typewriter and with word processors, learning and practicing revision strategies in both modes. Their work was evaluated in first- and final-draft stages by trained readers. This careful investigation found no evidence favoring either composition method: "the writing tool was apparently not the variable that influenced . . . success" (p. 15).

Thus, responsible experimental studies fail to support the thesis that word processing improves writing. Let me reiterate that I am not saying word processors are of no use to any writer, only that beyond the testimonial level I have seen no satisfactory demonstration of their worth as tools for writing improvement. Many reports and presentations supporting their use today are not much more sophisticated than the first I heard, some years ago, which cited as its evidentiary base the course evaluations from four students. If we cannot do better than this, we are putting vast expenditures of both our institutions' money and our own energies at risk in adopting the technology on a massive scale.

## Prewriting Programs

When we turn to evaluating another prominent kind of writing aid, the so-called "heuristic" or "prewriting" programs, a second uncertainty is added beyond that caused by polling users. It is not only that many such programs store half of an imaginary dialogue yet expect users to act as if engaged in a real one (see Waldo, 1984, pp. 317–319). As with so much computer-based assistance, an enormous burden of proof remains. The special burden of prewriting software might be called the "a priori problem." The development of these programs has been theory-laden from the start, from Hugh Burns's (1984) explicit use of Aristotle, Burke, Pike, Becker, and Young to the latest invocations of contemporary cognitive psychology. Evaluations of these programs' effectiveness may therefore pay more attention to how well they embody particular theories than to whether they actually work (see Petersen, Selfe, & Wahlstrom, 1984, p. 99).

Such a bias might be all right, of course, if the theories were known to work. But as recent critics have noted (Hashimoto, 1985; Dobrin, 1986), our understanding of heuristic thinking remains limited and controversial. Thus, evaluations of prewriting software based on theory must be considered partial until understanding grows and controversies are settled.

Our caution can, of course, be generalized to the full range of composition software, indeed, to much composition teaching with or without electronic aids, since our pedagogies are often long on theory and technique but largely unconfirmed by demonstrable results. Until there is solid evidence of the effects we hope to produce, we must maintain a show-me posture toward the promoters of computer-based writing tools. As programmers, as writing teachers, as users, or as all three, it behooves us to resist the continuing temptation to do everything we can.

## WHY USE COMPUTERS?

After presuming to call the whole enterprise of computer-assisted composition into question for lack of persuasive evidence that it produces better writing, I will end on a positive, even a constructive note. I do believe computers have at least a modest role to play in improving writing, and I think evidence of their effectiveness could be legitimately come by. The reason few seem to be gathering such evidence may be its high cost: since writing quality is not quantifiable (Cohen, 1987), measuring the effectiveness of writing tools calls for extended labor by expert readers.

By way of conclusion, then, let me describe briefly some uses of computers in writing that I think are appropriate, not because they have been proven newly effective, but because they are extensions of what most writing teachers have long practiced.

If only for their utility in making revisions swift and easy, final drafts neat and clean, writers will continue to flock to computers; and as teachers we should continue the effort to make word processing available to all our students. Because we simply do not know, and may never determine conclusively, the relative merits of pen-and-paper and on-screen composition, teachers and editors should emphatically not insist on electronic preparation of drafts from the start. On the other hand, it is no more oppressive to require that final drafts be prepared on word processors and letter-quality printers than that they be typed (assuming that some instruction is available with the machines), and we may do that in order to promote revision as well as neatness.

I have already suggested a word-processor-based exercise, creating a simple sentence list, that can aid in identifying poorly formed sentences and lack of variety in sentence structure. Most inexperienced writers will need help learning to apply the exercise.

Another reason to promote final-draft preparation on word processors is that it facilitates spell-checking. Young writers may be increasingly hampered in learning conventional orthography by their decreasing exposure to texts in our culture, but they can still be expected to submit essays relatively free of misspellings and typographical errors. The technology is available and easy to use in conjunction with word processing and, if it does not automatically correct the errors that are found, can be educational over time.

Software reviewers have often noted the inadequacy of usage checkers, though none has pointed out the reasons for it, and no one has noted that a solution may exist. As I suggested, the problem of usage checkers' limited coverage, however acute it may seem in the formal analysis I have outlined, is a matter of design rather than of conception. It is possible, by incorporating what programmers know as "wild cards" into a checker's list of problem usages (in other words, to wildcard the program's knowledge base), to multiply its coverage by a factor that brings adequacy back within reach. I believe my colleague Elaine Thiesmeyer and I (1987) are the only ones to have described this design possibility (novel in terms of database design theory, as well), which we have tested extensively over the past five years. Our current program, using a wildcarded database of more than four thousand entries, can typically identify over 75% of the mechanical errors and usage problems in student writing. Our hope is that users given feedback on a high proportion of the usage problems in their texts not only will not be betrayed by false confidence but also will eventually gain a sense of the most persistent usage problems they face, beginning to anticipate and avoid them and becoming more efficient in their efforts.

Like spelling checkers, then, programs properly designed to examine texts for usage and mechanical errors may have some use in writing. Until we can be more certain of adequate coverage, however (and perhaps even then), that use might still consist less in eradicating errors than in fostering certain principles of style. Of all the problem phrases a critical eye can flag in inexpert writing, only a fraction, perhaps a quarter, are outright mistakes. The rest are matters of judgment and taste: archaisms, empty intensifiers, affectations, gender-specific terms, slang and colloquialisms, jargon, trite expressions, vague words, clichés, and pleonasms (wordiness, redundancy, tautology, repetition). Editors, teachers, and readers would not agree canonically on a list of such judgments, and to choose a particular set of them for blame is undoubtedly to promote an idiolect of the chooser (though that is unavoidable, to some degree, in any editorial practice).

On the other hand, to adopt a policy of pointing out triteness or clichés whenever they occur, leaving it to the writer whether to revise, is to indicate that freshness is a desirable quality in writing. Similarly, to call wordiness and redundancy into question is to promote the general thesis that tighter is better. These are principles long held by composition teachers and editors.

I can cautiously recommend usage checkers, therefore, for several constructive purposes. But they should be nonprescriptive and designed to achieve adequate coverage. They should also allow their users to change or augment the lists of choices to be made, and should present themselves as aids to, rather than substitutes for, writers' judgments.

Well-designed text checkers can be useful even beyond their editorial function of marking up compositions. They can also be used in the study of writing, not by counting instances but by documenting them—by highlighting or listing them in context. A user warned about anaphoric *this* and *it* constructions can print a list of them by location in his or her next essay for leisurely contemplation. (See Geisler, Kaufer & Steinberg, 1985, for a formal discussion of this problem.) A teacher interested in studying "shun words" in texts (*-sion*, *-tion* endings, i.e., some forms of nominalization) can chart them similarly: no elaborate concordance program is needed. (For many such purposes the global-search facility built into a word processor might suffice, except that it may not provide printed records.) Much of this kind of careful research remains to be done, if only to confirm our prejudices about *be*-verbs, whiz deletions, passives, article ratios, prepositional phrases, and the rest.

I would even modify my stance against counting things in texts, to allow for a particular application I have found useful. A characteristic of dull writing is excessive repetition of particular content words, usually topical or thematic. A utility program based on concordance algorithms can count the uses of all words in a text, then provide a list of those used more than, say, four times per page; excluding the common function words, a writer can be encouraged to treat the rest as occasions for judicious use of a thesaurus and dictionary.

These relatively simple uses, and others which continuing ingenuity will find, make a modest case for the computer as a tool in composition. A thoughtful reader will see they are extensions of things teachers already do, of techniques editors use, not profound innovations destined to solve the writing problem once for all. As such, perhaps, they further the writing enterprise in familiar and justifiable ways.

## REFERENCES

Bermant, C. (1986, October 27). Xerox announces PC spelling checker. *Info-World,* p. 3.

Braden-Harder, L. (1986, May). *"Critique": A text critiquing tool based on a natural language parser.* Demonstration at the University of Pittsburgh Conference on Computers and Writing, Pittsburgh, PA.

Burns, H. (1984). Recollections of first-generation computer-assisted prewriting. In W. Wresch (Ed.), *The computer in composition instruction: A writer's tool* (pp. 15–33). Urbana, IL: National Council of Teachers of English.

Cohen, M. E. (1987). In search of the writon. In L. Gerrard (Ed.), *Writing at century's end: Essays on computer-assisted composition* (pp. 116–121). New York: Random House.

Cohen, M. E., & Lanham, R. A. (1984). HOMER: Teaching style with a micro-computer. In W. Wresch (Ed.), *The computer in composition instruction: A writer's tool* (pp. 83–90). Urbana, IL: National Council of Teachers of English.

Daiute, C. (1985). *Writing and computers.* Reading, MA: Addison-Wesley.

Dobrin, D. N. (1986). Protocols once more. *College English, 48,* 713–725.

Dobrin, D. N. (1987). Some ideas about idea processors. In L. Gerrard (Ed.), *Writing at century's end: Essays on computer-assisted composition* (pp. 95–107). New York: Random House.

Duffy, T. M. (1985). Readability formulas: What's the use? In T. M. Duffy & R. Waller (Eds.), *Designing usable texts.* Orlando: Academic Press.

Flower, L. (1985). *Problem-solving strategies for writing* (2nd ed.). New York: Harcourt.

Geisler, C., Kaufer, D. S., & Steinberg, E. R. (1985). *The unattended anaphoric "this": When should writers use it?* (CDC Technical Report No. 4). Communications Design Center, Carnegie-Mellon University.

Haas, C., & Hayes, J. R. (1986). *Pen and paper vs. the machine: Writers composing in hard copy and computer conditions.* (CDC Technical Report No. 16). Communications Design Center, Carnegie-Mellon University.

Harris, J. (1985). Student writers and word processing: A preliminary evaluation. *College Composition and Communication, 36,* 323–330.

Hashimoto, I. (1985). Structured heuristic procedures: Their limitations. *College Composition and Communication, 36,* 73–81.

Hawisher, G. E. (1986). Studies in word processing. *Computers and Composition, 4,* 6–31.

Hawisher, G. E. (1987). The effects of word processing on the revision strategies of college freshmen. *Research in the Teaching of English, 21,* 145–159.

Holdstein, D. H. (1987). *On composition and computers.* New York: Modern Language Association.

Hull, G. A. (1984). Computer-assisted instruction and basic writing: A proposal. In T. E. Martinez (Ed.), *The written word and the word processor* (pp. 125–136). Villanova, PA: Villanova University.

Hult, C., & Harris, J. (1987). *A writer's introduction to word processing.* Belmont, CA: Wadsworth.

Mace, S. (1986, June 16). Spelling aid works with ST GEM programs. *Infoworld,* p. 19.

Perry, W. G., Jr. (1984). Examsmanship and the liberal arts: A study in educational epistemology. In A. M. Eastman, et al. (Eds.), *The Norton reader* (4th ed., pp. 203–214). New York: Norton. (Original work published 1963)

Petersen, B. T., Selfe, C. L., & Wahlstrom, B. J. (1984). Computer-assisted instruction and the writing process: Questions for research and evaluation. *College Composition and Communication, 35,* 98–101.

Richardson, S. (1985, June). *Enhanced text critiquing using a natural language parser.* Paper presented at the Seventh International Conference on Computers and the Humanities, Provo, Utah.

Rodrigues, D. W. (1985). Computers and basic writers. *College Composition and Communication, 36,* 336–339.

Schwartz, H. J. (1985). *Interactive writing: Composing with a word processor.* New York: Holt, Rinehart.

Selfe, C. (1987, March 15). Personal communication.

Steinberg, E. R. (1986). A pox on pithy prescriptions. *College Composition and Communication, 37,* 96–100.

Thiesmeyer, E., & Thiesmeyer, J. (1987, July). Data bases for text checkers. Paper presented at the International Conference on Data Bases in the Humanities and Social Sciences, Auburn, AL.

Thiesmeyer, J. (1984). Some boundary considerations for writing-software. In L. Bridwell & D. Ross (Eds.), *Computers and composition: Selected papers* (pp. 277–291). Colorado State/Michigan Technological Universities.

Thiesmeyer, J. (1985). Teaching with the text checkers. *Collegiate Microcomputer, 3,* 299–306.

Thiesmeyer, J. (1987). Expert systems, artificial intelligence, and the teaching of writing. In L. Gerrard (Ed.), *Writing at century's end: Essays on computer-assisted composition* (pp. 108–115). New York: Random House.

Thompson, K. (1986, September 15). MORE: Mac outliner breaks new ground. *InfoWorld,* pp. 39–41.

Waldo, M. L. (1984). Computers and composition: A marriage made in heaven? In T. E. Martinez (Ed.), *The written word and the word processor* (pp. 313–322). Villanova, PA: Villanova University.

Wresch, W. (1984). Introduction. In W. Wresch (Ed.), *The computer in composition instruction: A writer's tool* (pp. 1–12). Urbana, IL: National Council of Teachers of English.

## Guide to Programs

*Electric Webster grammar option.* (1982). Albany, CA: Cornucopia Software.

*English spelling corrector.* (1985). New York: Houghton Mifflin.

*Grammatik II.* (1985). San Francisco: Reference Software.

*HBJ writer.* (1986). Chicago, Harcourt Brace Jovanovitch.

*MacProof.* (1985). Provo, Utah: Automated Language Processing Systems.

*Punctuation & style.* (1982). San Diego: Oasis Systems.

*Rightwriter.* (1987). Sarasota: Rightsoft.

UNIX *writer's workbench collegiate edition software.* (1985). Morristown, NJ: AT&T Information Systems.

# 6

# Computers and Basic Writers: A Critical View

Lisa Gerrard

Many of the benefits and drawbacks of computer-based composition have a special significance for basic writers. Although these students do not conform to a single profile, they are usually our most insecure and recalcitrant writers, with the least effective composing habits. These weaknesses make them especially likely to misinterpret the directives of poorly designed software or to fail to utilize the computer as an instructional tool. At the same time, the computer's capacity to invite experimentation, prewriting, revising, and collaboration—advantages for any writer—address several of the most pressing needs of this group. Depending on how they are used, computers, for good or ill, can transform the writing habits and attitudes of basic writers.

## THE COMPUTER AS A LEARNING AID

Though we may group basic writers in one English composition course, they do not necessarily share the same writing problems (Jensen, 1986). One advantage of computer-based writing is that it allows us to individualize instruction, tailoring it to the different writing processes and cognitive styles of different students. Computers can provide a range of different tools so that instructors can identify each student's needs and distribute the software accordingly (Melmed, 1986). Students sitting side-by-side in the lab can be engaged in entirely different tasks. The software itself also allows for some individualizing of instruction: Style analyzers and grammar tutorials offer a variety of syntactical structures to work on, and many grammar tutorials adjust the complexity of their exercises to the user's level of skill (see, for example, Epes, Kirkpatrick, & Southwell, 1979). Students can proceed at their own pace, backtracking or repeating parts of a routine without feeling self-conscious, and writers who need to repeat exercises can do so without embarrassment and without boring the instructor.

The computer can also help students control the writing process by dividing it into stages. A complete computer package with prewriting and revising aids can break the writing project into manageable steps, prompting students to explore their topic in one routine, guiding them through organization in another, and providing separate revising and proofreading exercises for additional drafts. The same effect can be achieved in a lab equipped with several kinds of invention and revision software. Students can choose the program appropriate to the status of their draft. This separation of activities helps basic writers, who are sometimes stymied by the multiplicity of tasks writing requires. In addition to keeping them from being overwhelmed by their project, the computer can offer them a new writing method. When invention and revising software complement word processing, guiding students from the onset of their project through proofreading, the software helps teach a recursive, process approach, particularly valuable for basic writers, whose writing processes are often unworkable. By assigning different computer activities at suitable stages of a paper's creation, instructors can help their students develop an effective writing process.

In addition to lodging separate phases of the writing process in separate routines, the computer also aids a writer in thinking through a topic by presenting prewriting questions or prompts in discrete steps. Ideas rarely unfold in a neat procession; more often they come in intermittent clumps, one idea entangled in another. This untidy process challenges proficient writers; less skilled writers may not even realize they've expressed several ideas as one. A planning exercise can present a single question on the screen, leaving the user's field of vision uncluttered by a previous outpouring of ideas or by additional questions to be answered. This feature allows writers to concentrate on one issue at a time and keeps them from being distracted by competing information.

Sequential presentations of data are among the things computers do best: They can easily be programmed to organize information and procedures in a linear, step-by-step system. Thus, it's relatively easy to produce software that asks the user to arrange ideas according to a linear system of logic. Many prewriting programs do just this: They teach the conventions of linear thought developing from a thesis. Sentence completion routines that ask for a thesis and supporting or opposing arguments, and idea processors, which allow writers to outline and rank their ideas, teach the logical development of ideas through clearly defined stages. Though such programs will not appeal to all writers or work well at the earliest idea formation stage, they can help students learn an important convention of academic writing: the pattern of a thesis directly followed by its subordinate ideas. Often basic writers are capable of generating complex and abstract ideas but lack the conventions in which to frame them. Such is the case for native English speakers who have never learned the written conventions of logic and for basic writers who are also English as a Second Language (ESL) students schooled in a nonlinear discourse pattern. (For a study of culture-bound rhetorical patterns and the teaching of foreign students, see Kaplan, 1966.)

Many basic writers are uncomfortable with written language, although they are at home with visual and auditory forms of expression. Students who have trouble seeing surface errors in their text can benefit from a voice synthesizer. After the paper is typed into the computer, the synthesizer "reads" it out loud, allowing the writer to hear errors his or her eyes missed (Lees, 1984). Students who think spatially rather than verbally can use graphics programs to diagram their ideas. (See Chapter 9 in this volume for a further discussion of the kinds of visual thinking that can be facilitated by graphics software.) These programs can create issue trees and idea clusters, or allow writers to design their own visual arrangements of ideas.

## EFFECT ON STUDENTS AND THEIR WRITING

Judging by writers' positive responses to computers, we can say that technology seems to have had a more discernible impact on writers than on their prose. Most of us immediately discover that our students enjoy using the computer, spend more time revising, feel more confident and in control of their writing, and socialize more with their classmates. Though we have less evidence that students' writing has improved correspondingly, these changes in attitude and practice provide conditions that foster learning. Writing difficulties, especially for basic writers, often have a psychological base. Basic writers are generally reluctant writers, who come to us after years of frustration, bearing the most pessimistic expectations of our courses. By making writing less painful, even at times enjoyable, the computer can reduce their anxiety about writing, decrease their resentment towards the course, and encourage them to spend more time on their papers. These observations, and others described in this chapter, are drawn from the results of approximately 200 student questionnaires as well as from my experiences teaching computer-based composition from 1980 to the present.

This change in attitude is fundamental to the improvement of these basic writers as students. Proud that they can operate the computer, they begin to think they can succeed as writers. They feel less stigmatized by their presence in basic composition and more confident of their writing. In addition, the communal lab socializes the class; unlike the traditional classroom with its centralized authority, the computer lab is an informal workspace where students share advice on how to use the computer. Proximity and the visibility of the text on the monitor steer these conversations into advice on writing. The result is spontaneous peer editing and other forms of collaboration, which quickly break the ice in workshop courses where writers must share their prose.

The communal atmosphere of the lab also alleviates the loneliness of writing, an impediment for some basic writers. Many of these students are especially gregarious, dislike studying in isolation, and don't relax enough to learn until they have made friends in class (Troyka, 1982). Even the computer itself reduces the solitude of writing. Many students are encouraged by its interactiveness—its prompt responses to commands—and talk to the computer as if to a friend. Some of my students personify the computer as their "pal," and one even wrote "her" a poem. A student in a class of my colleague's, for example, acknowledged the software by writing, "and thanks to WANDAH, the word processor, for helping me get started on my paper."

Computers can also benefit the writing processes of basic writers stymied by overly rigid methods. By making it easy to alter text, word processors encourage experimentation and disrupt the idea of a fixed text. The phosphorescent image is fluid: words are as easily produced as retracted or transformed. This tractability is especially encouraging for basic writers who are fearful of releasing anything other than their most polished utterance and who have never thought of writing as play. In their case studies of five advanced writing students, Bridwell and Duin (1985) reported that play was the only effect "that could be attributed purely to word processing" (p. 120).

By fostering experimentation, the computer has also been known to elicit longer sentences and longer papers from the students most likely to cut the writing task (and the paper) short. People who are highly anxious about writing find that their strain and discomfort induce them to find a quick escape. Selfe (1984), for example, found that the apprehensive writers she studied expressed this impulse by working at top speed. The fastest way to get a paper over with is to write short, choppy sentences with minimal elaboration. Students who are having fun with the computer are in less of a hurry to sign off, and many of the most stinting writers have generated longer papers containing longer, more complex sentences. These papers have not necessarily been more analytical, better organized, or less flawed than the earlier work, but they indicate a fluency and syntactical sophistication stunted by the previous composing method. The computer can thus help liberate skills the student's anxiety has suppressed.

Although these benefits are attributable to the computer, they do not happen in isolation but in concert with the instructor's guidance. The more closely the computer is integrated into other classroom activity, the more useful it is. Just as it would be hopeless to expect a rhetoric and handbook by themselves to teach writing, so it would be futile simply to hand students over to the computer. If not coupled with effective classroom instruction, the computer is unlikely to improve writing and may, in fact, do harm. We shall now consider the attendant pitfalls.

## DRAWBACKS OF REVISING SOFTWARE

### Mechanistic View of Writing

Revising programs offer the greatest possibilities for misuse. While word processing can encourage playfulness and flexibility, revision aids may do the opposite, enforcing rigid ideas about writing. Because of fear of failure, basic writers tend to cling to intractable and frequently erroneous rules about what a paper must contain, and in their anxiety about writing, seize on a mechanical formula as a mold to pour their ideas into. They labor so hard to fulfill the requisites of the rule or formula that they subordinate content to form. Recently, for example, one of my students could not revise because she had carefully enlarged or reduced each idea into five sentences—her rule for the prescribed length of a paragraph. To add or delete information would have disrupted her arrangement. Such inhibiting rules so frustrate the writing process that part of our task as writing instructors is to discover them and replace them with flexible alternatives (Rose, 1980; Sommers, 1981).

Style analyzers, however, can interfere with this effort; they can easily be misconstrued as offering a set of artificial rules. These programs typically identify potential stylistic flaws, such as forms of the verb *to be,* prepositional phrases, wordy or redundant expressions, nominalized nouns, vague words, and abstract nouns. They operate by matching every word the student types in against their own list of words or phrases. The computer, of course, cannot understand the paper or determine if these terms are problematic. It simply locates them in the text and leaves interpretation and correction, if need be, to the writer. Basic writers who are used to writing by rules are likely to misinterpret the purpose of this analysis and assume that the computer is offering a new set of rules: never use "to be," prepositional phrases, or any word the software designates. I have seen students automatically change all terms the computer flags, producing constructions they probably wouldn't have chosen in the first place. "Be" becomes "exist." Prepositions are arbitrarily excised. A paper on immigration twists into strange circumlocution to avoid the forbidden "-tion" word.

These efforts can be devastating not just to students' prose but, worse, to their notion of the writing process. Attempts to avoid "wrong" words support a mechanistic view of writing as a matter of wending one's way through a thicket of do's and don'ts. This view is reinforced by the mechanical nature of the computer itself. In spite of what we call their interactive nature, computers are just machines performing mechanical operations. That they do this so accurately, so consistently, is part of their utility. Unlike humans, computers can be relied on to find every preposition, every form of "to be," without getting bored in the search. As long as students regard the computer as a tool they manipulate to their ends, there is no harm in such precision. But if they take the computer's machinations as a model of the revising process, they are being misled. The very accuracy we prize in computers offers a model of revising as a rigid, infallible activity, a word-detection process, rather than a decision-making one. The computer's way of analyzing text is tidy, certain, and an appealing model for anyone overwhelmed by the unwieldiness of writing. But it falsifies the task: revising is a messy process with few certainties. Our basic writers, especially those addicted to formulas, need to accept this unfortunate reality before they can progress.

The computer's precision is most visible in its mathematical calculations, in the statistical information many style programs offer. These programs calculate such phenomena as the number of words per sentence, number of transition words, percentage of prepositions, average paragraph length, and readability scores. Used thoughtfully, this information can help students gain an objective perspective on their style and point out features to reconsider. Used mechanically, however, such calculations can teach unskilled writers that if they get the right formula—the right percentage of subordinate clauses, the right mix of long and short words—their paper cannot fail. Pages of printout showing a paper fragmented into its statistical components give visual support to the idea that revising means adjusting word counts and percentages.

## Superficial Revising

Even students who don't succumb to computer analysis as a model of the revising process may end up paying more attention to surface features of their text than to substance. Grammar tutorial programs can encourage disproportionate and premature concern with error correction. This is a particular problem for basic writers, many of whom already equate effective prose with correctness.

Style analyzers invite similar attention to surface features, suggesting that revision is local tinkering, not reconceptualizing. Although style programs are useful at the editing stage, when superficial tinkering is appropriate, they are not meant to replace rethinking and rearranging of content. In fact, the prototype for many of them, *Writer's Workbench,* was initially developed as an editing tool for technical writers at Bell Laboratories. Style analyzers and grammar tutorials by their very nature encourage students to focus on the surface of their text. Because the computer cannot understand the paper, it necessarily isolates matters of style and usage from their context. In separating form from content, it fails to show how error disrupts communication and how style constructs meaning. This separation encourages an unskilled writer to view grammatical and stylistic conventions as absolutes independent of content. Yet students cannot learn to read their own (or any) prose skillfully unless they see the relationship between content and structure.

Revision programs are also susceptible to other kinds of misunderstanding. Some programs flag commonly misused terms, like "affect" and "effect," "its" and "it's," although they cannot indicate whether the usage is correct. These programs usually provide on-line explanations of such terms and offer opportunities for writers to rethink their choices. But many students, accustomed to feedback when they do something wrong, assume that the computer wouldn't flag a term if it were correct. Even when they read and understand the rule, they cannot resist changing what they have written, often trading their correct usage for an incorrect alternative. This is a particular liability for basic writers, who usually view themselves as error-prone. With a history of failures in English, they are more likely than successful, confident writers to assume that a possible error is, in their case, an inevitable one.

## Misconceptions About Style

Programs that score prose according to readability can also mislead basic writers. These programs measure the complexity of style according to the number of long words and long sentences the computer finds. The more long words and sentences, the higher the readability score, and the more educated the reader must be to understand the text. By implication, readability scores also indicate the writer's level of education. While some basic writers—notably those wedded to short sentences and a choppy style—may benefit from such software, these programs can mislead writers into a simplistic notion of what a good style is. Indeed, it can teach them to imitate the worst of academic prose: serpentine sentences encumbered with long, Latinate words and an inflated style many already admire. Furthermore, readability formulas cannot measure real complexity in syntax, although this is what almost all basic writers need to develop. Nor can readability formulas consistently identify fragments and run-ons, though many basic writers need to learn the boundaries of a sentence. Rather than counting the words in their sentences, basic writers need practice constructing a variety of sentence types and developing a range of styles. IBM has been working on a sophisticated text parser that identifies sentence errors, including fragments and run-ons, but this system, called *Critique,* formerly *Epistle,* requires prodigious memory and, though impressively capable, is not as yet entirely accurate (see Heidorn, Jensen, Miller, Byrd, & Chodorow, 1982).

## Error-Correction Software and Student Passivity

Programs that work imprecisely create other problems for basic writers. Matching word lists, which is what most style programs do, is a relatively easy task for a computer. Other kinds of identification—finding words that should be capitalized, split infinitives, and determining subject-verb agreement—require more complex and fallible programming and are more susceptible to error. One of the advantages of software is that it can teach many parts of speech. When it locates "to be" verbs or abstract nouns, it shows the writer what these forms are. But while it is one thing to identify a "to be" correctly and leave it to the student to decide whether the verb should be replaced, it is another to misidentify a split infinitive and leave the student confused about what this syntactical phenomenon is. Basic writers do not need additional insecurities. If error identification software is not 100% accurate, it will misinform and frustrate these students. At best, they will distrust the software, rendering it useless (Thiesmeyer, 1987). At worst, it will affirm a conviction so many students hold: that assessments of their writing are capricious, and the computer, like the train of English teachers who preceded it, is yet another "subjective" judge.

Software that corrects errors also deprives students of the opportunity to learn from correcting their mistakes. It encourages passivity—a special danger for basic writers. Many basic writers have learned to depend entirely on outside authority for guidance and evaluation. Often they view writing as an activity outside their control and see successful writers as luckily inspired or innately gifted. These students need to gain confidence in their ideas, the skills they have, and their ability to grow as writers. Most of all, they need to feel in control. Yet our culture so venerates and empowers computers that students run the risk of relinquishing responsibility for their work and accepting the computer as the final authority. Software that makes decisions (e.g., automatically corrects misspellings, hyphenates, or capitalizes) may be useful for secretaries and executives, but it fails as an instructional tool.

## DRAWBACKS TO USING PREWRITING SOFTWARE

As passive learners, many basic writers accept feedback they don't understand, rather than questioning and learning from it. Just as their acquiescence can undermine their use of style analyzers, so it can interfere with prewriting. Most prewriting programs offer a single approach to thinking through a problem: They offer a framework for free association, ask guided questions, or prompt short summaries of the topic, purpose, or audience. Students who are restricted to a single invention program and who use it for every assignment may learn that there is but one correct way to plan a paper. Yet not all invention aids suit all topics or all students or all stages of a paper's evolution. Idea processors, for example, which allow writers to construct detailed outlines, may teach students to outline their ideas before they have fully conceived them (see Dobrin's, 1987, critiques of idea processors). Students need access to a variety of invention aids because writing and thinking are idiosyncratic processes, and the best software for one writer will exasperate or thwart another.

Though more software is being developed with a menu of prewriting or revising aids to choose from, most of the different approaches are lodged in separate pieces of software, many of which run on different systems. Few of us have the luxury of a large software library, and fewer still have access to several computer systems. At present, most classrooms provide one type of software for all students. This uniformity homogenizes instruction and limits the individual student's adaptations to the program's flexibility. Even in schools that can afford only one or two prewriting or revising aids, faculty may be exhorted to justify the expense (not to mention the cost of the hardware) by using them extensively. Students may find themselves required to use software that is incompatible with their composing style. This restriction is a particular liability for basic writers, many of whom are already locked into a single approach for planning or revising and who need to be introduced to a range of strategies so they can find the ones that work for them.

Even where a wide range of software is available, students will need help deciding which programs best suit them. Usually the software itself requires the instructor's guidance. To allow the student to think freely about a topic and also to remain applicable to many kinds of topics and many kinds of thinkers, much invention software is open-ended. It can ask general questions—the who, what, where, when, why, and how of the topic—or attempt to elicit a dialogue with the student or ask for a short summary of the student's ideas (see Burns, 1984; Rodrigues & Rodrigues, 1984; and Schwartz, 1984). Although this kind of software is meant to provoke and focus ideas, it sometimes prompts vague responses that generate little useful information. The summary, especially if it comes before the student has defined his or her topic, might look like this:

> The title of my paper is *consumer problems.*
> In this paper I wish to *describe the problems of being a consumer in today's society.*
> My primary readers will probably be *people interested in consumerism.*
> What I really mean to say in my paper is *that there are a lot of*

*problems with consumerism, some of which involve adver-
tising and the right of the public to accurate product information.*

A dialogue may leave the writer talking in circles:

What are you writing about, Gene? *consumerism*
Why do you think this subject is important? *We're all consumers.*
Could you elaborate on that? *We're all affected by consumerism.
We love to go to malls and spend money.*
Where is consumerism likely to be found? *In malls and any-
where people are parting with their money.*
Can you give me an example? *Everytime I go to the mall, I see
hundreds of people buying things.*

A student who gets frustrated with this dialogue may give up or respond with deliberate nonsense.


## ADDITIONAL PROBLEMS WITH COMPUTERS

Using the computer with basic writers poses other dangers that
instructors will need to forestall. Ideally, software should allow writers to concentrate on their text, not on the workings of the program. It
should postpone formatting until printing and offer enough on-line
help that students don't need to memorize complex commands or
interrupt their thoughts by consulting a manual. A program that is
difficult to use distracts writers from their writing. This would frustrate anyone but may well overwhelm basic writers.

Complicated formatting procedures may also encourage students
to focus on the appearance of their text to the exclusion of content.
This is a particular problem for basic writers, many of whom are
already excessively preoccupied with the physical appearance of their
text. Several of my students will not correct an error they detect in a
final draft when they don't have time for retyping: they cannot stand
to deface the page with handwriting. During timed writings, with an
hour to produce and polish a 500-word essay, many students meticu-
lously paint their exams with whiteout, then wait for the page to dry
before revising. These are the same students who routinely ask about
margin size, page length, and whether it's all right to use onion skin as
often as they ask about the assignment. Computers, especially those
with graphics capabilities, offer prodigious opportunities for altering

a text's appearance. Though computer graphics can be a useful adjunct to a well-wrought text, students should be discouraged from squandering their revising time on formatting, or they may come to value cosmetics over content and mistakenly assume their paper is as good as it looks.

The logistics of having to write on campus may pose problems for basic writers. The public nature of writing in a lab or classroom outfitted with computers may not suit all students, especially those who are self-conscious about their work or even their typing. The monitor displays their words to anyone who cares to look, and the beeps announce their mistakes. Though a public lab can socialize a classroom, it can also distract and embarrass students who view themselves as weak writers. These students can achieve some privacy by turning down the brightness on the monitor, but absolute solitude is just about impossible. It will take a new etiquette to control the human impulse to read over someone's shoulder; in a lab, looking at someone else's computer screen feels as normal as reading signs and billboards. We may also find that we cannot use our labs as fully as we would like. For some students, composing may be impossible in a noisy, distracting room. For others, busy schedules may limit their visits to the lab, interfere with their writing and revising on campus, and prevent them from finding time to explore fully the computer's capabilities. Likewise, these same students may not be able to afford a computer they could use at home or in their dorm rooms. Scheduling conflicts can be a particular problem for basic writers who are nontraditional students: their work and family lives are frequently more demanding than those of traditional students. Thus, basic writers often have limited access to technology despite attempts to provide university computer facilities for all students.

## SOLUTIONS

None of these problems is inevitable. We can make our assignments flexible so that no one is forced to compose on-line. We can carpet and soundproof our labs, adding carrels for privacy, if need be. We can teach students to exploit the computer's power rather than be exploited by it. We can show them how to analyze grammar and style in relation to content, forestalling any impression that good style is the absence of certain words. We can show students a range of powerful styles, many of them using to good effect the very terms we teach them to shun. Students need to know that there is nothing inherently right or wrong in "to be" verbs or short sentences and would do well to analyze pieces of effective and ineffective prose so they can see when a device weakens an assertion and when it reinforces it. We can teach our students that style analyzers and grammar tutorials perform a specific, worthwhile, but limited function for proofreading and polishing surface details and that these aids work best after the paper is thought through and developed.

We can be alert to all kinds of misunderstanding, taking care that the computer doesn't simply replace one set of restrictive formulas and misconceptions with another. If the software offers multiple exercises, we can help students decide which ones address their individual writing problems and best suit their particular stage in the writing task. We can help students attend more to composing than computing by writing our own operating instructions, paring down the user's manual to the functions students most need. If our store of invention software is limited, we can assure students that these are but a few of many possible ways to begin writing, and offer practice with many forms of non-computer-based prewriting. We can learn to teach effectively with open-topic prewriting aids by making sure students understand their purpose and by analyzing effective and ineffective models of completed exercises. In short, we can show students when, why, and how to use these programs.

Even the computer's most benign features require such instructor intervention. The often-praised flexibility of word processing is only an advantage if writers use it. If they regard the word processor as a formidable typewriter, they will not experiment with their prose—especially if they are tentative about writing and about the computer. Basic writers are often not aware that they have alternatives, that they are capable of saying the same thing in different ways. They need suggestions about how to experiment. The word processor itself will not produce experiments in prose, though it will facilitate them. In the same way, revision programs don't teach writers how to revise; they offer information writers can use in revision if they already know how to revise. Like more adroit writers, basic writers often sense that a sentence needs to be changed, but unlike skilled writers, they don't always know what to put in its place. In his study of the effect of computers on basic writers, Nichols (1986) found that the computer itself did not change his students' writing processes. (Significantly, during this study, the students received no instruction in composition.)

As important as instructors are to guiding students to successful computer use, we must also be sensitive to our students' writing processes and not foist computerized aids on them. In our enthusiasm, we may be disheartened to find that the computer conflicts with some students' preferred composing method: some like to work with pen and paper, notecards, or other tangible repositories for their ideas (Selfe, 1985). They should not be coerced into abandoning methods that work for them. Yet we may find ourselves in a conflict of interest with these students: having expended the effort to convince our department chairs that we need computers and the funds to acquire and assemble a computer lab, we may feel compelled to show large numbers of students at the keyboard. We need to remember that the computer is an additional tool in the classroom, not necessarily the primary one. Basic writers are especially vulnerable to how we mold their writing processes because their comfortable old methods haven't worked for them. They view themselves as poor writers—a view reinforced by the stigma attached to our courses—and therefore feel especially dependent on our advice. Those who are also passive learners may try to accommodate our suggestions even against their better judgment. By forcing them to compose on-line, we may paradoxically interfere with their development of an effective writing process. This interference, on top of restrictions already imposed by the writing lab on when, where, and how long they can work and distractions they might not encounter at home, makes it essential that we approach this new tool with flexibility. By understanding and accommodating the computer's limitations, we can best use its strengths to support our curricular goals in basic writing.

## REFERENCES

Bridwell, L., & Duin, A. (1985). Looking in-depth at writers: Computers as writing medium and research tool. In J. L. Collins & E. A. Sommers (Eds.), *Writing on-line: Using computers in the teaching of writing* (pp. 115–121). Upper Montclair, NJ: Boynton/Cook.

Burns, H. (1984). Recollections of first-generation computer-assisted prewriting. In W. Wresch (Ed.), *The computer in composition instruction: A writer's tool* (pp. 15–33). Urbana, IL: National Council of Teachers of English.

Dobrin, D. N. (1987). Some ideas about idea processors. In L. Gerrard (Ed.), *Writing at century's end: Essays on computer-assisted composition* (pp. 95–107). New York: Random House.

Epes, M., Kirkpatrick, C., & Southwell, M. G. (1979). The comp-lab project: An experimental basic writing course. *Journal of Basic Writing, 2,* 19–37.

Heidorn, G. E., Jensen, K., Miller, L. A., Byrd, R. J., & Chodorow, M. S. (1982). The *Epistle* text-critiquing system. *IBM Systems Journal, 21,* 305–326.

Jensen, G. H. (1986). The reification of the basic writer. *Journal of Basic Writing, 5,* 52–64.

Kaplan, R. B. (1966). Cultural thought patterns in inter-cultural education. *Language Learning, 16,* 1–20.

Lees, E. O. (1984). Using text-to-speech synthesis to assist poor editors. In L. Bridwell & D. Ross (Eds.), *Selected papers from the conference on computers and writing: New directions in teaching and research* (pp. 195–211). Houghton, MI: Michigan Technological University.

McDaniel, E. (1986). A comparative study of the first-generation invention software. *Computers & Composition, 3,* 7–21.

Melmed, A. S. (1986). The technology of American education: Problem and opportunity. *T.H.E. Journal, 14,* 77–81.

Nichols, R. G. (1986). Word processing and basic writers. *Journal of Basic Writing , 5,* 81–97.

Rodrigues, D. W., & Rodrigues, R. J. (1984). Computer-based creative problem solving. In W. Wresch (Ed.), *The computer in composition instruction: A writer's tool* (pp. 34–46). Urbana, IL: National Council of Teachers of English.

Rose, M. (1980). Rigid rules, inflexible plans, and the stifling of language: A cognitivist analysis of writer's block. *College Composition and Communication, 31,* 389–400.

Schwartz, H. J. (1984). SEEN: A tutorial and user network for hypothesis testing. In W. Wresch (Ed.), *The computer in composition instruction: A writer's tool* (pp. 47–62). Urbana, IL: National Council of Teachers of English.

Selfe, C. L. (1984). The predrafting processes of four high- and four low-apprehensive writers. *Research in the Teaching of English, 18,* 45–64.

Selfe, C. L. (1985). The electronic pen: Computers and the composing process. In J. L. Collins and E. A. Sommers (Eds.), *Writing on-line: Using computers in the teaching of writing* (pp. 174–190). Upper Montclair, NJ: Boynton/Cook.

Sommers, N. (1981). Intentions and revisions. *Journal of Basic Writing, 3,* 41–49.

Thiesmeyer, J. E. (1987). Expert systems, artificial intelligence, and the teaching of writing. In L. Gerrard (Ed.), *Writing at century's end: Essays on computer-assisted composition* (pp. 108–115). New York: Random House.

Troyka, L. Q. (1982). Perspectives on legacies and literacy in the 1980s. *College Composition and Communication, 33,* 256–257.

# 7

# Computers in Public Schools: Are We Being Realistic?

Andrea W. Herrmann

The recent proliferation of microcomputers in our society has catapulted education more swiftly into the information-age revolution than most of us ever anticipated. "Computer" has become the educational buzzword of the 1980s. Not long ago, if educators thought of computers at all, they thought of them in terms of math or business, not the humanities. Most English teachers never envisioned the possibility of ever using one themselves, much less teaching with it. All that has changed.

Ever since the microcomputer came on the market in the late 1970s, professional writers have written prolifically about their engagement with word processing. Indeed, word processing is fast becoming one of the computer's best known virtues. Teachers of subjects across the curriculum, as well as teachers of writing, are increasingly convinced that there is value in having their students write with computers. The growing number of journal articles stressing the advantages of computers in composition instruction during the last few years reflects the high expectations our profession holds for this tool.

But when we talk about computers in public classrooms, when we talk about computers replacing pencils, are we being realistic? Amidst the rising tide of enthusiasm, few reports point out the obstacles that composition teachers encounter at the front lines, when working with technology in the public schools. Yet, in moments of candor, English teachers sometimes admit they have lost more skirmishes in this computer revolution than they've won.

Therefore, in an effort to highlight potential problems accompanying the introduction of computers into English departments, the first half of this chapter looks at the struggles within public education, pointing out some of the reasons why computers are not being used effectively as writing tools in schools. The second half offers guidelines and recommendations aimed at helping schools successfully integrate computers into their writing curricula.

## PROBLEMS RELATED TO SCHOOL USE OF COMPUTERS

The major problems fall into four categories:

1. Problems inherent in our electronic age, an age requiring changes that upset traditional educational practices;
2. Administrative problems, including a lack of computer expertise among some administrators that results in their inability and unwillingness to assist teachers;
3. Teaching problems, including teachers' lack of experience with computers;
4. Application problems, even among teachers who are knowledgeable about computers, concerning the pedagogical approaches that are most effective in teaching writing.

Concerned educators must ask whether such problems represent mere inconveniences or whether they represent potential barriers to the successful implementation of computers as writing tools. If, indeed, the problems are potential barriers, then as educators we have a responsibility to understand their complexity and attempt to overcome them. Otherwise, effective computer applications in writing instruction may remain idiosyncratic, restricted to a limited number of teachers and schools, rather than becoming the norm.

### Problems Created by Our Technological Age

When we talk about pedagogical applications of computers, we're talking about change. Change is always unsettling but particularly so in our electronic age. The computer dramatically brings into question our traditional notions of what knowledge is and how education can best help children function in our evolving world. With the increasing quantities of information being made available within society, the responsibility of the educator is no longer to pass along a predigested package of "facts" for students to learn. Rather, schools need to help students (1) acquire appropriate data-gathering techniques using sophisticated technology and (2) learn methods for putting their information into a meaningful framework in order to determine its significance. The shifting needs of our information age underscore the importance of using computers for writing in the curriculum.

Society recognizes the need for change, but how capable are our schools of meeting this challenge? There is a love-hate relationship between innovation and tradition in our educational system. Our public schools want to do things within established guidelines, yet, at the same time, want to prepare children to live successfully in a rapidly changing world. This paradox is not easily resolved.

Marshall McLuhan, the prophet of our cybernetic age, depicted our changing world and the need for our educational institutions to take heed back in 1966:

> Centuries of specialist stress in pedagogy and in the arrangement of data now end with the instantaneous retrieval of information made possible by electricity. Automation is information and it not only ends jobs in the world of work, it ends subjects in the world of learning. It does not end the world of learning. (p. 300)

Just as education adjusted to the mechanical age of the assembly line, McLuhan reasoned, it must adjust to the electronic age.

> Our education has long ago acquired the fragmentary and piece-meal character of mechanism. It is now under increasing pressure to acquire the depth and interrelation that are indispensable in the all-at-once world of electric organization. (p. 310)

To be meaningful, education must be responsive to the "all-at-once world" taking place in society. And, to some degree, it has.

The Second National Survey of Instructional Uses of School Computers, which gathered information from more than 10,000 teachers and principals in a sample of over 2,300 U.S. elementary and secondary schools during the spring of 1985, reports that

- The number of computers used in elementary and secondary schools quadrupled from about 250,000 in 1983 to over one million in the spring of 1985.
- Three-quarters of the schools which had not previously used computers began to do so.
- During the 1984–1985 school year, approximately 15 million students and 500,000 teachers used computers as part of their school's instructional program. (Becker, 1986a, p. 1)

Increasing numbers of schools are purchasing increasing numbers of computers as our educational institutions attempt to respond to society's shifting needs. But what has really changed in the English classroom? Apparently not much. The Second National Survey reveals that, rather than tapping into the computer's power as an "instructional medium or a productivity tool," computer-related instruction in high schools is most often about the computer (Becker, 1986b, p. 3). This finding would seem to exclude the use of computers as tools for writing.

In fact, when we specifically look at the use of word processing for writing, we see how limited this application is. Word processing in high school most often occurs in business education courses (Becker, 1986b, p. 4), where students learn to copy and format documents, rather than in English classes, where instruction encompasses composing, revision, editing, and publishing strategies related to the creation of original pieces of writing. The report also notes that only 3% of K–3 students, 3% of 4–8 students, and 2% of 9–12 students use word processing in their English classes (Becker, 1986b, p. 6).

Yet despite the small percentages of high school English teachers teaching with word processing, those who do report highly positive results:

> Sixty-nine percent indicated that students had improved their writing, editing or proofreading skill by using computers—a greater consensus than for any other "effect" for any subject at any grade level. (Becker, 1986c, p. 13)

Thus, the problem is not that the schools are not buying computers but that in many classes, such as English, computers are not being used as effectively as they might be. What accounts for the fact that teachers who teach writing with computers believe them to be very beneficial, yet only limited numbers of teachers actually use them for that purpose? Could efforts to introduce computers as writing tools into English classes create stresses in public schools that work against instituting effective changes?

## Administrative Problems

Public schools are still traditionally paternalistic places. Authority, for the most part, is hierarchical: Administrators dominate teachers, who are rarely consulted about school rules, regulations, or changes.

Edicts come down from above, and teachers are expected to obey. Administrators in public education often take the attitude that they know more than teachers do, even in matters concerning the subject-matter expertise of the teacher. The few times teachers are consulted, it is often an empty gesture. An all-powerful administrative authority that lacks expertise concerning the pedagogical applications of computers can have devastating results, and many schools are learning this the hard way. Failure to include teachers knowledgeable about computers in the decision-making process has meant that districts must now devise creative ways to use the expensive, yet inappropriate, computer hardware and software they purchased without teacher input.

As part of a two-year ethnographic research project on a Pennsylvania high school writing class that I taught, using computers as writing tools, I interviewed the superintendent of a school district that had acquired a large number of computers through grant money the year before (Herrmann, 1985c). Although teachers were free to sign up to use the computing center, it sat idle most periods of the day. I asked the superintendent why there were no in-service programs, master teachers, curriculum coordinators, or other options available to help teachers learn effective ways of integrating computers into their courses. He responded, "If we encourage teachers to use this equipment, what do we do when we don't have enough computers to go around?" His fear that he would be unable to devise successful strategies for the allocation of this scarce resource encouraged him to do nothing toward helping teachers use the equipment that was already in place.

When I interviewed the principal of the high school, I asked him why he thought teachers were not using the computers. He replied, "There's no reason except they're afraid! Teachers are afraid to try anything new." Such fears might be well-founded, since teachers need opportunities to become comfortable with the equipment and to discover approaches that would meet their pedagogical goals before introducing computers to 30 or 35 students in a class.

I asked him what plans, if any, he had to assist interested teachers in gaining computer expertise. He replied, "If they want to, they're free to take computer courses at the colleges around here. If a teacher wants to learn to use computers, he'll figure out how to do it." Many teachers, of course, because of their anxieties, might not seek out such courses. Another part of the problem is that many administrators do not realize that word-processing software must be purchased if students are to use the computer as a writing tool. It is cheaper to purchase simple drill and practice software instead of the more sophisticated word-processing programs.

Take, for example, the situation in which a progressive school district in Arkansas had purchased enough computers for two computer rooms in its high school/middle school, one for programming and computer literacy and the other for word-processing and composition instruction. When the room intended for word processing sat unused, the administrators lamented that teachers were not teaching in it. Yet the school district had failed to allocate funding for the purchase of a word-processing program or printers. Nor had they taken steps to help the teachers gain any computer skills. The administrators had to learn that computers alone are not enough; word-processing programs, printers, and related materials also have to be available if computers are to become writing tools. Although the district eventually provided these materials, it was not until they promoted one of their computer-using English teachers to a position of specialist that word processing became a part of the English curriculum in any significant way.

Unfortunately, these are not isolated cases. During the 1986 National Council of Teachers of English Conference, at an advanced workshop in using computers in the English class, over half of the 50 participants indicated that administrators at their schools failed to support their efforts to integrate computers into English curricula (Bernhardt, Herrmann, Holdstein, & Hult, 1986). Without the knowledgeable cooperation of administrators, schools lack leadership and teachers lack support, including the allocation of necessary funds—all essential ingredients to the use of computers for writing in schools.

## Teaching Problems

Writing teachers confront their own difficulties in using computers as instructional tools. They need to learn how to use word processing for themselves before they are able to explore pedagogical approaches appropriate for their students. Teaching a graduate course in computers and composition has made me especially aware of the needs of teachers, particularly after conducting a qualitative study in one of the classes (Herrmann, 1987b).

Here is an example of one teacher's problems. Gloria, an intelligent, middle-aged graduate student, had used word processing for three years prior to the course. Yet she was still hesitant and fearful. I discovered she had only used the computer for keying in finished text.

In the class Gloria learned to risk making mistakes and to solve problems. She learned to compose while incorporating the unique and powerful procedures the computer offers writers into her writing process: inserting, deleting, moving blocks of text, merging files, and searching and replacing misspelled words. She gained self-confidence and flexibility as a computer-user, both critical traits of the successful teacher in an electronic classroom.

We see, then, that even teachers with word-processing experience may need instructional guidance. Writers need time to become comfortable with the range of possibilities offered by their word-processing program, especially to be able to call upon procedures automatically as they work. Integrating word-processing options, such as block moves, into one's writing process is facilitated with instruction, practice, and follow-up help. Until they feel confident using this technology for themselves, teachers are unlikely to teach others to use it. I stress this point because it is one of the principal reasons computers go unused in English classrooms.

But what about English teachers who have enthusiastic administrative support and who are comfortable with the use of computers as writing tools? Are their problems over? Unfortunately, no.

## Problems Involving Applications

Becoming comfortable with the computer is only the first step. Teachers need hardware and software that meet their minimum needs. They must decide what role the computer will play in their classrooms: Will it consist largely of computer-assisted instructional programs (cai) that drill students in grammar and mechanics in isolation from the process of writing? These programs are easy for teachers and students to use; however, such applications are controversial and increasingly questioned by writing theorists, researchers, and teachers (Herrmann, 1983).

Or will teachers concentrate on having students compose whole texts using word processing? If so, will the basics of the word-processing program be introduced in isolation from writing, or will word-processing and writing instruction be integrated right from the start? The teacher must decide what specific classroom activities will best serve his or her students' writing needs (Herrmann, 1985b).

Teaching students to write with a word-processing program is teaching two skills: word processing and writing. In the early stages of the course, this can turn into a juggling act for the teacher, who may worry that teaching students how to use word processing will engulf much of the available instructional time. Although word-processing programs vary as to complexity, the most encompassing programs allow the user a wide range of possible commands and procedures depending on what the writer wants to do. Programs are increasingly easier to learn, but it still takes time to incorporate effectively the various possible features into one's composing process. Furthermore, teachers who structure their writing courses around the use of word processing must still decide to what extent they will include additional software designed to support the writing of whole texts. Some programs, for example, assist writers' invention strategies, outlining abilities, and poetry and fiction writing skills. Others evaluate aspects of style, usage, and spelling.

Often programs intended as a support for writing are not compatible with any word-processing packages, making their use problematic. Some programs also take a good deal of time to learn. Others give students a complex array of information, which may not be helpful at their level of writing development. Teachers must be able to weigh the program's potential value against other factors, particularly the additional time students must spend using it. In many cases, the prudent choice may be to forego such programs in favor of maximizing students' time writing with word processing.

## GUIDELINES FOR INTRODUCING COMPUTERS INTO ENGLISH CURRICULA

Clearly, the greatest problem in implementing computers in the English classroom lies not in the decision to purchase computer equipment, since schools are doing this, but in the myriad issues surrounding the integration of word processing into the curriculum. Introducing computers into schools and classrooms is not enough. Administrators and teachers need to take steps to insure success.

First, they must acknowledge forthrightly that the computer brings changes. While creating new opportunities, the computer introduces new problems. In order to integrate computers as writing tools into the English curriculum, I recommend that school districts make the following changes:

1. Require administrators to become better educated concerning the educational applications of computers, particularly computers as writing tools;
2. Encourage administrators to work collaboratively with teachers, rather than maintaining traditional, paternalistic roles;

3. Create opportunities for English teachers to learn word processing and other computer applications related to writing;
4. Encourage teachers to foster collaborative learning in their classrooms, both among the students and between themselves and the students;
5. Provide additional support systems, including networking with computer-using teachers and a system of incentives and rewards, aimed at teachers who experiment with computers in their classrooms.

Each of these recommendations is discussed in detail in the section that follows.

## Administrators Must Be Educated About Computers

To begin with, schools need to require administrators to become more knowledgeable about the educational applications of computers. Integrating computers in schools is often seen solely as a problem of re-educating teachers. Certainly teachers need increased opportunities to learn how to use computers, but uninformed administrators are a more serious problem. Not every teacher needs to teach with computers, but the actions of just one unenlightened administrator can prevent the successful integration of computers within an entire school district or school. Because of their positions of power, including their control over financial matters, administrators can be serious impediments to educational innovation and change.

Administrators may need encouragement to break away from stereotyped ideas that value computers for mathematics over applications involving literacy. Superintendents, principals, vice-principals, curriculum coordinators, and department chairs should be expected to take courses involving the humanistic applications of computers, including the use of computers for writing. Those who are unwilling to become re-educated should be prevented from making and carrying out policies involving computers.

## Administrators and Teachers Must Collaborate

Since the computer brings about changes in the traditional dynamics of power and authority, it appears likely that success or failure at integrating computers in English classrooms will depend on the success or failure of the participants in adapting to the shifting role relationships our electronic age makes necessary. For the successful implementation of computers in English classes, the traditional hierarchy of power needs to be modified. Administrators and teachers need to work together collaboratively. Without effective collaboration with teachers, principals may find them unwilling to acquire the necessary computer skills or fearful of trying new approaches in their classrooms. Administrators will also fail to benefit from the teachers' specialized knowledge, namely their subject-matter expertise in relationship to their students' needs. Collaboration means that teachers will no longer be excluded from the decision-making process. A committee of computer-using teachers should always be included in formulating decisions that affect them.

It must be remembered that innovative teachers, not administrators, lead the way to reform by changing what goes on within their classrooms. Of course, enlightened administrators are clearly important, but classroom change cannot be mandated. Ultimately it rests with the teacher. Increasing the number of computers in a school may be one important step, supportive administrators another, but the real test of success will be what the teachers and students do together in their classrooms.

Our evolving educational world is becoming increasingly complex as a result of the availability of computer technology. Decisions are costly; mistakes are expensive and usually have long-lasting consequences. Formerly, writing teachers needed only a little ingenuity to make changes in their teaching approaches. Today, teachers need access to expensive equipment: computers, printers, various types of software programs, diskettes, fan-fold paper, printer ribbons, and other supplies. Teachers previously selected textbooks in keeping with their pedagogical goals. Now, purchasing computer hardware, choosing the software, deciding the location and layout of the computers, and other related matters are equally important. Collaboration between administrators and teachers should result in the purchase of equipment appropriate to teachers' needs; it should also provide them with another incentive to get involved in teaching with computers.

### Educational Opportunities Must Be Created for Teachers

School districts must create opportunities for teachers to acquire the skills needed to understand and use computer equipment effectively. If this is not done, only very dedicated computerphiles will have the necessary interest and expertise to teach using word processing and to make informed decisions about the selection and use of other computer materials for writing.

There must be an increase in in-service programs designed to be responsive to the needs of computer-using English teachers. Regular, substantive programs are necessary. An hour or two after the school day, once or twice a semester, won't do.

Preliminary investigations suggest the value of such educational opportunities for teachers. In one study, Hawisher (in press) interviewed experienced teachers after they participated in a four-week summer workshop and after they had returned to their teaching a semester later. She reports that a large percentage of these teachers became involved in establishing computer and composition curricula within their schools and that they also helped train other teachers to work with technology. Thus, it would seem that English teachers respond to the challenge of computers when provided with in-service opportunities.

I also researched and taught an intensive three-week graduate course for teachers in the use of computers as writing tools (Herrmann, 1987b). Six months after the course, eight of the eleven respondents reported teaching writing more. Many indicated using an expanded repertoire of writing activities and having their students do more revising and editing. Eight of the teachers indicated they now use word processing for their own professional and personal writing, and seven of the teachers use computers for writing with their students.

## Teachers and Students Need to Collaborate

Just as computers in schools require collaborative relationships between administrators and teachers, it appears that computers in classrooms work best in environments that foster collaboration between teachers and students. Collaboration, in fact, helps solve some of the problems that integrating computers into the English curriculum generates. Teachers familiar with the power and complexity of using computers for writing realize they will never have solutions for every problem that using computers generates. In traditional classrooms, teachers are expected to know, or at least pretend to know, everything. In collaborative classrooms, teachers are expected to explore along with students and to be a learner among learners. They are freed from the debilitating role of being the font of knowledge.

Collaborative classrooms benefit both teachers and students. Teachers grow when they are free to undertake classroom activities even in areas where they may not have all the answers or all the expertise. Class work is transformed. Teachers and students together confront and resolve real problems in need of real solutions. The opportunity for students to grow is also great. Their activities become true explorations in search of knowledge rather than rote exercises to please the teacher. The students may now become self-directed and involved.

Of course, the educational benefits of collaboration existed before the introduction of microcomputers. Mason (1972) argues in favor of it in his book, *Collaborative Learning:*

> The best learning is now most likely to happen where the itemized syllabus is abandoned and the distinction between teacher and learner is blurred to the point where, exploring together patterns of information new to both of them, the teacher's skill as a learner becomes apparent to the pupil and can be used as a model which need not be slavishly imitated but can be modified and elaborated. . . . This kind of collaboration should no longer be rare; it should be the basic teacher/learner relationship, the first aim, not the last. (p. 72)

Bruffee (1983) advocates collaboration as an essential aspect of the teaching of writing. He states:

> This necessity to talk-through the task of writing means that collaborative learning, which is the institutionalized counterpart of the social or collaborative nature of knowledge and thought, is not merely a helpful pedagogical technique incidental to writing. It is essential to writing. (p. 165)

Seymour Papert was probably the first to draw our attention to the value of collaboration in the teaching of writing with computers. As early as 1980, he offered the following:

> I believe that the computer as writing instrument offers children an opportunity to become more like adults, indeed like advanced professionals, in their relationship to their intellectual products and to themselves. (p. 31)

In the final analysis, Papert (1980) envisions the computer ''as a transitional object to mediate relationships that are ultimately between person and person'' (p. 183).

Preliminary evidence supports the idea that using computers for writing promotes this sort of collaboration. One study, conducted by Selfe and Wahlstrom (1986) at Michigan Technological University, found that the use of computers as composing tools intensified collaborative relationships among faculty and students by establishing new patterns of sharing information about writing. They report:

> Both teachers and students indicated that the traditional boundaries existing between the two groups began to break down when individuals came together to compose in a computer lab or workspace. (p. 290)

A similar result was discovered by Stephen Bernhardt and Bruce Appleby (1985) in a survey they conducted of professionals using computers for writing, 65% of whom were teachers. Much to the surprise of the investigators, they found that 13% of the respondents identified their students as "their primary collaborators on writing projects" (p. 34).

My own research, involving the high school writing class that I taught using word processing, also reveals that the role relationships between the teacher and the students, as well as among the students, changed to a more collaborative one (Herrmann, 1984, 1985a, 1985c, 1986).

> The interactional dynamics and the shift in our school work from using pencils to word processing necessitated making many transitions. There were transitions from a traditional, teacher-dominated classroom to an experimental, student-centered classroom; from the teacher as expert to the teacher as a learner among learners; . . . from writing as private and individual to writing as public and collaborative. . . . (1985c, pp. 324–325)

A greater degree of mutual support and a greater amount of collaboration, as opposed to the traditional hierarchies between teachers and students, are important changes that teaching writing with computers can foster. Knowing the value of a collaborative classroom environment may encourage teachers, who would otherwise hesitate, to risk introducing computers for writing into their classrooms. Schools need to help teachers see the value of collaboration and to support teachers who want to teach in such an environment.

### Support Systems for Teachers Must Be Increased

In education's rapidly changing world, novice and expert computer-using English teachers alike need support systems that will assist them in carrying out the activities that they cannot do alone. As we have seen, computers make new demands on teachers to make changes: to learn more, to create more collaborative classroom environments, to work harder, and to be more creative. The vast majority of teachers are already greatly overworked; they do not have the time necessary to meet these new demands. Support needs to extend teachers' evolving levels of expertise by making information and materials concerning computer applications available and by helping teachers cope with the problems an electronic classroom produces. This support involves changes in the environment where teachers and students work as well as changes in the personnel available to assist teachers.

If we want our students to do more than use the computer for drill and practice or simply as a fancy typewriter, schools must recognize the need to make changes in the classroom environment. English classes need regular access to computers, preferably in a computer center with a knowledgeable director available. The computers should be configured in such a way as to permit collaboration among students and to allow the teacher to move freely among students as well. The computer center should also be open to students and teachers on a drop-in basis before and after regular school hours and during lunch.

In addition to creating a positive writing environment, districts should create new positions of leadership and reconsider the qualifications and duties of existing administrative positions. There should be districtwide curriculum coordinators with expertise in the humanistic applications of computers, including computers as tools for teaching writing. Within each school there should be master teachers with computer expertise; these teachers should be given a reduced course load so that they can keep abreast of developments in the field and provide assistance to other teachers. The director of the computer center should be expert in the word-processing programs used by the English teachers. To fill at least some of these positions, computer-using English teachers within the school should be promoted or, if necessary, English teachers with computer expertise hired.

School districts should assist English teachers in creating networks with other computer-using faculty in their schools, in their districts, in their states, and nationally. Within the school and the district, computer-using teachers and administrators should be encouraged to form committees that meet regularly to formulate appropriate policies and to decide on the purchase of new hardware and software. Networking in the state and nation can be facilitated by newsletters, by subscribing to computer and writing journals, by using computers' telecommunications powers to network electronically with teachers and with students in other areas, and by sending teachers to workshops and conferences.

In addition, districts can encourage teachers to go beyond simply teaching writing with computers and to do research in their own classrooms (Herrmann, 1985c, 1987a). Encouraging teachers to become researchers will increase the individual teacher's understanding of the effects of this new technology on the learning of students. It will make these teachers important resources to the school and to the educational community in general. By investigating what goes on in their own classrooms, teachers arm themselves with the knowledge and power needed to maintain control over the pedagogical decisions that affect their students, their classrooms, and themselves.

An important ingredient in these recommendations, however, is that districts should not expect writing teachers to meet the extra demands teaching with computers makes on them without receiving adequate compensation. Districts need to provide incentives for teachers who are willing to take on the added responsibilities entailed in using computers. Such incentives might include providing teachers with released time; increasing their salary benefits; reducing the number of classes they teach; reducing their class size; and paying their expenses to workshops and conferences.

## VIEWING CHANGE AS LIBERATING

Schools can choose to view the changes brought about by computer technology as either threatening or liberating. Since word-processing programs are promising tools for communication in general and for writing in particular, accepting the computer as a writing tool in education should be viewed as a liberating change. Yet the optimum conditions for such change cannot be expected to happen automatically.

Education's successful leap into the technological age requires much more than the purchase of greater numbers of computers. Significant modifications must be made in the way things have always been done. As educators, we cannot remain insensitive to the complexity of the issues involved. We cannot refuse to address emerging problems. We cannot remain rigid in our traditional roles. Without the informed and collaborative efforts of administrators and teachers as well as of teachers and students in the use of computers as writing tools, it is unlikely that the conditions necessary for profound, rather than cosmetic, change will occur in our schools.

## REFERENCES

Becker, H. J. (1986a, June). *Instructional uses of school computers: Reports from the 1985 national survey* (Issue No. 1). Baltimore, MD: Johns Hopkins University, Center for Social Organization of Schools.

Becker, H. J. (1986b, August). *Instructional uses of school computers: Reports from the 1985 national survey* (Issue No. 2). Baltimore, MD: Johns Hopkins University, Center for Social Organization of Schools.

Becker, H. J. (1986c, November). *Instructional uses of school computers: Reports from the 1985 national survey* (Issue No. 3). Baltimore, MD: Johns Hopkins University, Center for Social Organization of Schools.

Bernhardt, S. A., & Appleby, B. C. (1985). Collaboration in professional writing with the computer: Results of a survey. *Computers and Composition, 2* (1), 29–42.

Bernhardt, S. A., Herrmann, A. W., Holdstein, D., & Hult, C. (1986, November). *The computer in your English class: Effective applications.* Post-convention workshop conducted at the National Council of Teachers Convention, San Antonio, TX.

Bruffee, K. A. (1983). Writing and reading as collaborative acts. In J. N. Hays, P. A. Roth, J. R. Ramsey, & R. D. Foulke (Eds.), *The writer's mind: Writing as a mode of thinking* (pp. 159–169). Urbana, IL: National Council of Teachers of English.

Hawisher, G. E. (in press). Reading and writing connections: A model for introducing composition pedagogy and word processing to English teachers. In D. Holdstein & C. L. Selfe (Eds.), *Issues in computers and writing.* New York: Modern Language Association.

Herrmann, A. W. (1983). Using the computer as writing teacher: The heart of the great debates. In *Proceedings of the Annual Summer Conference, The Computer: Extension of the Human Mind II* (pp. 25–37). Eugene, OR: College of Education, University of Oregon. (ERIC Document Reproduction Service No. ED 260 406)

Herrmann, A. W. (1984, November). *The computer in the English classroom: The changing role of the teacher.* (Cassette Recording No. 74329-012). Paper presented at the National Council of Teachers of English Conference, Detroit, MI. (ERIC Document Reproduction Service No. ED 255 943)

Herrmann, A. W. (1985a, March). *Collaboration in a high school computers and writing class: An ethnographic study.* Paper presented at the Conference on College Composition and Communication, Minneapolis, MN. (ERIC Document Reproduction Service No. ED 258 256)

Herrmann, A. W. (1985b, November). *Teaching strategies for introducing word processing into the writing class.* Paper presented at the National Council of Teachers of English Conference, Philadelphia, PA. (ERIC Document Reproduction Service No. ED 276 037)

Herrmann, A. W. (1985c). Using the computer as a writing tool: Ethnography of a high school writing class. *Dissertation Abstracts International, 47,* 02A. (University Microfilms No. 86-02,051)

Herrmann, A. W. (1986). An ethnographic study of a high school writing class using computers: Marginal, technically proficient, and productive learners. In L. Gerrard (Ed.), *Writing at century's end: Essays on computer-assisted composition* (pp. 79–91). New York: Random House.

Herrmann, A. W. (1987a). Researching your own students: What happens when the teacher turns ethnographer? *The Writing Instructor, 6,* 114–128.

Herrmann, A. W. (1987b, March). *Teaching teachers to use computers for writing across the curriculum.* Paper presented at the Conference on College Composition and Communication, Atlanta, GA. (ERIC Document Reproduction Service No. ED 280 032)

Mason, E. (1972). *Collaborative learning* (1st ed.). New York: Schocken.

McLuhan, M. (1966). *Understanding media: The extensions of man* (2nd ed.). New York: New American Library.

Papert, S. (1980). *Mindstorms: Children, computers, and powerful ideas* (1st ed.). New York: Basic Books, Inc.

Selfe, C. L., & Wahlstrom, B. J. (1986). An emerging rhetoric of collaboration: Computers, collaboration, and the composing process. *Collegiate Microcomputer, 4,* 289–295.

# 8

# Training College Teachers for Computers and Writing

Deborah H. Holdstein

Because of the lack of professional exchange among instructors interested in using computers in their writing classes, I shall discuss in this chapter some of the issues related to computer training for college faculty. In doing so, I shall point to some potential problems that might arise, posit questions related to work in computers and writing, and propose a training and follow-up program for college teachers.

## BACKGROUND

In the introduction to the 1976 edition of his excellent book, *Teaching Composition: Ten Bibliographical Essays,* Tate cites Paul T. Bryant's presentation at the 1973 meetings of the Conference on College Composition and Communication. In one of the earliest calls to writing specialists to establish their field as worthy of pursuit, Bryant indicts teachers of college composition for "not learning from the past and for not systematically accumulating a body of knowledge to undergird their practice" (Tate, 1976, p. vii). In response to the secondary status often accorded composition and its faculty in most traditional English departments, Bryant notes,

> Too often we behave as if there is no continuity in the teaching of composition, as if the subject has just been invented and every idea for teaching it is new at the moment. We fail to draw on the experience of colleagues. We learn neither from past successes, of which there have been a few, nor from past failures, of which there have been all too many. As a group, we are the living proof of the adage that those who do not know history are condemned to repeat it. (pp. vii-viii)

Bryant also argues that the teaching of composition is both a science and an art. As a science, the field demands that its instructors

> move ahead in the accumulation of . . . knowledge in a clearly linear fashion. . . . Every generation of composition teachers not only can, but is obligated to, stand upon the intellectual shoulders of the generations that have gone before. An historical, know-nothing approach to this type of knowledge is wasteful and stupid, to say the least. (p. vii)

Few would question the wisdom of providing some formal guidance for new instructors of composition at the college level. Yet a decade ago, several institutions with large freshman composition programs (and large populations of teaching assistants assigned to those courses) had only begun to add formal "seminars" in the teaching of writing to their lists of offerings for graduate students. Additional courses in rhetoric and composition, some reasoned, might detract from the graduate students' more important, intellectually trenchant purpose: the study of literature and critical theory.

Despite Bryant's reasonable call to arms, college instructors interested in the theory and practice of teaching writing have been tacitly, if not overtly, discouraged by many graduate departments of English from devoting time to preparing themselves as composition teachers. Graduate teaching assistants assume responsibility for many of the composition classes taught in university English departments, and many of them will carry sections of composition as part of their teaching loads as full-time faculty; nonetheless, some English department faculty to this day tolerate only subtle, inobtrusive forms of "supervision for instructors"—a seminar on teaching composition, perhaps, a departmental manual containing sample handouts and syllabi based on the agreed-upon text, a "teaching assistant–to–teaching assistant buddy system," or a more experienced graduate teaching assistant supervising a group of newcomers and observing their teaching. To acknowledge this "teacher training," that is, any preparation for instructors of writing, is to raise the dread spectre of colleges of education, of English education, of Masters of Arts in Teaching, of "inservice" and other notions outside the domain and interpretive community of English departments and their dedication to the study and teaching of literature and critical theory. Only in the last several years has the subject of rhetoric and composition become an appropriate focus of inquiry for instructors within the critical canon of a traditional department of English. And if English departments are slow to accept teaching writing as a worthy pursuit, think how slow they will be to accept teaching writing with a computer!

## COMPUTERS AND THE ENGLISH DEPARTMENT

It should surprise no one by now that the introduction of the computer to the English department writing curriculum has been met with new variations on this old theme of resistance. And if there is as yet no systematic "theory" on appropriate training of college instructors for computers and writing (or much theory on computers and writing), there is even less practice. Where it exists at all, training in computers and writing is often haphazard (particularly when we compare college efforts with those at the secondary level), often foiled by the myriad components of hardware, computer-center time, and interdepartmental cooperation.

The field of computers and writing demands its own intensive, planned, organized instructor-training effort, in addition to other forms of instructor support and supervision for teaching writing. Once computers are introduced to the composition curriculum, senior faculty teaching writing might well need the same training as graduate teaching assistants or junior faculty members. Since some English department colleagues disparage the idea of "training" to begin with, writing faculty capable of training their colleagues must first gain respect for their efforts in composition and computers. They must also gather support for the structured teacher training that will incorporate computers into the formal writing curriculum. (See Holdstein, 1986, 1987.)

Like so many Natty Bumppos on the prairie, individually forging new paths through a new frontier, those involved in computers and writing (and those helping others get involved) still represent a uniformly small, if vocal, band of pioneers. Dispersed at colleges throughout the United States, these instructors only occasionally meet through electronic computer conferencing or major convention conferencing. Even at these conferences the question most raised is not How can I help my colleagues get into this? but How should I convince my colleagues that I should be doing this at all?

So, despite the interest in computers-and-writing sessions at major conferences, the field is still relatively new in terms of having acquired a broad base of faculty expertise in either practice or theory. While publications concerning the role of computers and writing continue to increase, a significant number of colleagues interested in using the computer within their writing curricula still don't know where to begin, much less how to attract and train others to do the same.

And since the issue of instructor training at the college level has been largely ignored, faculty must frequently waste time reinventing

the wheel. They have little opportunity to learn from colleagues because the people involved in student-centered work with computers
and writing at the college level have been too busy with logistics to
conduct faculty training sessions as well. They have organized writing
laboratories, reviewed software, negotiated and argued for resources,
determined their own best methods for using the computer in the
writing curriculum, attempted to define "good" or "productive" or
"scholarly" research in computers and writing, with little time left
over for teaching and training newcomers (Holdstein, 1986).

In other words, they have been working towards firmly establishing the field for their own students and for their own professional
goals with little attention given to formally helping others do the
same. If these energetic faculty members could be encouraged to devote some of their efforts to training others, they would soon have
colleagues to share the responsibility for logistics, leaving themselves
more time for scholarly pursuit.

## TRAINING FACULTY

Even if all political and practical obstacles to using computers in
writing curricula can be overcome, another issue remains: the training
itself. Who should train instructors? How should they be trained? By
whom? How should one begin? Training efforts should be initiated
and supported by departmental hierarchies (if only to help instructors
deal with intrauniversity negotiations for computer time). No one
system of training will work for all universities and colleges: any
training program demands that faculty and administrative decisions be
based on their particular university context. The individual teaching
patterns, software selections, and writing lab setups at a small college
might not fill the needs or suit the population and resources at a larger
university, and vice versa. While efforts at other institutions might
serve as advisory, starting-off points, only by careful examination of
their own unique needs can departments be assured that their training
will provide a student-centered, teaching-supported context.

Even acknowledging the differences that exist from campus to
campus, most faculty members committed to implementing the computer within their university-based writing curriculum will find several things they can do—and several they should not—when beginning
to train other faculty. My remarks are primarily directed to the training
of novice computer users, a far greater challenge than a training ser-
mon designed for the converted. (Faculty charged with the training,

however, will find that there exist wide ranges of ability and interest in any faculty workshop.) I shall often overlap "what" things should be learned with "how" the instructional plan should be implemented; they are as inseparable to the writing specialist as "form" and "content" are to the literary critic.

One simple rule should be followed before faculty are encouraged to enter the lab with a writing class: instructors should be proficient and comfortable with whatever word-processing package students will use. Never encourage faculty to "leave all of the students' software instruction to the people in the computer lab." Why? Imagine a colleague who tries to teach *Romeo and Juliet* without having read the play, or imagine one who has given an assignment or examination borrowed from a colleague, and then turns the grading over to a colleague in physics. Hard to imagine? I've witnessed colleagues who didn't bother to learn the software and hardware first, either with others' help or on their own; they merely "observed" a lab assistant teach their students the rudiments of, say, *Wordstar,* and then, with no knowledge of any software's capabilities, told their students to "enter and revise their papers" or to "just free-write for a while."

Certainly some students might eventually master the computer's potential for revision in this instance, but such instructors will have generated mostly "busywork" when they could have instead achieved more significant results. Of course, the same general rules apply to any instructor given (or assuming) the role of computers-and-writing mentor (or trainer) to other faculty. In other words, instructors must know the software to be used in training other instructors just as they needed to master it for their own students.

To avoid potential abuses of computer laboratory time, and to disabuse instructors of their fears that the computer will control their classrooms and completely change their teaching methods, training leaders must first promote rethinking the roles of the computer and the instructor in the classroom. They must encourage instructors to

- Devise their own methods for teaching students to use the computer that grow naturally from their own, tried-and-true writing strategies, now enhanced by the computer
- Acquire the necessary knowledge to troubleshoot general questions about software for their students, who also must learn the software thoroughly lest the mechanical aspects of the computer impede their writing processes
- Become advisers to students as they write their drafts, a productive role only if the instructor can easily integrate knowl-

edge of the software's simple functions with suggestions to the student for revision.

Even more important than knowing what to do, however, is knowing what *not* to do. Colleagues and students are likely to be apprehensive, even hostile, toward the computer and eager to seize on any mistake by the trainer as cause for damning computers and computer-based writing. Here is a general list of what *not* to do in faculty training, and why. The list is devised from my own experience (Holdstein, 1987) and from conversations with others:

- Never try to teach colleagues information they won't really need, like graphics cards, motherboards, buffers, the promise of artificial intelligence, and so on. Until the participants have mastered the software that will form the basis for discussions on teaching, such information will be distracting and intimidating.
- Avoid the temptation to stage a lecture series on computers as the primary means of instruction. Small-groups, particularly with individual attention and hands-on experience, are most effective—just as they would be for any group of beginning, uncertain writers.
- Avoid making attendance at workshops mandatory. Gentle, behind-the-scenes persuasion along with a "strongly encouraged to attend" but "optional sign-up" policy will prove far more effective. A small, enthusiastic group is better than a large, frustrated one.
- Don't assume that everyone teaching composition has to learn to use the computer as part of her or his method of teaching writing. The computer is an enhancement tool, not a replacement for traditional methods that have worked well in the past. Trainers must be as open-minded towards others' effective teaching methods (which for good reason might not include the computer) as they want others to be about technology.
- Don't assume that you are the only one with anything worthwhile to teach. Even with a group of novices, learning is one-way only if the training is arbitrarily (and wrongly) separated from curricular and teaching issues.

Trainers will undoubtedly generate additional lists based on the dynamics of their own programs, departments, and universities.

## WHAT ELSE SHOULD TEACHERS KNOW?

The need for participants' grounding in the theory and practice of composition—and even in critical theory—becomes particularly important within a training program for composition and computers. For instance, Emig's (1977) assertion that composing is a way of learning works for both instructor and writing student. As teachers learn to write using the computer, as they move from using the computer as a typewriter to composing and revising at the terminal, and as they learn to integrate hard-copy/pencil editing with on-screen revising, they concurrently begin to envision teaching methods that are grounded in the composing process.

Moreover, workshops must focus on those skills and concepts that teachers can easily transport to their own classrooms; teachers must be able to transform these skills to suit their methods of teaching and their students' needs. For instance, Fish's (1980) notion of "interpretive communities," coupled with the social contexts of other recent reader-response, feminist, sociological, and composition theories (see, for instance, Bazerman, 1983; Faigley, 1986; Bartholomae, 1986; Bizzell, 1982; Showalter, 1985), encourages the close examination of texts within the influence and context of various "communities"— both inside and outside the classroom—and underscores such pedagogical strategies as draft exchange, critiques among teachers and students, peer revision groups, and so on. Through their familiarity with recent scholarship, then, instructors in a computers-and-writing workshop can transform good, theory-based, "traditional" pedagogy into appropriately wrought "electronic" pedagogy, often combining the best of both worlds.

Before they can effectively use computers within the curriculum, then, instructors must first be prepared to base their approaches in the process theory and practice of composition, only then acquiring computing concepts and skills to use within that theory-based context. As instructors become familiar with a word-processing package, previous readings in composition and process-based theory provide an informed context for experimenting with technology. For instance, we can use the word-processing package's filing system to support multiple drafting. We can generate methods for using networks, for sharing files, for initiating and conducting peer revision groups, and for critiquing and exchanging drafts.

Most important, we can learn to create prewriting "files": idea-generating questions for topics that we develop with our students in brainstorming sessions, another skill derived through social theory and composition-process theory. Using the computer's capabilities to support draft exchanges and critiques among peer revision groups, instructors also learn to conduct group evaluations of drafts in a projection classroom (one paper projected at the front of the classroom) or through networked computers in the "regular" computer classroom. Besides becoming familiar with social and process-based theory, instructors can look into reader-response and other recent critical theory to inform these aspects of classroom practice.

In sum, the context of an appropriate training program focuses on the give-and-take between theory and scholarship; it supports process-based teaching of composition and necessary practical skills—creating files, moving parts of text, generating hard copy, and using networks—in order to implement the technology that will best support the way we teach writing and the ways in which students learn it.

## A TRAINING PROGRAM

Word processing is taught best when the teacher uses it and understands its effects on his or her own composing, writing, and rewriting processes. Since individual instructors will approach even a department-wide syllabus with different emphases, techniques, and goals, faculty trainers cannot expect total agreement about one, specific, perfectly defined role for the computer. The good trainer will be quick to channel these many perspectives into fruitful discussion and "brainstorming" during the workshop.

How often should workshops meet? No one answer is appropriate for all situations. Given the diversity of faculty schedules and vacations, I've met with groups for only two intensive days during registration week; this immersion approach works, but, when practical, a long-term approach (after an initial, intensive day or two) with regular monthly meetings throughout the semester appears to be more effective for both faculty who have never used the computer at all and veteran computer writers. I stress that this is a possible approach when, due to time constraints, it is most feasible. A two-day, intensive approach, followed by four or five days with approximately six hours' training a day, would seem ideal.

In the rest of this section, I will describe a workshop I have developed as an example of one possible approach. First I want to emphasize a few general points. All meetings should take place in the computer lab, where there is always the opportunity for "hands on" work and illustration by example. Because workshop leaders can't always meet participants' different needs at the same time, I recommend training several graduate assistants in the word-processing program so they can help provide individual attention to faculty at the terminals. Initial instruction (loading DOS, turning on the machine, and so on) works fine at the group level as long as several trained assistants are available to tackle any individual problems. In addition, any trainer should warn participants that any new computer effort brings with it a guarantee that any and many things will go wrong: disks won't work ("boot"), terminals will die, work won't get "saved," and so on. Forewarned, participants are less likely to blame themselves and tend to be accepting, if vigilant, of foul-ups.

What follows is a general description of the workshop sessions. During the first morning session, called "Getting Started," we begin with very rudimentary instruction—finding the "on" switch, locating disk drives, loading DOS, formatting disks, and making sure that each disk is formatted only once, so that participants won't lose their saved text. (Since there is always a wide range of familiarity with computers in any given workshop, those participants most familiar with the computer and the software are enlisted to help those who are less so.) After participants load the word-processing package, they free-write or enter text they have brought along with them, allowing themselves to become comfortable with the keyboard and such functions as "insert" and "delete." We print out these texts—and revise with pen on the hard copy—before focusing on the capabilities of the software (moving text, for example).

During this time, colleagues write a document for use in a class: either a syllabus, a handout, portions of articles stemming from their own research, or another document already in progress. Producing something useful enhances the workshop and the participants' sense of its overall practicality, particularly in this early phase. Quite often, the morning activities extend to the afternoon, the instructors' own composing processes having prepared them to discuss their students' writing needs.

During the afternoon of the first day, we spend time reviewing and discussing aspects of composition theory and the ways in which it structures the work we do in class with our students. Called "The Computer in a Process-Based Classroom," the afternoon session gives us time to brainstorm and design assignments in small groups after participants have spent time in their revision groups going over the morning's hard copy with pen or pencil. Afterwards, the groups cluster around terminals and take turns discussing one another's documents and entering revisions, helping one another use the more sophisticated capabilities of the software. Afterwards, we do the same to write up group-generated assignments. If there is additional time during this first afternoon, we also look at different types of computer-aided instruction—tutorials, drill-and-practice—and discuss whether these might be adapted for some students in the process-based curriculum. (If time runs out, and it often does, we save this demonstration and discussion for the next morning.) We cap the afternoon's work by discussing which computer-based activities might be most fruitful for our own classrooms, together generating more ideas for process-based writing activities using the computer. This very lively exchange usually keeps us going past our scheduled concluding time.

During the morning of day two, called "More Practice and Process: Word Processing and Composing, Continued," participants continue the work they started the day before, revising classroom activities and assignments as well as their syllabi, handouts, and other documents related to their own research. All the while, participants become more comfortable with the software and its capabilities; the anxieties associated with word processing are eased by collaborative work within the familiar, process-based contexts of classroom work they already know. Most important, the computer becomes the medium that helps these instructors become aware of their own writing processes. As a result, instructors integrate the ways in which they create classroom materials to assist students' writing processes with the ways in which the instructors themselves write. During this time, we also focus on printing, using graphics in creating classroom-related documents, discussing other issues related to multiple drafting and revising, and analyzing ways of using networks for peer critiques and collaborative writing. Since there are usually issues from the previous day's discussion that require more time, the morning gives us the opportunity to reiterate what we've already covered while using these skills to introduce new topics.

The program for the afternoon, "More Applications," finds us still discussing methods for the process-based computer-writing classroom; we now, however, integrate these issues with ways to evaluate software, to use CAI, and to keep records of students' progress on the computer. We also take our discussion of networking to the projection classroom, delineating ways to use networked terminals and the projection screen for group commentary on drafts. At this point, as instructors become familiar and comfortable with methods and issues surrounding computer use in the writing curriculum, they are likely to raise issues of ethics and procedure: in this instance, the question of public versus private writing in the projection classroom. Our last hours, then, are spent discussing the ethical issues raised by computer use for writing as well as the political and practical considerations that instructors might later confront.

Although most participants enjoy writing their evaluations of the workshop at the terminal, this does not preclude our having thorough and lively discussions as well. In fact, after one workshop, participants' feedback encouraged certain changes from an earlier model, resulting in extra "free time" for devising classroom activities and generating classroom-related documents during the late morning of day two. In another workshop, participants shortened the lunch break to have additional time in the computer lab.

A week-long effort augments the two-day plan and includes the following (if incomplete) list of activities:

- Additional discussion of process-based readings in composition and technical communications, as well as in cross-disciplinary contexts such as sociology and philosophy
- Further brainstorming sessions to generate classroom ideas
- More practice with different types of software and word-processing software
- Additional teamwork (as before, colleagues, in pairs or larger groups, devising exercises, commenting on one another's work as practice for commenting on student papers and students' collaborative writing)
- Further discussions of access and ethics; issues in research; shortcomings of recent research; computer lab etiquette; critiques of computers and writing; and practical problems—scheduling, assistance, and so on

Whether the workshop lasts for two days or one week, the group and I always seem to complain that we have used our time well but that "there is too much unfinished business." There never seems to be enough time to discuss everything we want to discuss; as a result, I must plan for follow-up activities as I plan for the workshop, even if these concerns are not part of the formal workshop agenda.

## THE FOLLOW-UP: A WRITING COLLOQUIUM

I have used the computer workshop as the impetus for an ongoing "writing colloquium," a series of meetings that provides structure for regular discussions after the formal training process. These meetings are a forum for scholarly discussion in which all instructors, both learned and uninitiated, can participate; by holding meetings in the lab, I can encourage further brainstorming and discussion about classroom applications of the computer in both writing and literature.

Since the circumstances for using the computer within the writing curriculum might change, given the dynamics of a department or institution, the basic structure of workshops might remain the same while the content varies. Colloquium sessions allow colleagues to plan workshops and their content, debating the need for different emphases on particular issues or skills. Recalling Bryant's words, note that composition instructors have been guilty of having learned "neither from past successes, of which there have been a few, nor from past failures, of which there have been all too many" (Tate, 1976, p. vii). Within workshops and follow-up colloquia, then, we have the chance to revise our methods, to change our attitudes and tendencies, and to learn from the successes and failures of previous workshops and actual day-to-day implementation of our theories. Colloquia also allow us time to address the questions that come up during classes in the lab or as we think further about teaching- and research-related issues in composition and computers. Some questions that have arisen during monthly colloquia (and during the week-long training, when that scheme is possible) include the following:

- Why use the computer at all?
- Should students use style analyzers? How? Do they merely encourage cookie-cutter, uninspired, formulaic, prescribed writing, particularly in the wrong instructor's hands?
- Should word processing be a departmental requirement for students' outside papers, even if the instructor includes no formal computers-and-writing component within the syllabus?
- What about students who seem hampered rather than helped by classroom computer use?
- What are the ethical issues surrounding "public" versus "private" writing in the lab?
- What are issues of "equal access" for all students who are interested in using the computer for writing and their ramifications for the students in this department?
- What about gender differences that occasionally surface during student computer use?
- How should instructors balance word processing with computer-aided instruction? Should CAI be used at all? For what purpose?

- What if one instructor prefers certain software over the lab's or the department's choice?
- How many times a week should a class meet in the lab?
- How can instructors cope with the latest litany of computer-age excuses now given by students? (Replacing such old saws as grandmother's death or the dog's accidents.)

A point that bears repeating: as with any other type of classroom experience, those training instructors to use the computer for their writing (or literature) classes must allow for the differences among participants and the ways in which they teach. The relative youth of the computers-and-writing discipline notwithstanding, good workshop leaders will pattern the content of future workshops and follow-up colloquia the way they would pattern any other productive learning and teaching experience, allowing instructors to grow and change as, to again quote Bryant, they "move ahead in the *accumulation* of . . . knowledge" (Tate, 1976, p. vii; emphasis mine).

Topics in addition to the ones I've mentioned for colloquia and ongoing discussion will depend on faculty interaction in particular humanities or English departments, as will practical issues and procedures for evaluating instructors: for instance, whether or not instructors will be observed working with students in the laboratory and in the regular classroom (as students revise hard copy in peer groups, for instance); whether or not instructors will be observed by the director of composition and/or the training leader.

To insure goodwill within the department and within the college, I've invited administrators, who have often spent a good deal of money on computers and software, to the workshops. Many welcome the opportunity to see how faculty are using resources. And the dean's familiarity with departmental efforts, for example, won't hurt strategically when it's time for the department chair to negotiate for further computer or software resources, or when the dean presents the newest developments in her or his college to the rest of the university community.

## SOME FINAL COMMENTS

All of these exciting opportunities present options and risks to teachers of writing as they prepare for the future of computers and writing at the college level. It is clear, however, that developing programs in teacher training can lead to fruitful collaborations in pedagogy and research with other writing instructors; with colleagues in literature and theory; with instructors in other, related disciplines; with administrators throughout the university; with students; and with computer center staff.

As recent scholarship in technical communications has taught us (see Bazerman, 1983), contact with others involved in computers "across the curriculum" does not mean that writing instructors have to become computer scientists, or even computer "specialists"; nor does it mean that one will suddenly abandon scholarly work. Rather, flexible teacher training that acknowledges the problems as well as the possibilities of computers and writing emphasizes the unique contributions each writing instructor brings to the curriculum and classroom—and the essential emphasis on teacher and student interaction that must underscore any instructional or administrative decision regarding computers in the teaching and learning of writing.

## REFERENCES

Bartholomae, D. (1986). Inventing the university. *Journal of Basic Writing, 5,* 4–23.

Bazerman, C. (1983). Scientific writing as a social act: A review of the literature of the sociology of science. In P. Anderson, R. Brockmann, & C. Miller (Eds.), *New essays in technical and scientific communication: Research, theory, practice* (pp. 156–184). Farmingdale, NY: Baywood.

Bizzell, P. (1982). College composition: Initiation into the academic discourse community. *Curriculum Inquiry, 12,* 197–207.

Emig, J. (1977). Writing as a mode of learning. *College Composition and Communication, 28,* 122–128.

Faigley, L. (1986). Competing theories of process: A critique and a proposal. *College English, 48,* 527–542.

Fish, S. (1980). *Is there a text in this class?* Cambridge, MA: Harvard University Press.

Holdstein, D.H. (1986). The politics of CAI and word-processing: Some issues for faculty and administrators. In L. Gerrard (Ed.), *Writing at century's end: Theory and practice in computers and writing* (pp. 122–130). New York: Random House.

Holdstein, D.H. (1987). *On composition and computers.* New York: Modern Language Association.

Showalter, E. (Ed.). (1985). *The new feminist criticism: Essays on women, literature, and theory.* New York: Pantheon.

Tate, G. (Ed.). (1976). *Teaching composition: Ten bibliographical essays.* Fort Worth: Texas Christian University Press.

# Part III

# PROMISING DEVELOPMENTS: THEORY AND PRACTICE

In an important sense, the lure of computers is always what they promise for the future. The first part of this collection looked to the past in an attempt to establish what we have learned of the role of technology in composition classes and studies. The chapters in the second part identified problems that characterize much of our involvement with technology today and presented tentative solutions. This third part, then, looks to the future with an overview of some of the noteworthy developments—both theoretical and practical—in computers and composition.

As a profession, we are just beginning to realize how dramatically our work with computers could change the writing classroom and our concepts of literacy by providing alternative or complementary settings for traditional academic dialogue. Even now, for example, computer networks make conversations possible among writers and readers in different geographical locations, often for individuals who are handicapped and for those who do not find it possible, because of age or economic constraints, to attend traditional classrooms. Currently thousands of students each year participate in college or advanced education programs in "virtual," or on-line, classrooms rather than in traditional settings.

Classrooms, of course, are not the only parts of our writing programs influenced by advances in technology. Computers and desktop publishing have made it possible for small composition programs in individual schools to design, lay out, and reproduce high-quality documents. The advent of desktop publishing has resulted in more newsletters, more brochures, more documents of all kinds than were previously possible. An article in the *Christian Science Monitor* ("Study finds," 1988) attributes the fact that there were 265 more magazines published in 1987 than in 1986 directly to the increase in computer-based publication techniques. This immediate access to the power of the press, limited heretofore to wealthy publishing houses and newspapers, changes the nature and politics of communication and the publishing process—matters of critical concern to teachers of English.

Finally, experts claim that computers will, or have already, changed the ways in which readers and writers think: that computers allow for the integration of graphic and textual representations of the same material, that they alter our notions of conversation and information exchange, that they encourage us to establish connections we do not normally make. In a college graduation address, James Dickey noted:

> One constantly hears the computer referred to as a tool, as though this were reassurance of some sort. It is reassurance only until one remembers how the tool has shaped the human hand, and notes with a shock that this tool is shaping not the hand but the mind. A tool used as extensively as the computer cannot help influencing how we think. (quoted in "Melange," 1988, p. 3)

Implicit in the chapters in this last section is the assumption that working with computers will change and shape our educational system because technology does indeed affect how we think.

In considering these claims and their relation to composition studies, the authors in this section explore promising developments in computer use. Ron Fortune, in Chapter 9, explains how the computer's capabilities can allow us to integrate visual representations of information into our writing classes and claims that students can generally benefit from a graphic reinterpretation of their ideas. Computer graphics, Fortune suggests, can help us make meaning in ways that are not generally available to writers without technological support. He contends that easy-to-learn graphics software may allow us to test new methods of teaching writing that go beyond current pedagogy.

Billie Wahlstrom, in Chapter 10, describes the changes that desktop publishing has brought and will continue to bring to our teaching and to our work. In defining these changes, she discusses the theoretical, political, and legal implications of ordinary people's new capability to produce text of professional quality. This chapter establishes a connection between the process by which the word processor has replaced the typewriter and the process by which desktop publishing is replacing typesetting. But we still do not know, she argues, how these changes may alter our concepts of written communication.

In Chapter 11, Michael Spitzer continues to examine new developments in computers and composition by discussing the potential of computer conferencing. Spitzer describes how computers alter the essential nature and form of information exchange among participants in a conference by fostering a connectivity that is at once more immediate and more distant than traditional dialogue. He suggests ways in which these electronic conferences will change scholarly activities, ultimately affecting how our students learn.

In the final chapter of this book, Janet Eldred extends the concept of connectivity and argues that electronic communication allows us to focus on writing as a public rather than as a private activity. She contends that networked computers and databases can help teachers of English develop a socially based pedagogy that emphasizes students' ability to receive, synthesize, and incorporate others' ideas into an ongoing written conversation. This chapter provides a framework for considering ways in which we might structure our teaching to take advantage of the special environment provided by technology.

The ideas in this final section have only begun to influence the ways in which we both teach and perceive written communication. If, however, they are any indication of what the future holds for our profession and its use of computers, we have another challenging decade ahead of us.

## REFERENCES

Study finds increase in publications. (1988, February 26). *Christian Science Monitor,* p. 19.

Melange: Commencement 1988. (1988, June 8). *Chronicle of Higher Education,* p. 3.

# 9

## Visual and Verbal Thinking: Drawing and Word-Processing Software in Writing Instruction

Ron Fortune

Now that computers are finding their way into writing courses at all grade levels, there is growing interest in going beyond the computer's basic applications such as word processing and computer-assisted instruction. It is not that these basic applications have lost their value, but as teachers continue to discover the computer's potential, they want to find additional but perhaps less obvious ways in which the computer can assist the development of students' critical thinking and writing abilities. Some teachers focus on hardware configurations, as indicated by the many efforts to utilize local area networks to develop collaborative learning environments in writing courses. Others concentrate on specialized software, expert systems to assist writers in defining the problems they explore (Burns, 1986).

This chapter focuses on a widely available type of software that has not figured prominently in writing instruction but that could have a very positive impact on the development of students' thinking and writing abilities: drawing and graphics programs. Such programs are probably as numerous as word-processing programs but, with the exception of business and technical writing courses, there have been few attempts to combine these image-oriented programs with word-processing programs to teach writing. The same teachers who encourage students in a business or technical writing course to use visuals often see little use for graphics in less specialized writing courses. The materials covered in a business or technical writing course, teachers argue, invite the use of visuals because the writing in such courses stresses either representing numerical data in some graphic form or depicting the physical configuration of an object. Considering visuals in this narrow way, however, severely limits the dimensions of the rhetorical enterprise. The subject, to the exclusion of other aspects of the communication triangle, determines the relative suitability of visuals to a written text. To appreciate the potential of drawing and graphics software in a writing course, teachers should also consider the writer and the cognitive means he or she has available to articulate meaning regardless of the subject being addressed.

I argue for using drawing and graphics software in all writing courses. Given the widespread concern with developing students' writing and critical thinking abilities in all writing courses at all grade levels, we should consider how image-oriented software can make these objectives more readily accessible. Having established the theoretical grounds for using such software in a writing course, I shall then provide samples of student writing using this approach.

## BRAIN HEMISPHERICITY AND VISUAL AND VERBAL THINKING

A useful context for looking at the role of visual thinking in writing courses can be found in recent discussions of brain hemisphericity and the learning process. While these discussions raise as many questions as they answer about the nature of left-mode and right-mode thinking, they do suggest the complexity of the human brain and the variety of faculties it employs in dealing with problems, rhetorical and otherwise. Generally, studies of this subject associate left-mode thinking with verbal and linear reasoning and right-mode thinking with imagistic and visual perception, though even such a basic division of labor must be viewed tentatively (Gardner, 1980). However, teachers and researchers should not be deterred by this tentativeness from investigating issues related to brain hemisphericity and writing. Rather, they should continue to explore the subject, always remaining sensitive to its complexity and restricting themselves to conjectures for which there is some degree of consensus.

Accepting, even tentatively, the very basic distribution of cognitive labor that associates the left mode with linear and verbal thought and the right mode with intuitive and visual thought allows a variety of consequent questions involving why teaching and learning should include an emphasis on both visual and verbal thinking and how the two contribute to learning in general and to learning in specific disciplines. First among these questions is, If visual and verbal thinking, as operations of the left- and right-modes of thought, respectively, do contribute significantly to the learning process, how can they be culti-vated in classrooms at all grade levels? Answering this question de-pends in turn on an understanding of two related issues: (1) Why have visual and verbal thinking often been represented in opposition to one another? (2) How in fact do they cooperate in the development of an individual's knowledge and understanding?

## The Separation of Visual and Verbal Thinking

In a study of visualization, Samuels and Samuels (1975) present a historical overview of how visual and verbal thinking came to be perceived as being opposed to one another. At the heart of this oppo-sition is the greater efficiency of language in representing abstract meaning:

> The use and development of visualization has occurred in inverse pro-portion to the development of language and a written structure for re-cording it. . . . As language developed words came to serve not only to evoke images or experiences but to enable the speaker to establish dis-tance between himself and his experience. (pp. 13–19)

Samuels and Samuels then suggest that, in allowing language to become predominant over imagery to the point of dismissing the role of images in thinking, people have gained in communicative efficien-cy but have lost sensitivity to themselves and their world.

While Samuels and Samuels address the historical basis for the preeminence of verbal thought, Gardner (1980) offers a perspective on individual development, suggesting a parallel between historical and individual evolution. Gardner begins by asserting that "until the task of writing has been mastered, the system of drawing is the only one sufficiently elaborated to permit expression of inner life" (p. 155). By age nine or ten, children learn to achieve through written language what they used to accomplish through drawing. With children's emerging reliance on language, Gardner concludes, "the stage is set for the decline—or demise—of graphic expression" (p. 155). He goes on to suggest, however, that this erosion of the individual's reliance on graphics should be countered by a conscious effort in the educational system to cultivate the capacity to draw as an indispensable dimension of cognitive functioning.

In light of Gardner's last assertion, it is ironic that the educational system may instead be reinforcing and promoting the preeminence of the verbal to the detriment of students' learning processes. Edwards

(1979), for example, argues that schools are specifically structured to limit students' experiences with right-mode thinking, suggesting the "school systems in general are still structured in the left-hemisphere mode. . . . the right brain is lost in our school system and goes largely untaught" (pp. 36–37). This bias, she suggests, is reflected in the virtual absence from the educational system of instruction in visualization and perceptual and spatial skills. Adams (1986) argues that the de-emphasis on visualization in schools has had grave consequences for the development of students' problem-solving abilities. He reports that the "extremely verbal" group of students with whom he works at Stanford University are initially blind to certain aspects of the problems they address because of a formal education that virtually ignores the hemisphere of the brain that would see problems in spatial and holistic terms (pp. 94–95). Problem-solving, he states, benefits most from the ability to perceive a problem from a variety of conceptual angles.

## Reintegrating Visual and Verbal Thinking

To a degree, the educational system's emphasis on verbal over visual thinking proceeds from the widely held perception that verbal thinking reflects a more advanced stage of cognitive development than visual thinking, which it should replace. Often, this belief is based on the oversimplified application of models of cognitive and intellectual development. The model of intellectual development offered by Bruner, Olver, and Greenfield (1966) has been one victim of this tendency to reduce complex phenomena to simple formulations for the sake of instructional expediency (Bracewell, 1983). In this model individuals progress from an "enactive" stage of development through an "iconic" stage to a "symbolic" stage. The iconic stage is characterized by children's representation of the world through imagery. When they advance to the symbolic stage, they become able to use words as symbols, and their representations of the world reflect abstract relationships, including "categorality, hierarchy, prediction, causation and modification" (p. 47). Seeing the dynamic of this model in strictly linear terms, many educators interpret their primary task to be moving students from one level to the next by weaning them from a reliance on the imagistic and initiating them into a mastery of a symbolic system based on language.

Development does not occur as linearly and straightforwardly as this model and others have often tried to suggest, and in the last few years educators in individual disciplines, including composition studies, have learned to use developmental models in a less fixed and more dynamic way (Lunsford, 1986; Williams, 1984). Instead of relying on stage models as rigid and fixed representations of how individuals develop mentally, these educators have come to see that the intellectual progression implicit in development is complex and often circuitous. This means that cognitive development does not progress linearly but is cumulative and recursive. Individuals do not completely shed cognitive abilities developed early and replace them with an entirely new set. Instead, they transform the former as they develop the latter and, synthesizing the two, equip themselves with a richer range of abilities suited to increasingly varied and complex tasks they must learn to manage.

This richer, more dynamic perception of intellectual and cognitive development should have profound implications for the treatment of visual and verbal thinking in our schools. First, it should change the way in which the schools regard the relationship between "iconic" and "symbolic" thought so that students continue to develop both abilities throughout their schooling instead of learning to abandon one in favor of the other. Second, since educators will know that visual and verbal thinking should work together rather than successively, they should develop teaching approaches that cultivate a dynamic interaction between the two modes and show students how to bring the power of this combination to bear on the learning challenges they face.

Finding ways to stimulate visual and verbal thought processes to their mutual benefit requires knowing as much as we can about how the different modes of thought can work together. In his classic study of visual thinking, Arnheim (1969) draws a distinction between intuitive and intellectual cognition related to the differentiation made here between visual and verbal thought. He sees the role of intuitive cognition or visual thinking as the open and unrestricted exploration of interacting forces within a perceptual field. Intellectual cognition, on the other hand, involves isolating entities within the perceptual field, perceiving their special natures, and then articulating relationships among them. In effect, intellectual cognition, through the verbalization of propositions and principles, fixes and stabilizes the field apprehended dynamically and holistically through intuitive cognition. Although Arnheim is mainly interested in arguing against the tendency to place verbal above visual thinking, his comments also accentuate the interplay between the two modes of thought: "There is no necessary conflict, however, between intuitive and intellectual cognition. In fact, productive thinking is characterized, in the arts and in the sciences, by the interplay between the free interaction of forces within the field and the more or less solidified entities that persist as variants in changing contexts'' (p. 235). To Arnheim, thinking dominated by the verbal at the expense of the visual necessarily suffers from a kind of conceptual anemia.

While Arnheim focuses on the ways in which intellectual cognition operates on intuitive cognition, Edwards (1979) sees the relationship between visual and verbal thinking in terms of cooperative processing: ''We have learned that the two hemispheres can work together in a number of ways. Sometimes they cooperate with each half contributing its special abilities and taking on the particular part of the task that is suited to its model of information processing'' (pp. 31–31). The cooperative processing described here recalls the multivarious thinking that Adams (1986) associates with effective problem solving; that is, as the two modes approach the subject from complementary angles, they represent it in different ways, and this more complete representation allows the individual to use more of the subject field to deal with it. The result is a richer problem representation and a fuller solution in tune with the complete complexity of the problem.

## INTEGRATING VISUAL AND VERBAL THINKING IN WRITING INSTRUCTION

With this general understanding of the ways in which visual and verbal thinking can and should work together, it is appropriate to explore the role of visual thinking in writing instruction. Writing is so explicitly verbal that finding evidence of a need for visual elements in it can be difficult. Although many discussions of this topic seem general and somewhat indefinite, they nevertheless provide a basis for beginning to understand it; for example, Perl's (1983) intriguing notion of ''felt sense'': ''When writers are given a topic, the topic evokes a felt sense within them. This topic calls forth images, words, ideas, and vague fuzzy feelings that are anchored in the writer's body'' (p. 45). Implicit in her analysis, with its emphasis on both images and words, is a recognition of the balance between visual and verbal thinking in the writer's apprehension of his or her subject. Neither is given priority over the other; the full apprehension of an idea depends on the contributions of both.

A different view is offered in Bernhardt's study (1986) of the arrangement of information on the page as a manifestation of visual thinking. He suggests that the ways in which writers arrange their texts on the page constitute one form of graphic expression critical to effective writing. He thus asserts the importance of developing visual thinking abilities in writing instruction for teaching students to organize their ideas on the page. The effective use of white space, headings and subheadings, and indentations, for example, depends on students being able to see the graphic shapes their texts take on the page and to relate these shapes to the logical configurations of the ideas they discuss. Obviously, with the growing popularity of desktop publishing and the attendant emphasis on document design in technical writing programs, Bernhardt's comments are relevant to the education of future professional and technical writers. His comments also suggest, however, that teachers in all writing courses should help their students develop the ability to use page layout both to organize their ideas and to communicate those ideas more effectively to readers.

Most studies that focus on the role of drawing in the composing process deal with the composing processes of children. Nevertheless, these studies raise issues worth considering here. These studies generally examine the reciprocity between visual and verbal thinking in the writing of children who are moving from a predominant reliance on visual expression to a dependence on verbal expression. Two studies, one by Graves (1982) and the other by Newkirk (1982), echo the line of visual/verbal development described by Gardner (1980). Graves demonstrates that, for some of the seven-year-olds he studied, drawing was a necessary prewriting activity. His research also indicates, however, that as children develop they display a diminishing reliance on drawing and a growing attachment to written verbal expression in their composing processes. Newkirk (1982) stresses the need to get children to separate drawing and writing in their composing. That children fail to distinguish between writing and drawing, he argues, can be at least partly responsible for problems in their writing, especially problems related to the completeness of information in their texts. Moreover, children ultimately are driven from a reliance on pictures to a reliance on language by the exigencies of communication as they gradually realize that language is a more efficient means of communication than pictures.

While the Graves (1982) and Newkirk (1982) studies illustrate a common pattern that children follow or are taught to follow in handling drawings as a part of their composing, their observations also place the problem in a different light. The real issue in discussions of children's drawing and writing is not so much whether or not children should abandon drawing in favor of writing at a certain stage in their development but rather that the relationship between drawing and writing should be allowed to change as the children mature cognitively. This conclusion would seem especially appropriate in light of those arguments (e.g., Edwards, 1979) that children abandon drawing or do not integrate it well into their learning, including their learning to write, because schools implicitly if not explicitly encourage as much. Teaching students to write across grade levels may ultimately include learning how their developing command of language calls for new uses of drawing in their composing processes.

Dyson's (1986) study of writing and drawing in children's composing describes the various patterns of cooperation and tension that exist among speaking, writing, and drawing in children's composing: "The study documented differences in children's ways of weaving together pictures and talk, thus suggesting that the resources and tensions these other media create will vary in identifiable ways for different children" (p. 407). Although her study is concerned with a greater range of behaviors than is under investigation here, it is pertinent in its suggestion that, while teachers may generally promote the use of drawing and writing, they must also remain sensitive to necessary variations that will exist from writer to writer in employing the two media.

What is lacking in the various discussions of the role of visual thinking in writing is an analysis of how drawing can and should play a role in the composing of adolescents and young adults in high school and college. While some discussions (e.g., Perl, 1983; Bernhardt, 1986) indirectly assert the importance of visual thinking in all composing regardless of age group, and others (e.g., Graves, 1982; Newkirk, 1982; Dyson, 1986) focus on the direct use of drawing in the composing of children, very little is available on the role of drawing in the composing of older writers. If visual thinking is as important to everyone's conceptualization processes as Adams (1986) and Arnheim (1969) suggest, then more needs to be done in developing ways to work it explicitly into writing instruction for students at all grade levels. The computer provides an excellent opportunity to develop such approaches because of its ability to blend visually and verbally oriented software.

## DRAWING AND WORD-PROCESSING SOFTWARE IN WRITING INSTRUCTION

The most obvious question for writing teachers to answer before using the computer to promote visual thinking in conjunction with verbal thinking is: "Why does one need a computer?" Those who would grant all of the arguments supporting the cultivation of visual thinking abilities in a writing course might still argue that visual materials can be created more easily with a pencil and a sheet of paper than with a computer. Therefore, they would argue, the computer offers no special advantage and only creates the need for students to deal with a superfluous tool that interferes with, rather than promotes, thinking and writing. For elementary drawings, this argument has merit, and for such drawings, students could use a pencil and a sheet of paper. As drawings become more complex, however, the computer has three distinct advantages. First, even a basic drawing program often enables the writer to combine screens so that a relatively complex drawing can be created through the combination of several simpler ones. Second, just as word processing enables one to revise a text with greater efficiency than is possible with a sheet of paper and a pencil or a typewriter, so drawing with a computer makes modifying an image easier. Finally, using the computer for drawings allows students to maintain a "clean" image at all times, and this often affects their sense of accomplishment and satisfaction with their progress in creating the image and the text.

### Description of Hardware and Software Configurations and Examples from Student Writing

When considering using drawing and graphics software in conjunction with word-processing software in a writing course, one must examine the hardware and software configurations available. We shall consider three examples of student writing and the configurations used therein. In the first two examples, the configuration was quite basic; in the third, the configuration was a bit more sophisticated though still rather basic. The hardware for all three applications consisted of a Zenith PC-158 computer with a graphics card and an IBM graphics printer. The software programs for the first two applications were *Wordstar* (version 3.3) and a shareware "drawing" program called *PC Keydraw* (version 2.21). This keyboard-based drawing software was selected primarily because it does not require an elaborate hardware setup. It enables the writer to compose relatively sophisticated drawings without need of a mouse, light pen, or digitizer. The software for the third application consisted of *Publisher's Paintbrush* (version 1.52), and the hardware added a mouse to the configuration described above. (The third application required greater flexibility in the manipulation of the graphic image; *Publisher's Paintbrush* and the mouse provided such without substantially complicating the setup.)

A basic limitation of both of these setups, but one that could be readily overcome with different software, was that the software was not integrated. Thus, drawings and text could not be created together; they could only be combined once they had been generated separately. In any case, the principles informing the applications described below extend to virtually any hardware and software configuration capable of text and drawing production.

In his discussion of the need to develop students' visual thinking abilities more effectively in the educational system, Adams (1986) subdivides drawings into two broad categories: those done to communicate with others and those done to communicate with oneself. Obviously, both functions figure prominently in the composing process since writers often vary their attention throughout the process between writing for the self and writing for others. The student samples below, therefore, follow the same subdivision. The first suggests how a student used drawing and free-writing on a computer to discover what she understood about the subject she was addressing. The second illustration demonstrates how another writer combined drawing and text in an essay to communicate his meaning as fully as possible to his readers. The writer in the final example is closer to the second writer; his drawing represents a different kind of exploration of a perceptual field than does the drawing of the first writer.

All of the drawings included in the examples are relatively simple. My argument is not that computers and drawing software allow students to develop highly complex graphic images for their texts but rather that they enable students to combine text and graphics conveniently and thus allow students to approach their ideas and develop their texts with a richness of perspective not available in verbal expression alone. Simple graphics are as appropriate as more complex graphics provided they are suited to the rhetorical tasks students set for themselves. (The student samples included intentionally do not involve business graphics or CAD/CAM software. These types of software certainly are conducive to promoting visual and verbal thinking in a writing course, but both applications are specialized and rather obvious. Granted, using business graphics software enables students to explore their subjects visually. However, because line charts, bar graphs, and pie charts have such obvious applications in rhetorical situations involving numbers and percentages, it seems unnecessary to elaborate on these applications.)

As the following examples illustrate, when drawing and writing are combined in the early phases of students' composing processes, the dialectic they exhibit often reflects the dialectic Arnheim (1969) describes in his discussion of intuitive and intellectual cognition: The drawing tends to be an open and free-flowing investigation of the subject that becomes somewhat stabilized through the simultaneous and subsequent use of language. This is not to say that language itself is not to a degree free-flowing; indeed, even as language solidifies the relations inherent in the images the writer creates, it opens up new possibilities that can be further pursued both in drawing and in writing. Thus, while formulating the nature of the dialectic between drawing and writing is useful, too strict a formulation oversimplifies the rich and recursive interplay that can occur between the visual and verbal modes of thought.

The first example demonstrates the use of visual thinking in the prewriting and planning phases of composing. Produced by a student who was writing a paper on the conflict between school and work responsibilities among working college students, this visual exhibits the exploratory role visual thinking can play during composing. The student represented the problem visually and then generated text to articulate the understanding she achieved through the analysis of the diagram. She first drew two parallel lines, each representing a different side of the conflict. One line stood for the issues associated with her schoolwork; the other line represented matters tied into her work as a clerk at a local department store. She shaded the space between the two lines, but on the extreme sides of the lines she noted topics that occurred to her as she thought about the subjects affiliated with each line (see Figure 9.1).

The issues covered in the graphic and written down in the early stages of her writing reflected her own situation as a student and a worker. As she approached doing a formal draft, she was able to generalize these to other students in situations similar to hers, and her final draft embodies a more complex delineation of the issues represented somewhat rudimentarily in this drawing.

Perhaps the most interesting aspect of her visual and verbal thinking is that she envisioned the conflict she was dealing with in terms of that shaded space between the parallel lines. Solving the problem for her meant being able to connect items on opposite sides of the parallel lines. She did this by using lines to connect boxed items that she thought she could relate to one another in a way that might enable her to come to terms with her problem. In some instances, she grouped items on the same side of the lines before drawing the line that connected one item in the group to single or grouped items on the other side of the shaded boundary. Having done this, she began to articulate the ideas that allowed her to connect the items as she had. These ideas then became the key points she tried to work out in her initial draft.

Figure 9.1    Student's Visual Representation of Conflict between School and Work Responsibilities

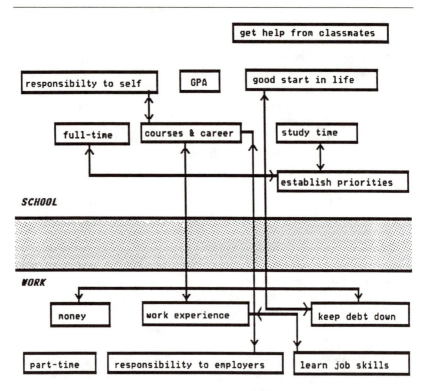

The visual and verbal thinking she did as a part of her prewriting, then, nicely illustrates the dialectic that Arnheim (1969) sees as characteristic of the interplay between intuitive and intellectual cognition. It should be stressed, however, that while this dialectic is embedded in one form or another in the prewriting of most students who are encouraged to combine drawing and writing, it is not always as evident as it was in this particular writing episode for this student.

This first graphic was not so complex as students' drawings often become. Even for this student, however, having composed it on a computer was advantageous because she could revise it easily as she progressed and as her understanding of the problem she was addressing evolved. Also, if she wanted to use all or any part of the diagram in her essay, it did not have to be redone for the sake of neatness; her first efforts were as neat as they needed to be and could readily be exported into her draft. Finally, although her drawing was not as involved as it might have been, the potential to extend it without having to start over was always there if the student needed it.

The second example, a flowchart, is a common form of drawing students use when they are learning to think visually for purposes of communication. They use flowcharts as Flower and Hayes (1980) did to depict a cognitive model of the composing process. In doing so, students create two complementary ways for the reader to process the information being communicated. For the left hemisphere, they offer the discursive explanation of their ideas; for the right, they provide a diagram of the same ideas. As readers process the text that includes both the discursive analysis and the pictorial depiction, they play the two representations off one another to check the accuracy of their understanding of each. Because they have this means of testing their evolving understanding of the concepts being presented, readers can process a text more efficiently and more effectively.

The flowchart in Figure 9.2 depicts the writer's view of how various considerations must be taken into account in managing time successfully. The essay in which the chart appeared was concerned specifically with time management, a problem that most college students struggle with, often throughout their collegiate careers. Although the chart was created to assist the reader with the flow of ideas presented discursively in the essay, it also had a positive influence on the writer's ability to isolate the structure and idea sequences to be covered in the essay. In fact, the writer worked out the flowchart during his prewriting; it had the same purpose there that the diagram described earlier had for the writer during her prewriting. The difference is that the second writer retained the diagram for communicative purposes in the final text whereas the first writer did not.

The drawing in the final example differs from the first two in that its form is freer and less prefabricated than the forms of the first two. Although the first two show the writers using visuals to explore and communicate their ideas, they are basic in the sense that both writers restrict themselves to the elementary visual elements of lines and boxes. They also are dominated by verbal expression to the degree that the lines and boxes are used to connect words and phrases. Neither example fully suggests the kind of freedom that can come with using visuals to explore ideas and concepts. In effect, the first two examples represent a first-level process of visualization, a level many students must begin with because of their acquired reluctance to use drawings in a writing course. The third drawing depicts a second-level process

Figure 9.2    Student's Flowchart Representing a Time-Management Strategy

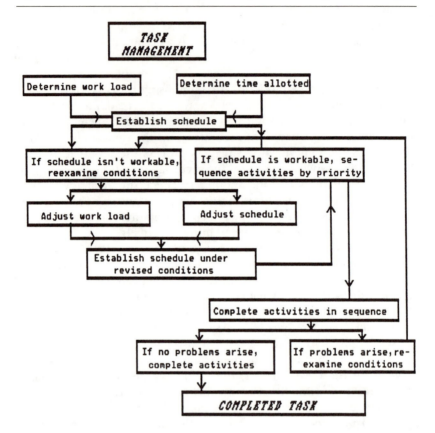

of visualization as the student graduates to more complex visual forms than lines and boxes and does not rely on verbal expression to explain the organization of his visual forms.

The drawing in Figure 9.3 was produced by a student having difficulty identifying a subject to write about; the student asked for suggestions and was given a variation on an assignment appearing in Edwards'(1986) *Drawing on the Artist Within*. This assignment had students draw an analog to the concept, "Human Energy" or "Power." Edwards found two dominant variations in student responses: an exploding image and rising triangular forms. The writer who drew the lightning bolt and the hand in Figure 9.3 exhibits the second variation but, significantly, adds to the "rising triangular form" a rough drawing

Figure 9.3    Student's Visual Analog for the Concepts "Human Energy" and "Power"

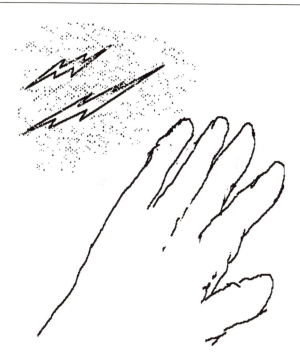

of the human hand, which becomes not only the focal point of the drawing but also the theme for the essay that followed. The essay itself focused on the human hand as a symbol for and critical mechanism in human progress.

Of the three figures, the third perhaps best illustrates Arnheim's notion of the relationship between intellectual and intuitive cognition. The student had been given similar tasks before starting this drawing assignment and had been unable to respond to them by writing. The drawing represents the student's open exploration of a field—triggered by the phrase, "Human Energy"—and then his "solidifying" what he sees through principles and propositions articulated in his essay. This student's experience reveals the value of combining drawing and word-processing software in a writing course: Stymied in his writing and lacking ideas to investigate in his paper, the student was able to use drawing as a means of freeing his creative potential and developing insight.

## CONCLUSION

The advantage to cultivating visual and verbal thinking in a writing course through the use of drawing and word-processing software should be apparent. Some instructors, however, will argue that their students need as much work with language as possible and that spending time to develop students' visual as well as verbal abilities detracts from the development of the latter. Such an argument misses the point. By developing visual abilities in conjunction with verbal, we may be providing students with a special means of extending their critical thinking and writing abilities more efficiently and more effectively than is possible if we restrict writing instruction to verbal expression alone. It is ultimately a question of helping students learn to take full advantage of all of the cognitive resources they have available to them. Failure to do this amounts to handicapping students in their efforts to learn to think and to write.

## REFERENCES

Adams, J. (1986). *Conceptual blockbusting: A guide to better ideas* (3rd ed.). New York: Norton.

Arnheim, R. (1969). *Visual thinking.* Berkeley: University of California Press.

Bernhardt, S. (1986). Seeing the text. *College Composition and Communication, 37,* 66–78.

Bracewell, R. (1983). Investigating the control of writing skills. In P. Mosenthal, L. Tamor, & S. A. Walmsley (Eds.), *Research on writing: Principles and methods* (pp. 177–203). New York: Longman.

Bruner, J. S., Olver, R. O., & Greenfield, P. M. (1966). *Studies in cognitive growth.* New York: Wiley.

Burns, H. (1986). The promise of artificial intelligence research for composition. In B. McClelland & T. Donovan (Eds.), *Perspectives on research and scholarship in composition* (pp. 214–228). New York: Modern Language Association.

Dyson, A. H. (1986). Transitions and tensions: Interrelationships between the drawing, talking, and dictating of young children. *Research in the teaching of English, 20,* 379–409.

Edwards, B. (1979). *Drawing on the right side of the brain: A course in enhancing creativity and artistic confidence.* Los Angeles: J. P. Tarcher.

Edwards, B. (1986). *Drawing on the artist within: A guide to innovation, invention, imagination and creativity.* New York: Simon and Schuster.

Flower, L., & Hayes, J. (1980). Identifying the organization of writing processes. In L. Gregg & E. Steinberg (Eds.), *Cognitive processes in writing* (pp. 3–30). Hillsdale, NJ: Erlbaum.

Gardner, H. (1980). *Artful scribbles: The significance of children's drawings.* New York: Basic Books.

Graves, D. (1982). *A case study observing the development of primary children's composing, spelling, and motor behaviors during the writing process.* (Final Report for NIE Grant G-78-0174. Project 8-0343/9-0963)

Lunsford, A. (1986). Research on writing and cognitive development. In B. McClelland & T. Donovan (Eds.), *Perspectives on research and scholarship in composition* (pp. 147–176). New York: Modern Language Association.

Newkirk, T. (1982). Young writers as critical readers. In T. Newkirk & N. Atwell (Eds.), *Understanding writing: Ways of observing, learning and teaching, K–8* (pp. 106–113). Chelmsford, MA: Northeast Regional Exchange.

Perl, S. (1983). Understanding composing. In J. Hayes, P. Roth, J. Ramsey, & R. Foulke (Eds.), *The writer's mind: Writing as a mode of learning* (pp. 43–51). Urbana, IL: National Council of Teachers of English.

Samuels, M., & Samuels, N. (1975). *Seeing with the mind's eye: The history, techniques, and uses of visualization.* New York: Random House.

Williams, J. (1984, May). *Critical thinking, cognitive development, and the teaching of writing.* Paper presented at the Institute on Higher Order Reasoning, Chicago, IL.

# 10

## Desktop Publishing: Perspectives, Potentials, and Politics

Billie J. Wahlstrom

Teachers of writing, teacher educators in English, writing lab directors, and directors of programs in scientific and technical communication have been slow to realize the impact of desktop publishing (DTP) on our work—which is not to say we have been slow in adopting the technology or silent on the subject, either. Desktop publishing magazines like *Publish* are flourishing; most of these publications, however, have dealt only marginally with theoretical perspectives and the implications of such theory for the teaching of writing. Scholars are only now beginning to explore this rich research area, and their observations are urgently needed. Writing teachers and administrators of writing programs, already faced with the arrival of DTP in their departments, need to know how to integrate DTP successfully into existing writing programs and individual courses.

The fact that we have not yet put DTP in theoretical perspective or developed a research agenda for it is not surprising. We found ourselves in a similar position only a few years ago when we discovered the extent to which process-based writing instruction on college and high school campuses used computers. Even now in the field of computers and composition, we are only slowly building the theoretical, pedagogical, and research understandings necessary to integrate this technology humanely and successfully into our curricula.

A merging of computer hardware, software, and printing technologies, DTP has come to teachers of writing from outside our profession. DTP's birth, like that of the computer, was midwived by people with training and purposes different from our own; it was designed primarily to serve business, writing teachers, and writing program administrators. With the introduction of DTP into the academic environment, as with the introduction of computers, we have to discover for ourselves just what role we want these new technologies to play in our writing programs and instruction.

DTP is spreading rapidly. The Seybold Report on Desktop Publishing noted that in 1987 60,000 software programs for systems were sold; it estimates that in 1988 the number will be 300,000 ("Desktop Publishing," 1988). For teachers faced with a multitude of decisions—from what DTP program software to buy, to how to do research on the impact of this technology on writers—there has been little useful discussion. Early journal articles on DTP confused products with processes and were so full of corporate acronyms as to be incomprehensible. Companies marketing DTP want to sell their products, not contemplate the philosophical issues emerging from them. As a consequence, companies like Apple have deluged writing teachers and writing program directors with flashy brochures and sent out invitations to demonstrations at which, somewhat anachronistically, they give away free pens. Even those of us who see promise in DTP have been cautious in exploring this technology.

Because of the lack of information on computers in the classroom, teachers of writing are still inclined to see DTP as just another writing tool and nothing more. Although computers hinted at the changes coming in communication, DTP is finally forcing us to deal with the depth and breadth of those changes. What the computer only hinted at, DTP makes clear: fundamental alterations in the word/print relationship resulting from digital communication technologies. Like it or not, DTP and the changes it brings are part of the writer's world, and so they must be part of the world of the writing teacher and the writing program administrator as well.

This chapter explores the nature of this technology and raises some of the questions we have to consider as we integrate DTP into our teaching, our curricula, and our understanding of the role that written communication plays in structuring society and individual lives. Although this is by no means an exhaustive list of issues we face now or will face, it suggests some of the philosophical, aesthetic, social, legal, and ethical issues associated with DTP that make planning for its impact on our curricula, research, and pedagogy difficult.

## COMING TO TERMS WITH DESKTOP PUBLISHING

### The Nature and History of DTP

Before teachers and administrators can make sound decisions about the use of DTP, we need to consider both its history of development and its nature. DTP is a way of streamlining and reducing the costs of the printing process. With a desktop publishing system, authors using microcomputers and readily available software can create documents that can be printed in-house on laser printers at modest costs when compared to printing the traditional way. DTP eliminates the need to send documents out to be typeset and, therefore, cuts the turnaround time needed to create a printed document. It allows companies, newspapers, colleges, and even amateur authors to produce in their offices or homes documents that look almost as good as those produced by complicated printing systems. DTP is being marketed as a tool of incredible promise and no problems: "An Apple Desktop Publishing System puts control in your hands. Money in your pocket. Time on your calendar. And quality within everyone's reach" (Apple Computer brochure, 1986). Control, money, time, and quality, however, are precisely those issues that affect our curricula and that make planning for implementation of DTP difficult.

Although at first glance DTP seems a technology suited to business and industry rather than education, no academic can afford to treat it lightly. Even if its only applications were in business and industry, DTP would still have a significant impact on those who direct scientific and technical communication or professional writing programs and on business writing teachers because part of our charge is to train writers to write well using the technology they will find in their work.

Because DTP is able to do some very remarkable things, however, its significance to teachers of writing and program directors goes beyond the simpler issue of training writers to use up-to-date technology. It provides, for instance, entry into the once-exclusive realm of the published word, and as a consequence highlights the transformation of information handling. Changes in the way information has been collected, stored, and distributed have profound implications for the way societies function and institutions are structured. Earlier revolutions such as the development of writing, the invention of printing, the telephone, and the computer were all accompanied by profound social changes that were scarcely predicted and even now are only imperfectly understood (Lancaster, 1983; Ong, 1977, 1982). The changes in information storage, retrieval, and manipulation that make DTP possible appear to be of this magnitude, and the consequences of these changes are likely to be far-reaching.

In many ways the claims made for DPT as another cultural revolution sound hyperbolic. How can a technology aimed at simplifying making documents produce earth-shaking changes? The answer lies partly in DTP's challenges to conventional notions about the power of the printed word and the idea that truth resides primarily in university libraries. Whether or not we care to face this fact, most of us involved in the teaching of writing have invested heavily in the printed word—both psychologically and professionally. Academia's rapid adoption of a new technology is in itself worthy of study, but that it is adopting a technology that alters the text/print relations upon which its institutional validity rests is an issue writing teachers and administrators can hardly afford to ignore.

DTP is having an enormous impact both inside and outside academia because it fills a huge and growing need to make more information available to more people quickly and cheaply and to have this information look good. The success of DTP underscores what we have known for a long time: the printed word carries more clout than does the nonprinted (handwritten, dittoed, or typed) word. And, if there is any doubt about the amount of information we are considering here, the Xerox Systems Group provides some perspective: "In 1984, American companies generated 2,500 billion pages of printed materials. Industry experts predict that by 1990, U.S. businesses will be producing more than 4,000 billion pages per year" (Corporate Electronic Publishing Systems, 1986).

Although it appears to have burst upon us suddenly, DTP represents the coming together of a number of technologies rather than the invention of a single new one:

1. Computers capable of replacing the analog storage of information with digital storage;
2. Computer software capable of joining the computer with typesetting equipment;
3. Computer programs capable of sophisticated word processing;
4. Inexpensive laser printers.

Because DTP is a digital technology, it can be involved in both the production of conventional print on paper and in the "generat[ion of] new electronic publications that virtually simulate print on paper" (Lancaster, 1983, p. 3). Paradoxically, then, DTP both supports an increase in the power of the written word because it allows for quick, neat, low-cost printing and undermines traditional print/text relationships because it also makes possible the creation of electronic texts that never appear on paper. DTP, as part of the family of electronic publishing technology, has the ability to generate *virtual texts,* texts existing only on computer monitors or television screens. Capable of being sent almost anywhere in the world over modems as desktop telecommunications (Decker, 1988, p. 5), these virtual texts need never find their way into a traditional print form and may be written, published, and discarded electronically. Documents formatted on the screen for the eye of the reader can be amazingly complex; moreover, like the Macintosh magazine *On Line,* they may never exist in a printed version. For teachers of writing this issue is critical, since we have almost no experience designing writing programs or courses to handle text that is written for the screen only.

DTP was originally designed to facilitate the creation of hard copy rather than virtual text, however. The electronic technology necessary to create DTP itself had to result from a merging of existing technologies. Until a means was found to join computer technology with the technology of typesetting, DTP could not begin to develop. Printing has always been a labor-intensive and time-consuming process. As electronic technology developed, it is not surprising that every attempt was made to bring that technology to bear on printing. For years printers used optical typesetting and Linotype machines to create camera-ready copy. This process required large investments of time and human energy, but at least printers could see the text that they were setting. The computer, when it came along in the 1960s and 1970s, promised to reduce that human investment by providing a means of running typesetting machines faster and more easily.

At that time, the biggest problem with using the computer to typeset text came from the fact that programming had to be done "blind." The typesetter could program the computer but could not see until the program actually ran what the text would look like. In 1961 the Cooperative Computing Center at M.I.T. passed a milestone in typesetting history by setting the "tail" from *Alice in Wonderland* using a computer program (Barnett, 1965). In Figure 10.1, we can compare the text with the computer program that created it. The printed tail was not visible to the typesetter until it was printed, however. Manipulating the program and observing directly the effects of those changes on the appearance of the text was not possible.

Although a second generation of more powerful programs was developed in the 1970s, they still did not allow the typesetter to see the finished product until it came out of the typesetting machine. DTP did not become possible until a third generation of typesetting programs solved this problem by *digitizing* the text, that is, reducing it to binary pieces of information rather than keeping it as letters and words. Digitizing both opened the way for the inexpensive creation of printed documents and established an electronic methodology for handling text that also freed it from its dependency upon print.

Figure 10.1 Excerpt from *Alice in Wonderland*

---

```
[indn77d12ls24st1,,36cnxs1]
EXCERPT FROM ALICE IN WONDERLAND
[nl1sl8]
December 6, 1961
[sp4st2,10,36st3,11,36st4,12,
36st5,13,36st6,14,36st8,16,
36st9,17,36st10,18,36ls14dl1xs2rl]
[sc19sc19]Fury said to
[xs3]a mouse, That
[nlxs6]he met
[xs7]in the
[xs8]house,
[xs9][sc19]Let us
[xs7]both go
[xs6ls12]to law:
[xs5dl9]I[dl1] will
[xs3]prosecute
[xs2dl9]you.
[nlxs3dl1] Come, I'll
[nlxs4]take no
[nlxs5]denial:
[nlxs7]We must
[nlxs8ls11]have a
[nlxs9]trial[sc47]
[nlxs10] For
[xs7]really
[xs6]this
[nl] morning
[nlxs8ls10] I've
[xs6]nothing
[xs5]to do.'
[xs4]Said the
[xs2]mouse to
[xs1] the cur,
[nlxs3][sc19]Such a
[nlxs4ls9]trial,
[xs3]dear sir,
[xs2] With no
[xs2]jury or
[xs1ls8]judge,
[nlxs2]would be
```

"Fury said to
a mouse, That
he met
in the
house,
'Let us
both go
to law:
*I* will
prosecute
*you.*
Come, I'll
take no
denial:
We must
have a
trial;
For
really
this
morning
I've
nothing
to do.'
Said the
mouse to
the cur,
'Such a
trial,
dear sir,
With no
jury or
judge,
would be
wasting
our breath.
'I'll be
judge,
I'll be
jury,'
Said
cunning
old Fury:
'I'll try
the whole
cause.

Of course, DTP involves more than the printing of documents. Part of its significance lies in its offering a complete package for developing documents from roughest stages through to their finished form. Therefore, another major stage in the creation of DTP was the development of computer programs designed to create documents, that is, software which handled the drafting, polishing, designing, and laying-out of documents.

In this stage, word-processing programs became capable of dealing with the types of problems faced by writers, such as revising and editing text, handling layout, and checking spelling. Word-processing programs have greatly improved over a very short time so that now such features as spelling checkers, automatic hyphenation and justification, as well as a host of glossary, footnote-making, and text-formatting options, are readily and inexpensively available. And because many documents include graphics and require a variety of type fonts as well as special features (bold letters, italics, underlining, super- and subscripts), document software borrowed heavily from developments in electronic printing, thus hastening the progress of DTP.

An additional stage in the creation of DTP involved the development of relatively inexpensive, better quality printers to replace the dot matrix or daisy wheel printers associated with microcomputers. The technology of laser printing provided the ideal solution. Laser printers produce a relatively high-quality copy at half the cost of traditional printing methods. In many cases, the savings is even greater.

A typical DTP system of the type found in universities, school systems, and small businesses usually has the following components:

1. A microcomputer (or several netted together), with monitors and storage devices, usually floppy disks or a hard drive
2. A variety of software for word processing, graphics, printer driver, page design, and composition
3. A laser printer (Although some systems may depend for a time on other kinds of printers available for computers, only when a laser printer is used are documents produced of sufficiently high quality to qualify for DTP.)

Modems and telecommunication software can be added to this list, if material is to be collected from other sites (as is typically the case in systems designed for newspapers) or if documents are to be transmitted on-line or sent to another location for printing as is typically done by large publishers.

Modems are also becoming more and more common in the English/language arts curriculum, as evidenced by a project in North York, Ontario, in which during the past two years charter public schools have created a North York English Telecommunications Network. This network tied to schools' desktop publishing systems is allowing students from all grades to participate in the writing of a book on the immigrant experience in North York. Schools tied into the net (over Bell System's gateway network Inet 2000 and the Educational Data Access Network, [EDAN], established by a joint project of the Ministry of Education and TVOntario) send student writing directly to the collection source, where it is added to the hard copy sent by schools without computer-networking resources and assembled (Decker, 1988, p. 5).

DTP is finding its way into the public schools because systems that can print credible documents are available at a cost under $10,000. Dedicated systems designed for book publishers cost as much as several million, but prices are falling rapidly. The system for a small company, school system, or university would include a printer like the Apple LaserWriter with a resolution of 300 dots per inch (dpi) and a printing rate of approximately 8–10 pages per minute for pages without graphics. The cost of the LaserWriter is less than $3,000.

## What DTP Offers

Despite whatever misgivings we may have about the system, DTP shows promise for writers, teachers of writing, and program administrators as well as for businesses that rely heavily on the printed word. It is highly adaptable, both to the needs of business and those of the writing lab. For a modest investment, a business user can publish newsletters, employee publications, forms, price lists, technical manuals, brochures, reports, recruitment and marketing materials, memos, and all internal documents—all in the office and in a matter of hours.

The laser printer uses plain paper, which eliminates expensive and problematic phototypesetting chemicals, a real issue for schools with print labs. And, the fact that it uses plain paper also makes it attractive as a teaching tool; students can experiment with a variety of layouts on a given document and print each experiment inexpensively. These then can be discussed with the teacher or in peer groups. Indeed, a DTP system in the computer-writing lab provides the teacher with an opportunity to have students do the same writing tasks that will be expected of them after graduation using equipment similar to what they will find at the work site. Student writers can produce projects that look good and contribute to the writer's self-confidence and growing sense of mastery of language.

DTP also offers teachers and students the very great advantage of being able to print diagrams and figures as well as text in their documents. This fact is especially attractive to student writers who must do lab reports in science and engineering and who are now able to produce creditable papers without handmade graphs and charts glued onto their final papers. For student writers in engineering and the sciences, DTP becomes an incentive to write because the final product more nearly reflects the amount of effort the students feel that they must put into incorporating graphic material in their reports in order to get good grades.

DTP's affordability is also especially attractive for public schools, colleges, and universities, especially those offering printing, design and layout, publications management, and scientific and technical communication. Students in English classes can create their own books and newsletters; students can publish creative writing magazines. DTP allows (given a school's budget constraints) for the publication of much more student writing to a larger audience than just the class in which it is written. Some school systems sell collections of students' writings from throughout the district. DTP's ease of use, in fact, encourages students from more than one class to combine their writing. Students in journalism, publications management, and scientific communication also enjoy the added opportunity to see their works in print. Additionally, these students can have firsthand experience with state-of-the-art equipment. Students in these curricula can be assigned real projects for real clients because their laser-printed products will satisfy the needs of most businesses and community agencies. We shall explore later the issues that this raises with respect to universities competing with small businesses.

In addition to stimulating new student publications, existing student publications can take on a whole new look that both instills (for a modest cost to the institution) a sense of professionalism in students who will be involved in some aspect of information transfer when they graduate and gives a college or university external visibility. For example, after Michigan Technological University (MTU) acquired its DTP system, the Society for Technical Communication chapter at MTU printed their award-winning newsletter, *Communiqué,* with the new equipment and used the money that would have been spent on typesetting to buy higher quality paper. The result was a document of such quality that it is used to recruit new students and faculty.

DTP is also attractive to academia because it facilitates instruction. In a communications program such as ours at MTU, it is important to produce materials for instruction that establish a standard of professionalism like that we hope to instill in our students. DTP provides an inexpensive means for teachers to produce professional-looking syllabi, overheads, assignments, and other daily instructional material. It also enhances the quality of faculty presentations at professional meetings, and can make a difference in the life of the teacher and administrator who must turn out professional-quality proposals, reports, grants, newsletters, memos to the higher administration, and when all else fails, resumés and job letters.

Book companies using larger electronic publishing systems report that there is also a great saving in human resources, a saving that, to some extent, teachers using DTP also experience. Lippincott, one of the first major users of computer-assisted publishing systems, has learned to appreciate DTP because it eliminates "redundant keyboarding," gives the editors another systematic way to "provide the author with a record of the changes that have been made in his [or her] manuscript," and allows them a "ruthless enforcement" of spelling because of spelling checkers built into the system (Frank, 1986). The elimination of redundant keyboarding is attractive to both the teacher and student alike who value the process approach with its many drafts. For many of us who require students to use DTP to produce their writing assignments, the ruthless enforcement of spelling is handled by the system's software (albeit, not without limitations), and papers come to us with margins, headings, and other features, which often (though not always when we deal with novice users) make our job as readers much easier and more interesting.

Almost all of the DTP systems allow people to print in a variety of typefaces and type sizes. A typeface is a set of letters of a particular design. A typical system includes a wide variety of both serif and sans serif designs as well as special purpose faces, all of which are available in a wide range of sizes. The Apple DTP system allows users, with appropriate software, to print documents with letters as small as $1/20$ inch and as large as 10 inches. Type sizes are usually expressed in points; one point equals approximately $1/72$ of an inch. A particular typeface in a particular size is called a font: 12-point Helvetica, for example. This flexibility in type fonts allows for a great deal of freedom in designing attractive and effective documents. The fact that there is sufficient memory in these systems to store both foreign language characters and mathematical and scientific symbols is also a large attraction for writers.

One of the most useful advantages of DTP over earlier typesetting programs is that it lets users see what the page of text will look like before it is printed. The user can experiment with a variety of design options on the monitor, thus saving the time and expense of printing each one out. This feature is what makes DTP a remarkably effective tool for those teaching document design, and it allows amateurs great latitude for experimentation.

These programs are called WYSIWYG—("Wizzy Wig," what you see is what you get) programs. More accurately, only large electronic publishing systems allow users to see *exactly* what they will get when a page is typeset so that they can lay out and evaluate all the elements of their documents—graphics, text, and headlines—before printing (Chauncey, 1986, p. 79). Smaller programs of the sort found in most companies, school systems, and universities are called WYSIMOLWYG, or "what you see is more or less what you get." The screen provides the user with a proportional representation of what the page will look like. This is more than adequate for most small publishers. Already, though, manufacturers are moving toward making WYSIWYG programs available to even smaller users. The Macintosh now supports the Radius Full Page Display peripheral, for example, which allows users to see the full page layout rather than just the screen that they are working on and to manipulate all of the elements of the final document before printing it. Peripherals like the Radius Full Page Display are appearing in computer-writing labs because of their great usefulness and affordability. They allow the teacher to interact with students during various stages of the writing process, exploring and experimenting with headings of various sizes, typefaces, and layout.

## GOING DIGITAL: *DTP* AND THE BIG PICTURE

### Digital Messages: The New Language of Information

Even though the advantages of DTP seem apparent, there are still many reasons why we are only now beginning to understand the potential impact of this technology on our theory, research, and pedagogy. For most of us trained outside the sciences, the relationship of

DTP to the so-called information revolution is unclear. We are not certain what the social, cultural, theoretical, or pedagogical implications of the technologies we are making increasing use of will be.

Desktop publishing is part of a major transformation in information handling. This transformation has been called "going digital," and it means that we are rapidly replacing all traditional analog transmissions of data with digital transmissions. In analog transmissions, variations in the original "sound or visual wave forms are transformed into related variations in electrical impulses on a wire or in electromagnetic disturbances in the air" (Williams, 1984, p. 168). Digital information processing refers to the representation of information by binary patterns of "yes/no" (or "on/off" or 0/1) electrical impulses read by computers.

Analog transmissions are not efficient because they use a fixed amount of signal space, whether or not that part of the space is carrying a message. They are also subject to interference, or noise, as anyone who has experienced static on the telephone line can attest. In contrast, digital transmissions require less space per message; digital signals can be easily multiplexed for efficient use of transmission channels and can be transmitted with less distortion. Additionally, because the messages—whether audio, video, text, or graphics—are all encoded in the same binary pattern, they can all be read by computers which can edit, manipulate, route, and "reconstitute" them in their original form on the receiving end.

When not in use, the binary data can be stored on hard disks, floppy disks, compact disks, magnetic tapes, videodiscs, or any of a variety of other storage devices. When put into an appropriate playback device, an exact clone of the original message—audio, video, text, graphic, or photograph—is recreated. Ostensibly, the computer has made it possible for human beings to encode all information in binary messages and, in that form, to send it everywhere. This ability to reconstitute exact copies is significant to administrators and teachers considering the implementation of DTP in their curricula and will receive more attention shortly.

## Creating the Vast Interconnect

Coupling the digitalization of information with inexpensive but powerful computer hardware and software, and adding high-speed, broadband communications from satellites, cable television, fiber optic, telephone, and microwave systems has created a vast interconnect. This interconnect allows people access to other humans and to computers so that they can create, receive, and store a wide range of information products in a rapid and economical form (Nanus, 1983). The system at North York described above is a small but real version of what happens when English and language arts teachers explore the power of DTP and desktop telecommunications. And many institutions like MTU are discovering the enormous impact local area nets (LANS) are having in their departments as faculty and students send messages to each others, exchange papers, engage in electronic conferences, and work together collaboratively on the same assignment and the same time but on different computers. Students within even our own relatively small department routinely exchange information and assignments with teachers and with each other in print, on disk, or electronically over a LAN, or transfer their written or graphic material via an interface to videotape.

If we consider larger nets, information exchange does not have to be localized. It can be transmitted to homes as well as to offices, plants, schools, and universities. Already, many school administrators have committed resources to making certain that their entire institutions are netted locally and through larger nets with other schools nationwide. *Electronic publishing,* of which DTP is part, uses computers to create documents which can be broadcast to home television screens as teletext or cablecast to televisions or computers as videotext or sent to a local printer who can use the electronic data to typeset them. In some cases, students from a variety of schools exchange writing assignments over these networks with students elsewhere in the school system or in the country. Faculty are also making use of large networks (e.g., BITNET and MERIT) to exchange drafts of their papers with colleagues at institutions elsewhere and to access library resources unavailable on their own campuses.

DTP is part of a transformation that includes, among other things, electronic mail, databases, and interactive educational systems, or "virtual classrooms" (Hiltz, 1986). It is one of the developing systems that provide information and services to those who need or want them. The digital revolution means more than a deluge of information: Digital communication technology, including DTP, means that more *exchange* of information can occur and that more opportunities for interaction among people is possible. As a consequence of the rapid exchange of information allowed by these systems, new communities are created. Burt Nanus, director of the Center for Futures Research at the University of Southern California, calls these groups of communities linked together over the globe an "infosphere" (1983, p. 17).

## HUMANISTIC ISSUES AND DESKTOP PUBLISHING

DTP is an exciting development in the history of words on paper, but, like all communication developments, it is not without consequences. These consequences are of special concern to the people who will teach writing using DTP systems and those who have to make administrative decisions about its role in programs and curricula. We must confront the problematic issues of control, money, time, and quality glossed over in the Apple brochure mentioned above. In addition, we must consider other legal, ethical, and aesthetic issues seldom raised by teachers of written communication.

### "Who Says?": Questions of Authority

Recently, in a class discussion on DTP, one of my students said, "Wait a minute. If you don't know who published something, how will you know whether or not to believe it?" This is an interesting question, because DTP does affect our concepts of authority. Traditionally, we have invested words on paper with the power to speak the truth. We feel strongly about the truth of the printed word and privilege written texts above other forms of information in our educational institutions. We have burned and banned books we felt violated our trust in the printed word. As teachers of writing, we keep the tradition of reverencing print alive.

Print has derived its authority from a number of sources. Part of its authority lies in its frozen nature. The spoken word is mutable, existing in time only at the moment of utterance. This temporal element of words was replaced by permanence when we became literate. The text, then, took on the authority that had previously been invested in the memories of the wise men and women of the community. Additionally, the publication process itself, involving the process of using experts to create texts that are then validated by other experts such as publishers and marketing moguls, transfers authority from the wise people of the community to the printed word. As teachers of writing, we have validated this system and, through our teaching, have invited students to embrace a certain set of cultural values that privilege text and reward those who can write well enough to have that material validated by appearing in print.

With DTP, virtually anyone can publish. Information can now be assembled in anyone's basement and will come out looking almost as authentic as anything coming from a typesetter. In the past, information in media that were the farthest removed from printing (dittos, handwritten notes, etc.) came to be associated with nonauthoritative voices. Authority alone spoke in print. This tradition is ingrained strongly in our entire culture. The Supreme Court and the FCC, for example, only speak in print. Verbal opinions are not official or binding. With the technology of print in the hands of any who can afford or have access to DTP, how will we be able to judge the truth of print when anyone can speak through it?

Like most important questions, this one has no easy solution. On one side, DTP is potentially an enfranchising technology, opening the door for more people to a powerful technology. On the other, DTP still costs money, and those that have access to such technology have access to a powerful tool for shaping opinion. The question is always how this tool will be used, and, once again, money and power are related.

It is hard to question authority with respect to the printed word. Maybe this will change in time, but for many people there are deep psychological convictions associated with print. This was brought home to me as a teacher of writing recently when I realized how difficult it was for me to mark errors on a student assignment which had been printed with the laser printer. The paper looked polished and perfect. Marking it made me feel as if I were defacing a book. I have since overcome my aversion to marking these papers, but that the reaction occurred at all illustrates how complicated the issue of authority and print is even on the level of individual psychology. One cannot deface a book because it seems to be public property, bearing as it does the literal imprimatur of a whole social group. The fact that almost anyone can now produce printed documents does not at this time much alter a deeply ingrained response to the printed word.

### Philosophically Speaking

DTP raises more questions than the issue of authority. It and its related technologies challenge what is *real* and *true* as well. As we have noted, DTP relies on digital processing of data, and in this realm questions about the nature of reality surface. These issues are not only of interest philosophically but legally: as we shall see, DTP challenges copyright laws by confusing our ability to distinguish easily between originals (the mainstay of copyright) and copies (the issues of infringement).

Through digital processing, information is reduced to binary patterns. Once in this state, such data can be manipulated easily by computers. In his article on the serious implications of digital image processing, O'Connor (1986) reports how photographs, once they are in digital form, can be "corrected" prior to printing. He points to an ad in which the "moon was slightly repositioned" and to the classic case of the May 1985 *National Geographic* cover in which the pyramids at Giza were moved a few inches in order to make the picture fit the magazine's vertical format.

No harm done here, perhaps, but what does one say about the fact that the *Orange County Register* "is said to have routinely altered the skies in photographs of the Olympic Games to print as 100 per cent cyan" (O'Connor, 1986, p. 127)? Is not filtering the smog out of its public relations photos a form of misrepresentation? Should we ask questions of the increasing numbers of publications (including *Time, USA Today, New York Times, Newsweek,* and *Reader's Digest*) that routinely use new digital information processing technologies?

Most professional communicators have formal codes of ethics to which their professions subscribe. Even with these codes in force, some of the ways in which digitized information is being manipulated is questionable. What might be the result of such a powerful technology in the hands of amateurs? of the unethical? People intuitively believe that seeing is believing. How will a person be able to defend himself or herself against a photograph that someone has silently "slightly repositioned," for example?

This issue is not limited to professional writers, of course; the digitizing of information in the DTP systems available in school systems allows students to perform the same "adjustments" to data. It is not always possible to know if silent alterations have been made. Now that many computer writing labs have scanners which can digitize virtually any visual material from photographs to charts, the problem is more complicated and more serious.

## Human Costs

New technologies invariably change human lives. In *Goodbye, Gutenberg,* Anthony Smith (1980) writes about the impact of the computer on such day-to-day newspaper activities as story gathering, editing, and printing. The existence of *electronic morgues* (computer files in which background material is stored) makes the clipping of articles obsolete and makes gathering of reference material much easier. The compatibility of computers and phone lines makes on-line editing a reality and allows for both *flextime* (people do their work at their convenience and leave it on the computer for the editor to examine) and *flexiplace* (people work at home and send their writing to the office over phone lines).

Smith (1980) also chronicles some of the more disturbing effects of these technological changes. He points out that we are caught in a time of transition. The electronic morgue, for example, sounds like a great idea, but in fact it only stores articles written since the introduction of the computer into the company. Without a tremendous investment of time spent in putting the older, print documents on-line, the morgue is next to useless for anyone seeking data more than a few years old. This is the exact problem that many libraries are having as they begin to come on-line. Current materials are listed on computer databases, but it is difficult to find the money and time to go back and recatalog materials acquired in the precomputer age.

The introduction of computers into printing has had a negative impact on many workers. Many people have lost jobs as computers have been used to carry out routine activities. Everything from actually printing the paper to stuffing inserts in the Sunday edition and bailing papers for distribution has been taken over by computers. Although flextime and flexiplace have been hailed as giving more freedom to workers, no one is sure what effect they will have on people's lives. As people spend more time working at home and less time interacting face-to-face with colleagues, isolation may be one ironic effect of the freedom brought to us by computers.

Many of the issues raised by Smith (1980) apply as well to DTP because DTP is part of the electronic publishing revolution. DTP threatens the jobs of many workers in the publishing field from typesetters and book designers to editors. Printers have already begun to take a stand against DTP, arguing that the relatively poor resolution of laser printers (300 dpi) as opposed to high resolution printing (1,200 plus dpi) is leading to a serious drop in the quality of the printed word. This is the issue that is raised on our own campus as we begin to solicit contract work for students in support of our communications programs. Each project that students print inexpensively, even at a lesser degree of resolution, serves their need for realistic learning experiences, but takes money away from small, local businesses.

There is also the additional problem of "skilling down" or "de-skilling" that DTP suggests. Skilling down means that since all design and layout can be done in-house instead of by expert practitioners outside, the overall quality of printed projects is liable to decline. Evidence of this is beginning to turn up in industry where technical and business writers are now being asked to make uninformed decisions about such issues as typeface and layout. The ultimate result is cheaper, but less readable and usable, documents. Teachers, enamored of DTP, are likely to encourage the same skilling down if they require students to make decisions about the documents they create when the students lack the theory and rhetorical training to do so wisely.

We simply have no idea what effect increasing amounts of information prepared by amateurs without the technical or ethical background of professionals will have on us. On a more positive note, some critics argue that because DTP decenters power, more voices can be heard, and these multiple voices are essential to a participatory democracy.

## Aesthetic Concerns

There are also a number of aesthetic issues growing out of DTP and related technologies. One major concern is that of typefaces. Digital manipulation of information allows for the designing of new faces; frequently, however, these typefaces are difficult to read. Designing good digital letters is especially critical at the low-resolution level found with DTP. The problem is exacerbated by the way letterforms are currently designed:

> Characters displayed or printed by personal and office computers are usually generated right in the machine's hardware. Most often the same engineers who developed the hardware designed these typefaces. The engineers "didn't think of the letterforms as important," says designer Charles Bigelow. "They thought the hard part was getting the machine to work." (Chauncey, 1986, p. 28).

Low-resolution monitors and printers contribute to the problem because high-resolution—1,200 or more dpi—monitors and printing are needed to approximate analog letters (Chauncey, 1986).

Digital information creates other aesthetic problems as well. It is easy to create a collection of "clip art"—widely sold, commercial software containing pictures, borders, and graphics—and boilerplate text. These graphics or pieces of text are reusable, which offers a saving in time and money, but also a temptation to take the easy way out by relying on the hackneyed but readily available inserts. The existence of these collections of images also means that there is often less of a perceived need for original art and design work and that people who make their living by doing this work may find their careers stalled. And, because copies are no longer inferior to originals, there is no longer any reason to prefer an original image or passage in place of the pat solution. The result is likely to be an almost endless number of look-alike documents. This phenomenon is something we already have found among students using the DTP system at Michigan Tech; the same graphics, borders, and designs recur as some students opt to let the software selection limit their creativity in document design.

Not surprisingly, there is a flip side to this issue of redundancy. DTP systems readily provide students with the opportunity to produce standardized, predictable, and readable documents. Within certain contexts, the products of DTP are pleasing to teachers who have to read them and to the students who are proud of having their work published. The danger for teachers of writing is that because students can produce such nice-looking documents, we will be distracted from deeper issues of content by the new set of surface features provided by the DTP system.

Still, although in some ways DTP systems seem to limit creativity, in other ways they may encourage creative acts. Some DTP systems permit users to develop type fonts as needed, and, for the first time in the history of print, fonts are coming into being that are not based on analogs. Editor Caroline Chauncey (1986) provides some perspective for that change: "Traditional letterforms are analog: the movement of the pen or the impression of metal type creates a smooth line . . . but in digital typography . . . each character is composed of a series of dots like the letters in a stitched sampler" (p. 26).

## Legal Issues

Digital information carries with it more than aesthetic problems. Because material is so easily stored and reused, the question of originality is hard to answer. If information is manipulated slightly—the pyramids are moved a few inches, for example—is the resulting image new and original? Is using this image a violation of the ownership rights of the person who created the first image? These problems do not even begin to touch the difficult issues involved in evaluating people's reputations. If a graphic designer, for example, creates an image and someone else alters that image in such a way as to destroy the intent of the design, what recourse will the graphic designer have?

All DTP documents printed are virtually the same. Copies and originals are indistinguishable, presenting legal issues never before faced either by writing teachers or, for that matter, the Supreme Court, which is struggling to interpret digital technologies in terms of the 1978 copyright law. Computer-writing labs that have adopted DTP and begun to purchase scanners as part of their systems face unsolved legal issues. Scanners digitize the information in drawings, photos, and other graphics and break down the information into a mosaic of pixels which appear on the computer screen. From there, the information can easily be altered and used. At what point an altered image becomes a new image is not clear as far as the legal system is concerned. This confusion makes it increasingly difficult to determine what is original; as a consequence, it is difficult for an author to establish copyright infringement of designs, drawings, or graphics.

Copyright law states that things have to exist in a tangible form in order to receive copyright protection. This presents problems when we are dealing with digitized information. As one of our graduate students recently wrote in a paper about the use of scanners in a computer writing lab, "the current copyright law doesn't address the electronic pulses of digital technology. When information is digitized, the image or page of text is transformed into electronic pulses, [and] . . . enters into an electronic 'limbo land,' a land unexplored by copyright law" (Guitar, 1988, p. 2). One consequence of this legal ambiguity is that those of us running computer-writing laboratories with DTP systems cannot be certain that our equipment is always being used in a legal and ethical fashion.

Copyright law was established to protect the rights of the author as well as "to promote the Progress of Science and useful Arts." In many ways these ideas are in conflict, for if we protect the rights of authors to their original creations, we restrict the progress of science and the arts. Copyright law hoped to strike a balance between protecting writers' rights to profit from their original works by providing a mechanism whereby they could be shared safely. With the digitalization of information, the word *original* no longer has its original meaning.

Because of the ease with which digitized material can be manipulated, legal questions arise when one asks how many pixels of an image have to be altered before one original image is transformed into another original? If a student takes an illustration or photograph, digitizes it on the writing lab's scanner, alters a few pixels, and then incorporates it in his or her document, has he or she infringed on someone's copyright or created a new original? Although the law recognizes that a certain amount of effort and creative judgment would result in a new original, the legal system finds it difficult in many cases to determine what is new, what is derived, and what is original.

A further complication for writing teachers lies in the fact that, when dealing with DTP, all printings are originals. In the past, photo-copying technology made it clear whether we were dealing with an original or a copy of a student's paper. With DTP, we can no longer tell at a glance if we have the original paper, a copy of someone else's paper, or a paper the student has used in another class. Thus, even teachers of writing are likely to develop an appreciation of the tangled legal aspects of differentiating between copy and original. In this area, we may eventually need to call on our university lawyers as we plan computer-writing lab policies, especially those involving use of the scanner.

## THE FUTURE

### The Enterprise of Ideas and Information

We look toward DTP as a time- and money-saver, a way of putting publishing on the desk of anyone who wants it, but at the same time, we are coming to realize that like the rest of the communications revolution, DTP is likely to have significant effects we cannot yet pre-dict. Some forward-looking scholars, among them F. Wilfred Lancas-ter (1983), see DTP as a brief stop in our transition from print on paper toward exclusively electronic text. These scholars argue that the print-ed book has only been around for a mere 500 years, an instant in the history of human communication, and that to assume its supremacy will continue is to be incredibly myopic. Lancaster, as cited by Seiler and Raben (1981), also contends that the logical outcome of DTP will be the replacement of existing print-on-paper publications by elec-tronic counterparts, a phenomenon already underway in the early 1980s. Libraries with their eyes to the future are already preparing to access these on-line publications. Others argue that books will never disappear by "conjuring up the nightmare of trying to curl up under a comforter on a winter night with the words of Tolstoi on a video screen" (Compaine, 1983, p. 12).

Perhaps the most farsighted scholars of all recognize that life is not static, that change is inevitable. What we find happening with DTP, that is, the transformation of publishing from a skilled guild activity to an easily accessible process, is happening all around us. This revolu-tion is cutting across all communication media. Home video, for example, has undergone the same sort of transformation. New camcorders with built-in microprocessors allow people to create videos of remarkable sophistication complete with computer-generated graphics and titles. The Amiga is the first computer to generate an RGB signal that allows people who also have VCRs and home video equipment to produce and put on tape animations that were beyond the reach of the most specialized video houses only a few years ago.

The issue of authority and truth that DTP raises is also raised by other media. Just as we saw authority in print, so too have we come to expect truth from television. The evening news anchor represents to many Americans their only source of news and information. As DTP has opened print to amateurs, so have public access channels opened television to the same amateurs. The digital revolution has put computers and video equipment into the hands of amateurs who can now create professional looking communications. The digital revolution has opened many channels of communication—cable systems, computer nets, and satellite communication systems—that were closed to all but professional communicators. Not only can people create professional-looking communications, but also they can distribute them more widely than ever before. As teachers and program administrators, it is important for us to convey to our students the social and cultural implications of the equipment and communication techniques they are using, implications we found much easier to ignore when we taught writing using the more conventional pen and paper.

Clearly, to deal with phenomena like DTP we need to discern and focus on the issues of lasting concern. We need to put change in perspective. W. Bradford Wiley, chair of John Wiley & Sons and a publisher of Melville and Poe, recently said: "To describe our business as one that traffics in paper, ink, and type is to miss the point entirely. Our real enterprise is ideas and information. . . . Until now our medium has been the bound book; tomorrow our medium will expand to include (computer stored) data banks and videodiscs" (Compaine, 1983, p. 12). Wiley's attitude is a good one. As scholars interested in how technology affects communication and as teachers of writing, we need to keep in mind our real enterprise, the realm of ideas and information.

## DTP in Academia

Keeping in mind the realm of ideas and information is the job of schools and universities, and it is here as well as in business and industry that the future of DTP is being shaped. At Michigan Tech, we have one of the largest undergraduate programs in Scientific and Technical Communication (STC) in the country with approximately 170 majors as well as a graduate program in Rhetoric and Technical Communication (RTC). As a consequence, we have been concerned with how to capitalize on the promise DTP offers for inexpensive document design and printing. In 1985, Michigan Technological University established the Center for Computer-Assisted Language Instruction (CCLI) primarily to support word processing in our writing-intensive courses but also to help support the graphics and text integration and document-design needs of students in the STC and RTC programs.

In 1985, the Humanities Department, which houses the CCLI, also began to develop desktop publishing facilities to support the STC and RTC programs. This facility is in addition to our traditional print laboratory. We currently have three Macintosh SEs, two enhanced Macintoshes, two Radius Full Page Displays, a scanner, two laser printers, and other printers—all netted with TOPS. Students have mastered the equipment easily and the machines are in use every hour that the CCLI is open and booked days ahead. Use of the DTP system is required for courses in graphics and publications design, publications management, and technical writing.

Once students and faculty have experienced the power of the DTP to produce attractive printed documents, they turn to the system for a variety of tasks. Regularly, students print their resumés and job application letters on the DTP system, convinced that the printed look will make them appear more serious candidates when they apply for jobs. From what we already know about the power of print, they are likely to be correct. The DTP system is used by faculty for printing departmental forms and to publicize colloquia and symposia. A member of our Theatre Department even used our laser printer to create original designs to publicize plays and then silk-screened the designs on T-shirts.

We, and many other schools, colleges, and universities, have made a substantial commitment to DTP. We know that we cannot afford to send our STC and RTC students out into the workplace without first-hand experience with this new technology. We know that DTP is an important technology, and we are just now beginning to formulate research questions regarding it. We are asking how DTP affects concepts of authority and how we should incorporate ethical and aesthetic issues into our print lab and publications management courses, and we have begun to raise these issues in new courses in communication law and communication ethics. We are starting to explore the human questions involved as we find ourselves asked to do more and more contract work for the community.

Although we can ask questions, we cannot predict the impact this technology will have on our department, the students, or the world at large. We would not have guessed that laser-printed T-shirts and overheads would become staples of the department or that the technology would be so easily mastered that students would use it to make custom valentines to sell as they did one year. We would not have been able to predict either that the undergraduate demand for access to this equipment would be so great, or that the addition of the graduate program to our department would put such an incredible additional burden on our system. Now that the IBM network in our computer laboratory can communicate with the Macintosh desktop publishing system, we have found ourselves in a state of gridlock. Students want 24-hour access to the equipment, and we simply cannot staff our laboratory that way all year round. Recently, the CCLI director was called at 8 A.M. one Sunday morning by an irate student who discovered the lab was closed.

We also cannot predict what will happen as the electronic networks continue to expand, when our students will be able to share work with distant collaborators as many of their teachers do over BITNET and other networks, when student publications may very well involve the efforts of students on a variety of campuses instead of just one. What new patterns of etiquette will emerge? How will the idea of professionalism change? What will such concepts as collaboration, plagiarism, and copyright mean?

DTP is only one of many changes brought about by the digitization of information and the computer. Those of us who are teachers must be careful not to define our concepts of literacy too narrowly. DTP may foretell a time when there will no longer be print-on-paper publications. In the meantime, we need to design new courses dealing with praxis, ethics, and aesthetics. We have to think about how we will grade projects created electronically by students working at terminals hundreds of miles apart, enrolled in different universities. We will have to adapt, but changes in the media of information exchange shouldn't matter as long as we remember that it is our task to prepare students and ourselves for the realm of ideas and information, regardless of the medium in which they appear.

## Acknowledgments

The author would like to thank Art Young and Marilyn Cooper for their suggestions on an earlier draft. The improvements are theirs; the failings remain mine.

## REFERENCES

Apple Computer, Inc. (1986, March). You may never go back to the drawing board again [brochure].

Barnett, M. P. (1965). *Computer typesetting: Experiments and prospects.* Cambridge, MA: M.I.T. Press.

Chauncey, C. (1986, Feb/Mar). The art of typography in the information age. *Technology Review,* pp. 26–31, 79.

Compaine, B. (1983). The evolution of the "new literacy." *National Forum: Phi Kappa Phi Journal, 63* (3), 10–12.

Corporate Electronic Publishing Systems Show and Conference. (1986). Brochure.

Decker, T. (1988, Jan/Feb/Mar). Use "desktop telecommunications" and "desktop publishing" to make your own books. *ACE Newsletter,* p. 5.

Desktop publishing continues to mushroom. (1988). *STC Intercom, 33* (6), p. 6.

Frank, J. P. (1986, September 5). Lippincott learns to love the "system." *Publishers Weekly,* pp. 76, 78–79, 82.

Guitar, S. (1988). Copyright laws and scanners. Unpublished manuscript. Michigan Technological University.

Hiltz, S. R. (1986). The "virtual classroom": Using computer-mediated communication for university teaching. *Journal of Communication, 36* (2), 95–104.

Lancaster, F. W. (1983). Electronic publishing: Its impact on the distribution of information. *National Forum: Phi Kappa Phi Journal, 63* (3), 3–5.

Nanus, B. (1983). Restructuring the information ecology. *National Forum: Phi Kappa Phi Journal, 63* (3), 17–18.

O'Connor, M. (1986, Mar/Apr). The serious implications of digital image-processing. *Print,* pp. 51ff.

Ong, W. J. (1977). *Interfaces of the word.* Ithaca, NY: Cornell University Press.

Ong, W. J. (1982). *Orality and literacy: The technologizing of the word.* New York: Methuen.

Seiler, L. H., & Raben, J. (1981). The electronic journal. *Society, 18* (6), 76–83.

Smith, A. (1980). *Goodbye, Gutenberg: The newspaper revolution of the 1980s.* New York: Oxford University Press.

Wicklein, J. (1983). How to guarantee diversity in the new communications. *National Forum: Phi Kappa Phi Journal, 63* (3), 14–16.

Williams, F. (1984). *The new communications.* Belmont, CA: Wadsworth.

# 11

# Computer Conferencing:
# An Emerging Technology

Michael Spitzer

Computers have been proliferating in education as they continue to prove their value on many fronts. Yet we are only beginning to recognize the potential uses of computers. In this chapter, I shall describe one application of computer technology that deserves to be better known and more widely adopted: computer conferencing. This technology overcomes the limitations imposed by geography and makes it possible for users to communicate easily with one another regardless of where they are located. All too often, researchers at universities struggle in isolation as they pursue their specialized lines of work. While scholars at other institutions may be interested in the same academic specialty, only in the largest universities is it likely that several individuals will share the same research interests. Generally, scholars communicate by phone and mail with colleagues at other institutions, and perhaps meet such colleagues once or twice each academic year at professional conferences. For the most part the life of the scholar is a lonely one, lacking the sort of constant feedback that stimulates thought and helps maintain enthusiasm. It is now possible, however, for colleagues in different regions of the country to communicate regularly and easily. With computer conferencing, these scholars can even collaborate on research projects in ways that would otherwise be impossible.

The advantages of computer conferencing are available to students as well as to their teachers and may help in breaking down barriers that exclude many potential students. We live in a time when technological and economic changes require that many people become better educated or re-educated. Some professions, such as medicine, require continuing education. Yet the nature of educational enterprise in the United States dictates that nearly all students travel to campus in order to benefit from education. For many people, this necessity has been inconvenient; for others it has been an insurmountable obstacle. Potential students with physical handicaps or employees whose jobs require that they travel a great deal have been unable to attend regularly scheduled courses. Other potential students live too far away from a campus to commute on a regular basis. As our society ages, more and more elderly people with increasing leisure time might find college courses attractive if access to the courses were convenient. Correspondence courses have provided an alternative to attending classes on campus, but correspondence courses typically have very high attrition rates because they require enormous personal motivation and perseverance.

These individuals can now enroll in courses that approximate the interaction that was once thought possible only in a classroom setting. They can take these courses without ever leaving their homes, doing the necessary work at times that are convenient to them. Through computer conferencing, they can participate in what Hiltz (1986) calls "the virtual classroom," a classroom that exists in an electronic environment rather than in a particular physical space.

## DESCRIPTION OF FEATURES

A computer conference allows people to carry on a discussion over a computer network. Using microcomputers with modems from their homes or offices, participants dial a telephone number that connects them to a host computer. Once connected, they can read messages stored in the computer's memory or write and send messages of their own. Computer conferencing is similar to electronic mail and to electronic bulletin boards, but it has features that make it more powerful and flexible than these communications media.

Electronic mail permits the user to send messages to individuals, whereas computer conferencing permits messages to be addressed to individuals or to a conference, all of whose members can read and respond to the message. These conferences can be public, with membership open to every member of the system (as is the case with a bulletin board), or access can be restricted to specific individuals who are admitted to membership by the person who starts, or organizes, the conference. Thus, computer conferencing provides for privacy, so important to create the mutual trust needed for the most productive conference activity.

Additional features help make computer conferencing a successful communications medium. Users can search the database created by the flow of correspondence for specific messages or for key words. They can profile other users and read the personal descriptions they have entered into the system. Participants can write messages on-line or compose them off-line and then upload into the conference. Users who compose notes on-line can use an editor to correct typos or revise text. Messages sent to an individual or to a conference in which an individual is a participant appear in that person's "in-box," so when users log on, they can tell at once how many new messages have arrived, and if these are personal notes, or notes in particular conferences. These notes take many forms, depending on the conference and topic under discussion. Often they resemble the informal talk of a telephone conversation; at other times they are closer in content and conventions to the discourse that appears in professional English journals or popular computer periodicals. Senders can mark personal messages as "urgent" and can also request "receipts" to show that recipients have read specific messages. After reading notes, users can file them for later reference.

The person who starts a conference can control what goes on in that conference. The organizer has the power to add and remove members. Every user can delete notes he or she has written, but the organizer can also delete messages written by other members or delete the entire conference. The organizer can restrict the rights of any individual conference member, for example, by limiting that individual to read-only or write-only privileges in the conference. This feature can be especially important for faculty who use computer conferencing to teach a course. It is also possible to create a poll, so that conference members can be asked to vote on specific issues. The organizer can permit users to see the votes of other members or can restrict the results so that the voters cannot see other votes until after voting themselves, or can keep the poll results private for as long as the organizer sees fit.

Several computer conferencing systems are available, and they all offer most of the features I have described. (For a description of the development of computer conferencing and a discussion of the features of various conferencing systems, see Meeks, 1985.) In higher education, the three principal applications are EIES (Electronic Information Exchange System), PARTICIPATE, and CoSy (Conferencing System). EIES was developed by New Jersey Institute of Technology, and PARTICIPATE was designed by Participation Systems, Inc. (since acquired by Network Technologies, Inc. [NETI]). PARTICIPATE is available to members of the Source and on Bread Net, and a version of this software was jointly developed by the company and New York Institute of Technology to run on Digital Equipment Corporation's (DEC) hardware. CoSy was created at the University of Guelph in Ontario.

Computer conferencing systems permit asynchronous communication, so that users need not be on-line at the same time. EIES and CoSy are linear, so that all notes follow sequentially one after the other. The New York Institute of Technology PARTICIPATE system is branching; it permits new discussions to grow organically according to the desires of users.

## Branching Conferences

Often, when several people discuss a specific topic, their discussion veers towards another, related issue, or to a subsidiary idea. When this occurs in a branching computer conference, it is easy to create a subconference dedicated to that subsidiary topic, so that all discussion on the issue can be gathered in a single place. A branching conference permits its users to pursue individual topics, setting up sub-branches, so to speak, from which new topics of discussion may emanate. The notes are often numbered to indicate which note in the original conference the new notes are a response to. In a conference devoted to a discussion of using computers to teach writing, for example, many of the branches organically evolved this way: Figure 11.1 shows some of

Figure 11.1    A Branching Conference

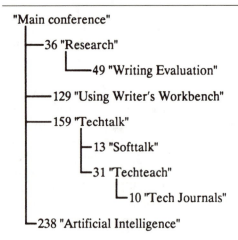

"Main conference"

—36 "Research"

    └—49 "Writing Evaluation"

—129 "Using Writer's Workbench"

—159 "Techtalk"

    ├—13 "Softtalk"

    └—31 "Techteach"

        └—10 "Tech Journals"

—238 "Artificial Intelligence"

the branches as they developed. (The number preceding the conference name identifies the number of the note in the main conference from which the branch conference was created.) This organizational structure helps focus attention on the subject and makes it easier for participants to refer back to earlier discussion.

It is also possible to structure the conference in advance, so that conference members know that material on topic A should be sent to one branch, and material on topic B should be sent to another. For example, Figure 11.2 shows the structure of a conference and its branches for a course I am teaching to distant-learner students.

These examples are of relatively simple branching conferences, yet they reveal the way discussion can be organized and suggest that complex structures can be tailored for specific purposes. In a very real sense, a conference can be thought of as an outline: the main conference presents the subject, and each of the branches represents the major subdivisions of the topic. Each of these, in turn, can be subdivided further.

## A NEW MEDIUM—VIDEOTEXT

Computer conferencing is different enough from other methods of communication to constitute a new medium, and users soon become conscious of this fact. A person new to computer conferencing is like the new kid in a neighborhood, hesitantly approaching the

Figure 11.2   A Conference for Teaching

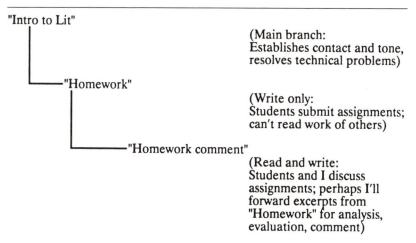

"Intro to Lit"

(Main branch:
Establishes contact and tone,
resolves technical problems)

"Homework"

(Write only:
Students submit assignments;
can't read work of others)

"Homework comment"

(Read and write:
Students and I discuss
assignments; perhaps I'll
forward excerpts from
"Homework" for analysis,
evaluation, comment)

playground and observing the behavior of the other kids, clinging to the fence, lurking in the shadows, then approaching the monkey bars tentatively, but reluctant to climb on. New users are almost always reluctant to send notes or messages. While they may be uncertain of how to use the technology, they are also insecure about how their messages will be received and what kind of response they will provoke. Will I be ignored, they wonder. What will the others think of me, they seem to say to themselves. Will I look like a fool, they worry. Batson (1985) of Gallaudet University had this to say about his first experience with the conference:

> It took me a week of reading the back notes before I risked writing something. I was very nervous about making a mistake. Once I had entered my text and had sent it, the next couple of days were tense as I awaited a response. Had I been brilliant? Could I fit in with this stellar group? I was welcomed with open arms.

I know other people feel the same way because I remember with what trepidation I sent my first message and because many other people have confessed to the same fears, no matter how articulate they are. For example, one conference is composed of some seventy college English professors. Its members are all articulate, and almost all are accustomed to speaking publicly to groups. Many of them are published authors and experienced teachers. Nonetheless, they are fearful, and I believe they are so because they are dealing with an unfamiliar medium, one for which none of their prior experience has prepared them. They are not sure how their text will be received because they have never communicated in this way before.

Most users overcome their initial fear and start writing. They gradually become comfortable, and then, especially if they are thoughtful people, they start to think about the nature of this new beast. Computer conferencing is a new medium that resembles and overlaps other, more familiar media. Most people think of computer conferencing as analogous to print because it is written text. Feenberg (1984) wonders whether it is closest to letters, memos, or telegrams. Levinson (1986) compares it to the holographic or mosaic style of Marshall McLuhan. Users of the NYIT conferencing system have compared the medium to "talking in writing," a "panel discussion in slow motion," and "writing letters mailed over the telephone." (The quotations I've included here are from, respectively, Dawn Rodrigues, Michael E. Cohen, and Jim Girard, and are taken from notes sent to the NYIT computer conference. See Spitzer, 1986, for a fuller discussion of the nature of computer conferencing text.)

Like print, computer conferencing consists of linear text. Yet the text is less palpable and permanent than print. Like telephone conversation, computer conferencing feels conversational and temporary. Yet it creates a written record that can be retrieved at any time. So what kind of medium is computer conferencing? The term "videotext" seems to describe it appropriately since it embraces several visual and text media. As one composes or reads text on the screen, the medium feels fluid and informal. It is generally spontaneous and has the temporary flavor of a phone conversation, although it is most often more like a conference call than a two-party interchange. Although it disappears after it has been read, it can be recalled for review or printed out as text. It is more extemporaneous than writing, more carefully planned than speech. It takes place over time but can be read as a continuous discussion. One can join in the middle yet not feel like a late arrival at a party. It is a visual medium, and messages can be designed to capitalize on graphic characters and screen layout, something along the lines of concrete poetry. When certain terminals are used, characters can be made to appear briefly and then disappear, and some users have experimented with dancing poetry on the screen. By making a sequence of letters appear, disappear, and then reappear, these users have created the illusion that the words move across the screen.

Because computer conferencing leaves a permanent record and is asynchronous, it is recursive. If your modem breaks down or you go on vacation, the discussion may seem to pass you by. Your colleagues may have moved on to a new "hot topic" in your absence. When you return, the messages you missed are waiting for you, and the content is both fresh and continuous, not stale as it might have become for others. If you choose, you can comment on the earlier topic, the one everyone has left. By so doing, you may spark new ideas among those who have moved on, or new users, and so that topic is resurrected with new vigor. In computer conferencing, topics become "hot" like this all the time.

## PROFESSIONAL APPLICATIONS

As we have seen, computer conferencing is a valuable medium whenever it is desirable to have an ongoing, seminar-like discussion among people who cannot be at the same place at the same time. As a result, it is appropriate for colleagues at different institutions who want to communicate with one another regularly. One such conference, supported by funding from the Exxon Education Foundation, is called "Fifth C." It links college English teachers at campuses in more than thirty states who share an interest in using computers to teach writing. Statements by the participants reveal the value of such communication:

> My research has benefitted because of the exchange of criticism from people who would probably never have gotten to look at my work so soon after it was done. Everything has been speeded up and made more efficient.

> Information is in the "medium" as much as in "messages": to know there are others, and to see the variety of projects they're involved in, is almost as valuable as the specific information imparted. It's especially important to find others with similar prejudices!

> The information I get here is more objective than my usual sources of information; I am getting information from people doing what I am doing; I am sharing in a network of people who know what they are doing; there seems to be a real commitment to truth-telling and mutual support on the network.

> Conferencing opens my world. In the middle of Iowa, one can become pretty provincial. "Fifth C" takes me out of the biases of one campus.

> By discussing my work and concerns with other professionals in the area, I have learned about what other people are doing and gotten valuable criticism of my own work. In addition, it's a great morale booster to know that other people share your concerns and feel strongly about the work you do.

> Done at my own convenience, with all "good" time—not part of it being tired, etc. Able to respond at my leisure and not under pressure. I feel I know people better than from a paper at a conference.

Of course, not everyone is so completely enthusiastic. Here is a dissenting view: "A three- or four-day conference would permit more serious and sustained monolog and dialog than 'Fifth C' does. . . . I recommend more time for thinking about what we read and write."

The previous comments come from responses to specific questions in a "survey" conference (Spitzer, 1985), one in which I asked people to evaluate their participation in the "Fifth C" conference. The construction of the survey itself gives an example of the power of computer conferencing: respondents were able to vote on specific questions and were able to write extensive comments. None of the respondents could see anyone else's answers until after their own responses were recorded.

The "Fifth C" conference is only one of many professional uses of computer conferencing. Engineers throughout the country are engaged in a conference on hypersonic aircraft. In New York, various units of the State Education Department are experimenting with conferencing as a means of linking educators throughout the state in discussions on specific topics related to their disciplines or job categories. Professional writers in several states have an ongoing, on-line writers' workshop, to which they submit original works of creative writing for constructive criticism and feedback.

## EDUCATIONAL APPLICATIONS

At New York Institute of Technology, faculty are experimenting with computer conferencing to promote collaboration among students and among students and faculty. For example, two colleagues work together to help students write research papers in an adolescent psychology course. The professors jointly moderate the conference, with the psychology professor giving advice on subject matter and the English professor giving advice on organization, style, and writing mechanics. Both guide students in proper documentation and research techniques (Kremers & Haile, 1986–87). Similarly, students in a chemistry course can contact their professor via computer conferencing to ask questions about assignments in the course.

This use of conferencing is more than merely a convenience. Students have always been given some academic support, of course, but what they often can't get is support when they need it, especially if they hold off-campus jobs. Scheduling problems can prevent a student from seeing a professor for several days. With the conference, students can get help within twenty-four hours. The conference, then, is a means of overcoming the constraints of time and space.

New York Institute of Technology also uses computer conferencing as a means for providing education to distant learners. More than two hundred students are registered for courses in which their primary contact with the teacher is electronic. Some of these students mail in their homework assignments, and others submit their work directly to the conference, but for all of them class "discussion" takes place through the conference. For students who cannot attend regular classes, computer conferencing can eliminate the barriers of time, distance from campus, and physical handicaps. Other differences disappear as well: no one can notice an individual's age, sex, race, dress style, hair length, or other distinguishing characteristics. As a result, instructors are more likely to attend to the quality of a student's work.

I have used the conferencing system to conduct two courses: an experimental one open to faculty, administrators, and a few interested people from outside the college, and a regular course offered to students for college credit. In the experimental course, called "Poetry," members read and discussed a number of well-known poems of the sort found in most college-level anthologies. Thirty-six people took part in this discussion and, in a period of 50 days, wrote 93 notes. The number may seem small, but many of the notes were long, some as long as 500 words. Most participants were faculty or administrators with training in science, social science, or engineering. They seemed to enjoy the discussion a great deal, and brought to it a perspective I had not anticipated. More than one person indicated that he or she logged onto the system during lunch hour every day for a stimulating change of pace. I invited Jim Girard, one of the "Fifth C" members and himself a professional writer and poet, to read through the conference, and he (Girard, 1984) commented on it as follows:

> I just finished reading through this conference, and found it moving and exciting (not only because the poems you chose are all among my favorites).
>
> One of the things I was attracted by was the emotional rather than intellectual quality of the discussion. It has been a long time since I have heard a serious discussion of such poems conducted by anyone other than English department faculty types or poets themselves. It was wonderful "hearing" from people who clearly had never read the poems before, reacting not in terms of their familiarity with the poet's canon, or with the tradition in which he was writing, etc., but just in terms of their reactions to the poem itself. It reminded me of my younger days, when I thought I wanted to be a poet because I thought that's the way people read poems (before I had much exposure to college English departments). I thought, reading this conference, that *this* is the way poets really want their poems to be talked about, these are the people they want to read them (excluding those poets who write only for each other—a very large group, nowadays, I think). I think this must be the way people talked to each other about poems back in the days when poetry was a popular art. If this medium could make poetry as accessible to everyone as rock music is, it would have more than paid its own way in cultural terms.

The success of the "Poetry" conference led me to agree to offer an introductory literature course to distant learners on the system. Since this new conference would be a college course, with college credits to be awarded and with deadlines and assignments due on a regular basis, we limited the enrollment to three students.

The course is not going as well as the "Poetry" conference did, perhaps because there are so few students, perhaps because the students see the course more as an obligation than as an intellectual challenge. One of the first notes I received asked me to explain how much the midterm, final, and conferencing activities would count in determining the final grade for the course. (At least I don't have to answer that question more than once; I can refer all future inquiries to my initial response.) Perhaps students' conventional attitudes towards school, schoolwork, and grades prevent them from entering into the spirited exchange that characterized the earlier discussion of poetry. Still, the conference allows me to do many things that a typical correspondence course does not permit. I have taught a few students via correspondence, and the process is slow and tedious: they mail in their assignments, I read the assignments when I get around to them, and the cycle of mailings seems to go on forever. In fact, it can go on for nearly a year, if the student completes the course. It is no wonder that the percentage of correspondence students who complete their courses is so low.

With the conference, I can maintain almost immediate contact with students. When I receive a homework assignment, I use the system to ask questions, reinforce perceptive comments or approaches, and, on one occasion, chide students when they seem more interested in finishing than in learning. I have a dialogue going with them and have established a tangible presence. The students will not drop out, for they are working productively. The retention rate has been much higher in computer conferencing courses than for traditional correspondence education, and I feel safe in concluding that computer conferencing is responsible for this success.

While computer conferencing as I have just described it can overcome distance, it has other, less apparent, advantages. Some teachers employ an overbearing lecture style that makes them appear unapproachable, especially by shy students. Some professors who are very dynamic in a lecture are themselves shy when it comes to talking individually to students. Computer conferencing can help overcome these problems. In a conference, both teacher and student have a chance to think carefully before writing, to compose their messages with deliberation, and to remember to say all they want to say. Thus, it is possible to argue that computer conferencing has some advantages over classroom instruction, and is not merely a means of hanging on to students who would otherwise be lost.

While computer conferencing can substitute for class attendance, it may have wider application as an adjunct to class, especially for students in writing classes. There are several projects now under way that use this electronic medium to enable students in different locations to communicate with one another. All these projects are based on the premise that writing can best be taught when the writer has a real audience and a legitimate purpose for writing. One project, called RAPPI, connects students in Canada with their peers in Western Europe: students in approximately 75 schools in four countries are participating (Hart, 1987). The Breadloaf School of English at Middlebury College sponsors a computer conference called Bread Net. A teacher and his students in a Pittsburgh suburb communicate with peers on an Indian reservation in South Dakota and in an agricultural community in Montana (Burton, Fisher, & Schwartz, 1986). Al Rogers has created the San Diego School Networking Project, with nodes in Nebraska, New York, Pennsylvania, and other states. Students in several New York City public schools are preparing to correspond electronically with students in England, as part of the "Global Education Project." New activities of this type are blossoming with increasing frequency.

In each of the projects mentioned, similar activities are under way. Students write to peers in other locations. They create and edit class newspapers, comment on topics of local interest and exchange perspectives on national and international issues. Students prefer the writing they prepare for electronic transmission to the artificial writing required by most school assignments. They have something to say to one another, a reason for writing, and a legitimate audience. When they correspond with peers, they can use their natural voices and their natural language. They get rapid feedback, so if their writing is confusing or imprecise, they will soon find this out. All these factors contribute to transform student writing into the meaningful, purposeful communication it should be.

## A LOOK AHEAD

In the preceding pages I have described some of the characteristics of computer conferencing and some of its current applications. Before expanding these applications and achieving the potential of computer conferencing, we need to overcome some of the barriers to wider use of this technology, and these are not minor barriers. Computer conferencing requires access to a computer and a modem, and often some technical know-how if users are to find their way through the labyrinth of dip switches and parameter settings that must sometimes be adjusted. In some cases, users must also master mysterious and perhaps idiosyncratic telephone systems. Conferencing requires an expensive mainframe computer to serve as host, and it is costly to transmit messages across long-distance phone lines.

New software will simplify using a modem, and increased volume might lead to lower transmission costs. Computer conferencing is still a medium in its infancy, and the applications that have emerged to date are only the first steps in its development. The growth of computer conferencing appears to follow a pattern common to the development of other new technologies in that the technology is first used to accomplish familiar goals that were more germane to other media. The earliest films were enactments of stage plays, and so too were the first television shows. When the telephone was invented, people thought of it as a novelty, not as an instrument they could use to communicate with others. Only gradually did these media exploit their individual potentials. The same, I think, will prove true of computer conferencing.

Within a few years, every faculty member who chooses to do so will be able to keep in almost daily written contact with a group of peers. Researchers will be able to discuss with one another in depth their current research activities, and not have to wait a year or more for some journal to publish an article that is virtually obsolete before it reaches print. Students will be able to take courses without setting foot on a campus, yet still benefit from the stimulation and discussion that are now possible only in a classroom. Those students who do attend traditional classes will be able to communicate electronically with their teachers as a supplement to their regular instruction, at the convenience of both students and teachers. Students in one community will be able to correspond routinely with students living elsewhere, creating for themselves a real audience and an authentic sense of purpose for their writing, elements that are all too often lacking in the writing assignments created by their teachers.

Some of these uses of computer conferencing may seem farfetched and futuristic, but all these applications have already been tried, at least experimentally. These activities will certainly become more commonplace as the technology becomes better known and its cost more reasonable. We can only speculate about the new applications that will emerge as our familiarity with computer conferencing increases. We are just beginning to learn what this medium can do and how it can be used. Exciting times lie ahead.

## REFERENCES

Batson, T. (1985). Note sent to New York Institute of Technology (NYIT) computer conference.

Burton, H., Fisher, A., & Schwartz, J. (1986, Winter). Writing from the banks of the Ohio to the summits of the Continental Divide. *Sewickley Speaking,* pp. 10–12.

Feenberg, A. (1984). *Moderating an educational teleconference.* Unpublished manuscript, Western Behavioral Science Institute, La Jolla, CA.

Girard, J. (1984). Note sent to New York Institute of Technology computer conference.

Hart, R. (1987). Towards a third generation distributed conferring system. *Canadian Journal of Educational Communication, 16,* 137–152.

Hiltz, S. R. (1986). The "Virtual Classroom": Using computer-mediated communication for university teaching. *Journal of Communication, 36,* 95–104.

Kremers, M., & Haile, P. (1986–87). Teaching writing by interdisciplinary computer conference. *Journal of Educational Technology Systems, 15,* 213–219.

Levinson, P. (1986). Marshall McLuhan and computer conferencing. *IEEE Transactions on Professional Communication, 36,* 9–11.

Meeks, B. (1985, December). An overview of conferencing systems. *Byte,* pp. 169–184.

Spitzer, M. (1985). [Survey of "Fifth C" Electronic Conference, PARTICIPATE]. Unpublished raw data.

Spitzer, M. (1986). Writing style in computer conferences. *IEEE Transactions on Professional Communication, 36* (1), 19–22.

# 12

# Computers, Composition Pedagogy, and the Social View

Janet M. Eldred

In the October 1986 issue of *College English,* Faigley identifies and labels three "competing" views of composition theory that have emerged in the last 25 years: the expressive, the cognitive, and the social. Faigley describes these three schools paradigmatically, demonstrating how all fit loosely under the large umbrella term "process." In this article, Faigley builds a conceptual framework into which we can place much of the information appearing in recent issues of composition journals. However, his inclusion of the social with the other two perspectives collapses many important distinctions between these competing views; most notably, the social emphasizes form ("product") as well as process, and in fact, differs from the expressive and cognitive because it reduces the exclusive focus on process and restores a concern for product. But the product/process pair is not the only binary of concern here: We can also see in Faigley's categories a rift between a romantic/aesthetic view of writing and a social/communicative one. In fact, if we shift the emphasis in Faigley's article from a paradigmatic evaluation to a syntagmatic one, we see more clearly the gradual progress of writing from a personal and private means of creative expression to a social act that helps define an individual's place within a given culture or subculture.

Composition scholars thus need to evaluate how emerging social perspectives in writing theory and microcomputer technology can be combined to create informed, effective pedagogy. Following this premise, the first part of this chapter accounts for emerging social theories and practices. The second demonstrates how instructors might use the microcomputer to complement social theory and pedagogy.

## DEVELOPMENTS IN COMPOSITION THEORY

A brief summary of movements in composition theory can help us to understand better the emerging social view of writing. As Faigley (1986) notes, the expressive view developed in response to the current traditional paradigm, a paradigm that Hairston (1982) argues stressed the completed product and ignored the composing process. Advocates of the expressive view focused on the process of writing, particularly on prewriting, on ways in which a writer can develop ideas and facilitate the flow of words to the paper. Perhaps just as importantly, they saw writing as an *individual* and *personal* means to sincere, authentic, original expression. In fact, as Faigley (1986) notes, they often argued for the kinds of writing that would make academics "relevant" or that would serve as "therapy," an appealing thought within the context of the late 1960s and early 1970s.

Soon researchers interested in cognition, in the mental activity of the individual as she or he writes, brought psychological frameworks and case study methodology to composition research. As Faigley (1986) observes, Emig's (1971) study of twelfth graders' composing sparked interest in the cognitive process of writing. The later, "problem-solving" research of Flower and Hayes (1981) made this line of questioning even more visible. They proposed that writing was not one process, but instead a set of distinctive thinking processes which writers, motivated by specific goals, organized or orchestrated. In short, those studying cognitive processes of writing search for underlying, universal composing patterns by observing individuals as they write. Perhaps influenced by the expressive view, these scholars focus almost exclusively on writing as an individual act.

We can see a similar history if we contemplate early work in the area of computers and composition. The preoccupation with editors, spellers, and the like reflects the traditional composition paradigm and its emphasis on product. The expressive and the cognitive views, on the other hand, with their emphasis on the mental activity of the individual, contribute to invention and revision software and study composing processes with the microcomputer. With this emphasis on process follows (by tradition, not necessity) the concern with the individual, the private. Not so coincidentally, the marketing history of the microcomputer parallels this shift from an emphasis on personal use to the social and public. IBM's product name—the "PC"—solidifies the idea: computers are *personal* tools, instruments to aid the individual with private, personal tasks. It is not until we encounter electronic networking that computers move into the arena of the public.

Process pedagogy developed in reaction to a "product" pedagogy; hence, these pedagogies represent two extreme positions, one stresses the individual's writing activity and the other the finished social text. Clearly, we need pedagogy that balances these two extremes, one that accounts for writing as a social as well as an individual activity and for the computer as a social as well as a personal tool.

## THE SOCIAL VIEW DEFINED

The social view, as Faigley (1986) asserts, is "less codified and less constituted" (p. 534) than the expressive and the cognitive because it arises out of the work of several disciplines. This social view of language is also more difficult to define or pinpoint because much of the work in the area is relatively new, only beginning to challenge and reshape our conceptions about writing theory and pedagogy. Before 1985, articles advocating a "social view" appeared only occasionally in major journals, but thereafter an issue rarely appeared that did not unfold some new dimension or new argument for a social view of writing. Faigley in October of 1986 identified four areas out of which this social view emerged: poststructuralist interpretive theory, the sociology of science, ethnography, and Marxism. Two months later, in the December 1986 issue of *College English,* Bruffee demonstrated that the social view was supported by yet another area, philosophy, and particularly philosophic thought as influenced by Wittgenstein and Heidegger. As Ferguson (1986) pointed out, feminist theory and criticism has from its beginning taught us that words are not "innocent," that all language carries with it the values and power structures of the culture.

Indeed, the idea that language informs and is informed by social context is now such a commonplace that it is difficult, if not impossible, to locate any single most influential source. Nonetheless, I will mention here several anthologies or review articles (in addition to the articles by Faigley, 1986, Ferguson, 1986, and Bruffee, 1986, I have already noted) that can serve as starting points for more extensive research on which to base a social view of writing. *Language and Social Contexts* (Giglioli, 1980), a book that has gone through several reprintings, serves as an introduction to the history of sociolinguistics (what Faigley refers to broadly as ethnography) and contains excerpts from researchers such as Labov, Searle, Bernstein, Goffman, and Hymes whose work has influenced composition studies. According to Giglioli, sociolinguists base their work on that done by Durkheim,

Mead, Sapir, and Whorf, and now study the speech act in all its social dimensions. Giglioli then proceeds to outline two strands of research: one that stems from linguistics and one from the ethnomethodologies of sociology and anthropology. Indeed, if one looks at the new four-volume *Handbook of Discourse Analysis* (Van Dijk, 1985), one can see that the trend continues; structural linguistics and sociology serve as two ends of a spectrum included under the umbrella term *discourse analysis.* What holds these diverse interests together is the idea that the social dimensions of language are proper subjects of investigation for both the linguist and the sociologist.

In the fall 1986 issue of *Freshman English News,* Harned demonstrates how two poststructuralist critics, Derrida and Foucault, have contributed to composition studies. Summarizing such concepts as Derrida's *différance* and Foucault's "discursive formations," Harned's (1986) article serves as a good starting point for research in poststructuralism and composition theory because it takes into account work already done in this area, and because he draws from the anthology *Writing and Reading Differently: Deconstruction and the Teaching of Composition* (Atkins & Johnson, 1985). Surprisingly, though, Harned makes no mention of the work of M. M. Bakhtin, whose contributions to literary theory have been far-reaching and whose name appears more and more frequently in work done in composition. Probably the most accessible (and brief) overview of Bakhtin's theories of "heteroglossia" is Wayne Booth's (1984) introduction to *Problems of Dostoevsky's Poetics* (Bakhtin, 1984). The essay "Discourse in the Novel" has thus far proved the most influential piece by Bakhtin (1981), but the more recently published "Problem of Speech Genres" (1986) presents many of the same ideas in a broader context (i.e., without reference to the novel).

For contributions from Marxist critics, MacDonnell (1986) summarizes concepts from Althusser, Marx, Pecheaux, and others. Likewise, the last chapter of Eagleton's *Literary Theory: An Introduction* (1983) might prove of interest to composition scholars, particularly those who argue for composition and literature to be housed under the general study of rhetoric. In the sociology of science, Greg Meyers (1986) reviews work in Britain that studies "the functions of talk and writing in . . . the construction of scientific facts" (p. 596). Meyers argues convincingly that this work has much to offer proponents of the social view as well as advocates of writing across the curriculum.

All of these areas of thought have influenced our ideas about the individual's relationship to social languages. We see that a social view of writing is not one easily categorized or defined at this time. As long as we do not attempt to form rigid (and finally incomplete) classifications, we can, as Faigley (1986) demonstrates, begin to locate some of the major issues and positions or stances within this large and eclectic camp in composition theory.

This cursory discussion has suggested the potential for researching and constituting a social view of writing within the contexts of work done in related fields, all of which share a concern for language and its social dimensions. What I would like to look at now are more specific ways in which this vast body of knowledge has affected the way composition scholars think about and teach writing. Most significant for composition studies has been the idea that each specific community or group has its own discourse or rhetorical conventions. In order to enter a community successfully, an individual must learn its discourse conventions. In composition studies, Patricia Bizzell (1978, 1982, 1986) has argued convincingly that students, and particularly basic writers, should be taught to think reflexively about discourse communities. They should know, for example, that academic discourse is just one of many conventions, that academic writing is appropriate and valid within its context, but that academia does not present the best or the only "correct" way to write. David Bartholomae (1986) agrees, adding, though, that teaching basic writers "expressive writing" is politically irresponsible. Basic writers, like other freshmen, need to learn the conventions of the academic community in order to do well in their undergraduate studies. Writing-across-the-curriculum proponents take the idea of discourse communities one step further, asserting that no one academic standard exists, that each different field forms a community with discourse conventions specific to its members.

Another position within a social view of writing is that written knowledge is dialogic (or better yet, polyphonic), that new texts are generated through interaction with previous texts. Charles Bazerman (1980) uses the metaphor of spoken conversation to suggest that writing entails "conversing" with previous written texts. Bazerman's 1980 article is one of the earliest to assert that we learn by synthesizing and rearranging the bits of knowledge surrounding us, that we do not produce good writing in a vacuum. Poststructuralist criticism, as Harned (1986) reminds us, confirms this idea: Grounding their arguments in Derrida's work, many composition specialists argue that "students will grow as writers . . . by looking to the practice of other, more experienced writers" (p. 12) and that new texts are generated through students' engagement of other texts. Porter (1986) summarizes the poststructuralist view that texts only make sense within the context of work that has come before them: "We understand a text only insofar as we understand its precursors" (p. 34).

The social view of writing also asks that terms such as "authentic" and "original" be reexamined. Expressive writing pedagogy insists that students write in "their own voice," in a voice authentic to them: They will then, so the argument runs, produce original essays. But at the heart of the social view is the premise that individuals have not one authentic voice, but many; we all speak not one language, but a chorus of languages (Bakhtin, 1981, 1984, 1986). Arguing from sociolinguist Bernstein's (1980) "restricted" and "elaborate" codes, Bizzell (1982) reasons that writers need to be able to shift codes, to speak several discourses to succeed in the university. Later work by Bizzell and others relies on the arguments of Derrida and Foucault, who share, as Harned (1986) demonstrates, some basic assumptions about authenticity and originality, about the individual's relationship to social voices. Composition scholars who argue from this poststructuralist perspective refute the notion of original as creation ex nihilo. Rather, "original" entails synthesizing available ideas into a new whole.

Finally, the social view rejects a model of human development that describes a movement from an egocentric individual to a social or communal person, a model that Piaget's early work fostered in education departments and that the popularity of Freud in English departments reinforced. Perhaps most influential in the toppling of this individual-to-social model is L. S. Vygotsky, a contemporary of Piaget, who in *Thought and Language* (1962) reviews Piaget's early work and arrives at a different conclusion. Based on his own research and on the work of his colleagues, Vygotsky posits the idea that "the true direction of the development of thinking is not from the individual to the socialized, but from the social to the individual" (p. 20). To put the issue in slightly different words, Wayne Booth (1984) paraphrases Bakhtin in this way:

> We come into consciousness speaking a language already permeated with many voices,—a social, not a private language. . . . We grow in consciousness by taking in more voices as "authoritatively persuasive" and then by learning which to accept as "internally persuasive." Finally we achieve, if we are lucky, a kind of individuality, but it is never a private or autonomous individuality . . . we always speak a chorus of languages. (p. xii)

The social view of writing, then, rests on five concepts:

1. Groups ("discourse" or "rhetorical" communities) define themselves and are defined by a discourse specific to that group.
2. To enter a discourse community successfully, a person must be familiar with and competent in the discourse conventions.
3. Written knowledge is polyphonic, "conversational."
4. Each person has not one "authentic" voice, but many. People create original texts by synthesizing and rearranging bits of knowledge available to them.
5. Humans develop by hearing, speaking, and using a variety of social voices. They become individual only by selecting the discourses in which they will participate.

## THE SOCIAL VIEW AND COMPOSITION PEDAGOGY

With the social view established, I would like to move on to review composition pedagogy that has emerged from or that is consistent with this social theory. Composition theorists such as Patricia Bizzell and David Bartholomae have located political and pedagogical issues concerning the basic writer. Indeed, this social view of writing has coincided with a larger political movement to combat the problem of adult illiteracy, a problem which composition scholars are beginning to address. And, in fact, some of the best social research in writing has stemmed from those interested in helping the basic writer, the "uninitiated," complete schooling in a university environment where they constantly feel their difference. Proponents have argued for an end to drill pedagogy, an end to the exclusive focus on sentences and paragraphs, and an end to expressive writing assignments. Instead, they call for the integration of reading in the writing classroom and for instruction in the rudiments of academic prose.

At least three other movements in composition pedagogy rest on the assumption that students should be taught the conventions of discourse communities, both within the university and outside of it. The rise of business and technical writing classes and programs suggests that writing in the business arena or in the field of engineering differs significantly from the one "correct" way of writing enforced in the traditional paradigm. Likewise, although we have conceived of writing largely as a solipsistic act, some are suggesting that a great deal of writing outside (and indeed inside) the university is collaborative. By implication, then, students need to learn to write collaboratively as well as individually.

Perhaps most strongly, writing-across-the-curriculum programs testify to a commitment to the idea of discourse communities. Writing across the curriculum rests on the assumption that each discipline or major area of study defines and is defined by rhetorical conventions specific to its group. Moreover, most writing-across-the-curriculum proponents would argue that each discipline should take the responsibility to educate and initiate its own members into both the discipline's content and conventions (including writing skills). For example, the chemistry professor should teach the novice chemist the higher level literacy skills specific to this field of study.

One other area of composition pedagogy stems from this commitment to a social theory of writing: "academic" or source-based writing. Source-based writing seeks to help students read critically a wide variety of public voices, evaluate these sources for knowledge, synthesize various bits of knowledge and finally formulate their own ideas, which at once incorporate and depart from the ideas of others. This theoretical model translates into syllabi that stress critical reading, paraphrasing, quoting, summarizing, synthesis, analysis, research, and collaboration. While recognizing the claim of writing across the curriculum—the claim that each discipline communicates through conventions specific to itself—proponents of source-based writing argue first that critical reading, reasoning, and synthesizing skills are essential to all fields within the university and even most outside. For example, if an employee were asked by a firm to write a report to help the board purchase a computer, that employee would first need to collect the necessary information, and then read critically, selecting the most appropriate information and synthesizing it into a concise report form. Source-based proponents would also argue that the one-semester or two-semester freshman composition course cannot alone teach students to write all of the myriad forms of nonfiction: writing instruction for specific disciplines or tasks needs to continue beyond the freshman year, and the responsibility to teach students these conventions must be shared by colleagues across the disciplines. Thus, source-based or "academic" writing pedagogy does not compete with, but rather complements, writing-across-the-curriculum programs.

The social view, therefore, has emerged from theories across the disciplines and has resulted in pedagogy that recognizes and accommodates the differences in various discourse communities within and outside the university. Figure 12.1 presents a visual summary of composition theory and practice from a social perspective.

Figure 12.1    Composition Theory and Practice from a Social Perspective

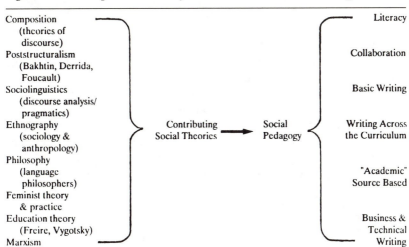

## COMPUTERS AND THE SOCIAL VIEW

In composition theory, where emphasis was once placed on writing as a personal, expressive process, writing is now viewed as a social act; a similar transformation has occurred in the literature (marketing and informative) surrounding the microcomputer. When the microcomputer was first introduced, it was touted as a personal tool. But a major benefit of a computer is its capacity to locate and access public information more quickly and easily than traditional methods. Highlighting these benefits, most of the literature focuses now on communications features, on how to make these personal tools more social. Networks (local area and broader), modems, electronic bulletin boards, public domain powerhouses: these are the topics that fill the columns of *PC Week, PC Magazine, Byte*, and the like.

Briefly stated, computers make tasks more social by inviting in public information, public texts. Those studying the effects of the computer in the workplace discover still other ways in which computers foster new social environments. Cynthia Selfe and Billie Wahlstrom (1986) argue that just the presence of a room equipped with a number of microcomputers and word-processing software encourages collaboration and results in the development of new speech communities and rules of conduct for writing in public settings. In a computer lab, they observed the dissolving of traditional divisions between teachers and students when members of the group raised questions and others volunteered answers. Such communal writing places alter the romantic image of the isolated writer by making both writers and their texts accessible and public.

The popularity and rapid growth of network systems in which the participants never meet face-to-face suggest that this socialization is not dependent on housing computers in one shared space. Indeed, the concept of on-line communication redefines (much like the telephone does) our notions of space and intimacy. Kiesler, Siegel, and McGuire (1984), for example, comparing the social and psychological effects of face-to-face group communication with a networked computer counterpart, arrive at three hypotheses:

1.  The networked group reached consensus more slowly.
2.  In the group of networked participants, no one individual is apt to influence or control the members.
3.  The networked communication and electronic communication, in general, seemed to depersonalize the message and direct attention away from the writer's audience.

These hypotheses have implications for the writing classroom equipped with networked systems. On the positive side, quick consensus is not so important to educational settings as it is to businesses. In fact, group discussions are usually meant to sustain, develop, and open up a conversation, rather than to achieve resolution of some issue. Moreover, the democratization of the participants seems conducive to classrooms trying to decenter the teacher and to involve some silent minority. (When we combine, in fact, this hypothesis with the observation that female students speak less frequently than males in the typical college classroom, we find that the computer might add significantly to feminist pedagogy.) The third hypothesis, the idea of "depersonalization," might, if we are not careful, prove problematic. Of course, writing is not a "face-to-face" speech act, so the computer in this case only intensifies the given situation, making more prominent the fact of the absent audience. The writing instructor's job is to make students more aware, not less, of audience. With careful pedagogy, word processing combined with composition instruction can achieve this heightened awareness of audience. Daiute (1985) suggests that "setting writing in such conversational contexts as corresponding, collaborating, conferencing, and self-questioning helps writers take the readers' points of view" (p. 42). Teachers from urban Pittsburgh and from rural Montana "used computers, modems, and tele-phone lines to facilitate the transmission of writing across the 2000 miles that separated [the] towns and to bring two quite different cultures into immediate communication" (Burton, Fisher, & Schwartz, 1986, p. 12). In doing so, they found that this network increased student awareness of audience; high school students from urban Pittsburgh began to imagine what life in rural Montana might consist of and vice versa. They learned that their specialized speech repertoires might not prove meaningful in different geographical and social contexts. Likewise, from their study of collaborative writing and word processing, Bernhardt and Appleby (1985) discovered that the computer facilitates the peer review process because text can be easily transmitted. This "process of continual peer review appears to heighten a writer's sense of audience because of the immediate feedback from the collaborator" (p. 38).

Even from this brief discussion, then, we have seen that innovations in word processing and communications can enhance any of the social writing pedagogies charted in Figure 12.1. In this final section, however, I will focus on academic or source-based writing pedagogy and specifically on how the use of computers in the classroom can enhance "dialogue" involving written texts and written knowledge. A classroom or lab equipped with computers can facilitate a source-based writing class by deemphasizing the computer as a private workspace and highlighting its potential communication functions.

### Information Access and Storage

Computers allow for convenient storage of and easy access to public and private information. Instructions for assignments or additional information usually provided on photocopies or dittos could be "filed" in a logical directory or designated space on the hard disk. Similarly, hard disks could be used to create *text bases* (on-line libraries of student or professional writing) so that students can have easy access to writing by their peers or professionals. Students, then, could read, synthesize, and use this knowledge to increase the sophistication of their own thinking. A text base, complete with index, would allow students to locate an essay, call up the essay, read or print it, or even load the essay into the bottom half of a split screen. Thus computers enhance the source-based classroom by inviting in a wealth of social, written texts.

In general, then, greater storage capacity allows for easier use of different applications and for the creating and maintaining of data-

and text bases. For the composition classroom, greater storage capacity means using the computer to facilitate a variety of writing tasks and creating data- and text bases from student or professional writing so students may easily acquire additional information. Moreover, when students find their own work becomes part of a text base, they understand more fully the notion of "intertext": the idea that their work is integral to a network of knowledge available to augment and increase the knowledge of others. Text bases can help students understand that any given speaker/writer "is not the Biblical Adam, dealing only with virgin and still unnamed objects, giving them names for the first time" (Bakhtin, 1986, p. 93).

But just how much text, how much potential knowledge can one machine hold? Greater storage capacity seems to be one of the research and marketing priorities for the microcomputer. The introduction of the CD-ROM (compact-disk read-only memories) to the market will allow for storage capacity far greater than the hard disk can offer. Developers of CD-ROM, inspired in part by the success of its cousin, the audio compact disk, are making rapid progress in their work, and reports now suggest that this technology may soon be ready for mass marketing. Indeed, according to Laub (1986), "CD-ROM, introduced early in 1985, is already the heart of some serious businesses based on electronic publishing of encyclopedias, reference works, professional directories, and other large databases" (p. 161). The immediate success of the CD-ROM might seem a bit farfetched, but one need only recall the rapid success of the audio compact disk to imagine how its computer relative might fare. (For a quick overview of the CD-ROM and its potential, see Laub, 1986, "The Evolution of Mass Storage.")

## Split-screen Capability

Greater storage capacity is certainly one area in which technology for the microcomputer could help in the implementation of a social writing pedagogy. But even if one has a room full of computers with no fixed drives and a budget that will never allow for a CD-ROM, features of the word-processing package alone could help in the teaching of a source-based approach. The ability to split the screen and to load two different files at once seems to encourage the integration of other sources. This synthesizing of the writer's own ideas and those from other texts is at the heart of the source-based classroom. With split-screen capability, students can compose a text in the top half of the screen and at the same time be able to view their notes (summaries and responses to readings or other texts) in the bottom half of the screen.

They can easily transfer words, sentences, paragraphs, even entire papers from the bottom half of the screen to the top. For example, if a student is writing a paper about Martin Luther King and his role in the civil rights movement, she might read several sources (either on-line or in print), including King's own works and essays and articles about King. After writing summaries and responses for several of the sources, she can then split the screen, using one half to compose the essay and the other to review, delete, and add to her notes. If she finds in her notes a paragraph or a few sentences that she wants to include in the final essay, she can easily transfer or copy the information from one part of the screen to the other. Using applications with split screens, students can compose and at the same time view and have access to information from outlines, notes, summaries, drafts, and other essays.

The split-screen feature is now standard for many word-processing packages. Both *Microsoft Word* and *WordPerfect,* for example, offer split-screen capability. But these are powerful, expensive, and relatively difficult programs to learn. Still, a program like *HBJ Writer*—a program that has the advantage of being both reasonably priced and of being created especially for use in writing instruction—has split-screen capability (as well as prewriting and low-level editing programs). *HBJ Writer,* of course, has its share of drawbacks. First, it requires its own data diskettes and yet another special disk to initialize or prepare the data disk for use. And, unlike the split screens of *Word* or *WordPerfect,* to split the screen with the *HBJ Writer* requires several keystrokes. Moreover, because of the copy protection scheme that the company has chosen, *HBJ Writer* cannot run on computers with fixed disk drives.

## Networking

Further possibilities for social writing pedagogy in the composition classroom are provided by Local Area Networks (LANS). Linking together individual machines in a network that allows communication between all workstations reinforces the idea that computers allow us easy access to the public voices or sources so important to what Bazerman (1980) calls *informed writing.* With a local area network, students can send files to the instructor and to other students. Moreover, software and printing devices can be shared by all users on the network system. With a network, an instructor need only load files or programs onto one hard disk drive. The information from this "server" can now be shared by all other units on the network. (Without the network, all applications or data files must be copied one by one onto the individual machines, and this process is time-consuming and tedious.) Likewise, all units can have access to a quality printer; a "spooler" next to the printer can accept the files to be printed, put the files into a queue, and print the files at the first available moment.

In terms of the classroom, LANS can facilitate the planning and execution of lessons. For example, the instructor can load an essay question onto the server. (Without the network, remember, the instructor needs to load the file individually onto each student's hard disk or pass around a set of floppies that contain the relevant file.) Students then respond to the question, store their files, and send them to the printer. At the end of the class session, the instructor has a handful of printed in-class essays. As Bernhardt and Appleby (1985) note, peer editing can also be enhanced by a network system. Students can send files to and retrieve them from their classmates. After reading and peer editing, they send the files back. Local area networks also link machines within the same building. Thus an instructor with a PC in the office could receive student files from a lab and return them to the lab.

A network, combined with a data- or text base, offers still more possibilities for the composition classroom working to make writing more of a public act. From their own terminals, students can review information in the text base, retrieving the files that piqued their interest (a read-only attribute would prevent users from changing information in the text base). Schwartz (1984, 1988), for instance, has developed a computer program called SEEN that consists of a task-specific heuristic, an electronic network, and a small text file in which the student stores successive drafts and peer comments. Using SEEN, Schwartz's students use the computer to explore topics and formulate thesis statements. Once students formulate ideas, they can list them on the class's electronic bulletin board and other students can read and comment on them. Students thus communicate and refine their ideas through this electronic medium.

Teachers can take Schwartz's method one step further. Using a network and database, students can incorporate a paper written by one of their peers as a source in their essay. For example, I have conducted a research project (Eldred, 1985) in which students study a nonfiction writer of their choice. The project stresses research as collaborative knowledge, knowledge shared and advanced by peers. Thus, students are encouraged to consult not only sources in the library, but also a text base of 300 or so student research papers. Of course, just as with published information, if they incorporate the ideas or words of another student, they must cite or credit the source. In this way, research is truly research, a system of knowledge shared and advanced by a group of peers. The only difference is that the research is facilitated by an electronic network.

Despite the promise of LANS, they bring with them a host of potential problems. Software and hardware need to be carefully coordinated for them to work successfully. Some applications work as "resident" or "pop-up" programs; that is, the application is loaded but does not appear on the screen until a key is pressed. Resident programs are handy because they allow a user to use two programs at one time, but these resident programs often bring networks down and render the network inoperative. Moreover, a problem with one machine can disable the whole network. Nevertheless, businesses and universities are finding LANS valuable for sharing data. As more composition teachers experiment with LANS, they will most likely reach the same positive conclusions, even if the data are more often in the form of text than numbers.

It should also be noted, of course, that the concept of "connectivity" applies to more than local area networks. Modems, through the telephone lines, connect one PC to another or a PC to a mainframe. For example, a modem can connect the PC at my home to the University of Kentucky Library: I can dial the library database, search for books, charge them, and have them sent to my office. Students can do the same in a computer lab equipped with PCS and a modem. Modems can also connect users to bulletin boards, where messages can be exchanged. In fact, using a modem or just a LAN, students can set up "local composition bulletin boards," where they can leave messages requesting and offering help and advice. A bulletin board thus helps to establish a collaborative work environment by fostering communications between students.

The largest (and oldest) educational network system is PLATO, developed by the Computer-based Education Research Laboratory (CERL) at the University of Illinois. Invented in 1960, PLATO is now a worldwide system with thousands of users. PLATO offers some programs for writing instruction, mostly computer-assisted, on-line drills or exercises. But, perhaps more promising for writing instruction, PLATO allows for three different kinds of dialogues between users: (1) mail, (2) electronic bulletin boards for groups, and (3) open conferences for anyone on-line. These electronic dialogues demonstrate just how extensive and varied educational computer systems can be.

Between the mammoth PLATO and the smaller LANS (like Schwartz's SEEN) lie other network systems, varying in size and scope. One that deals specifically with writing instruction is Bread Net—the national, rural networking system established by Middlebury College. Bread Net sets up a system of communication for teachers and students of writing, and, in fact, is the network system mentioned earlier that connects urban Pittsburgh students with those in rural Montana.

"Connectivity," then, whether through modems, LANS, or mainframes, has much to offer the composition classroom, particularly to one operating from a basis of social composition theory and pedagogy. As we have seen, social composition theory emerges from our "connections" with thinkers in various disciplines: philosophy, education, literary criticism, sociology, anthropology, and linguistics. As increasing concern for literacy and interest in business writing as well as writing-across-the-curriculum programs demonstrate, social theory develops into pedagogy that connects composition instructors with those inside and outside the university. Along these same lines, connectivity with the microcomputer facilitates finding, receiving, and incorporating public knowledge essential to informed, academic writing. Connectivity—in writing theory or in microcomputer innovations— stresses that knowledge does not emerge from a vacuum. It helps to establish a collaborative environment. All these networking devices link not just terminal with terminal, but individual with individual or groups, mind with minds. With increased storage and particularly with networking, the "P" in PC comes to mean public as well as personal.

## Acknowledgments

Since my essay argues the importance of knowledge-making as a collaborative enterprise, it seems fitting that I acknowledge the many people without whom this piece would not have taken shape. In addition to the editors, I want to thank Pam Patton, University of Illinois; Frank Solomon and Chris Cetrulo, University of Kentucky; and Rick Powers, novelist and free-lance consultant.

## REFERENCES

Atkins, D. C., & Johnson, M. L. (1985). *Writing and reading differently: Deconstruction and the teaching of composition and literature.* Lawrence: University of Kansas Press.

Bakhtin, M. M. (1981). Discourse in the novel. In C. Emerson & M. Holquist (Trans.), *The dialogic imagination.* Austin: University of Texas Press.

Bakhtin, M. M. (1984). *Problems of Dostoevsky's poetics* (C. Emerson, Trans.). Minneapolis: University of Minnesota Press.

Bakhtin, M. M. (1986). The problem of speech genres. In C. Emerson & M. Holquist (Eds.), Vern G. McGee (Trans.), *Speech genres and other late essays* (pp. 60–102). Austin: University of Texas Press.

Bartholomae, D. (1986). Inventing the university. *Journal of Basic Writing, 5,* 4–23.

Bazerman, C. (1980). A relationship between reading and writing: The conversation model. *College English, 41,* 656–661.

Bernhardt, S. A., & Appleby, B. C. (1985). Collaboration in professional writing with the computer: Results of a survey. *Computers and Composition, 3,* 29–42.

Bernstein, B. (1980). Social class, language and socialization. In P. P. Giglioli (Ed.), *Language and social context* (pp. 157–178). New York: Penguin.

Bizzell, P. (1978). The ethos of academic discourse. *College Composition and Communication, 29,* 351–355.

Bizzell, P. (1982). College composition: Initiation into the academic discourse community. *Curriculum Inquiry, 12,* 197–207.

Bizzell, P. (1986). On the possibility of a unified theory of composition and rhetoric. *Rhetoric Review, 4,* 174–179.

Bizzell, P., & Herzberg, B. (1987). *The Bedford bibliography for teachers of writing.* New York: St. Martin's Press.

Booth, W. (1984). Introduction to *Problems of Dostoevsky's poetics* by M. M. Bakhtin. (C. Emerson, Trans.). Minneapolis: University of Minnesota Press.

Bruffee, K. (1986). Social construction, language, and the authority of knowledge: A bibliographical essay. *College English, 48,* 773–790.

Burton, H., Fisher, A., & Schwartz, J. (1986, Winter). Writing from the banks of the Ohio to the summits of the Continental Divide. *Sewickley Speaking,* pp. 10–12.

Daiute, C. (1985). Issues in using computers to socialize the writing process. *Educational Communication and Technology, 33,* 41–50.

Eagleton, T. (1983). *Literary theory: An introduction.* Minneapolis: University of Minnesota Press.

Eldred, J. M. (1985). A research paper for the rhetoric/composition classroom. ERIC Reports #ED 263 606.

Emig, J. (1971). *The composing processes of twelfth graders.* Urbana, IL: National Council of Teachers of English.

Faigley, L. (1986). Competing theories of process: A critique and a proposal. *College English, 48,* 527–542.

Ferguson, M. A. (1986). Feminist theory and practice, 1985. *College English, 48,* 726–735.

Flower, L., & Hayes, J. R. (1981). A cognitive process theory of writing. *College Composition and Communication, 32,* 365–387.

Giglioli, P. P. (Ed.). (1980). *Language and social contexts.* New York: Penguin.

Hairston, M. (1982). The winds of change: Thomas Kuhn and the revolution in the teaching of writing. *College Composition and Communication, 33,* 76–88.

Harned, J. (1986). Post-Structuralism and the teaching of composition. *Freshman English News, 15,* 10–16.

Kiesler, S., Siegel, J., & McGuire, T. (1984). Social psychological aspects of computer-mediated communication. *American Psychologist, 29,* 1123–1134.

Laub, L. (1986). The evolution of mass storage. *Byte, 2,* 161–172.

MacDonnell, D. (1986). *Theories of discourse: An introduction.* New York: Basil Blackwell.

Meyers, G. (1986). Writing research and the sociology of scientific knowledge: A review of three new books. *College English, 48,* 595–610.

Porter, J. E. (1986). Intertextuality and the discourse community. *Rhetoric Review, 5,* 34–47.

Schwartz, H. J. (1984). SEEN: A tutorial and user network for hypothesis testing. In W. Wresch (Ed.), *The computer in composition instruction: A writer's tool* (pp. 47–62). Urbana, IL: National Council of Teachers of English.

Schwartz, H. J. (1988). SEEN [software]. Iowa City: Conduit.

Selfe, C. L., & Wahlstrom, B. J. (1986). An emerging rhetoric of collaboration: Computers, collaboration, and the composing process. *Collegiate Microcomputer, 4,* 289–295.

Van Dijk, T. A. (Ed.). (1985). *Handbook of discourse analysis.* Orlando, FL: Academic Press.

Vygotsky, L.S. (1962). *Thought and language* (E. Hanfmann & G. Vakar, Trans.). Cambridge, MA: M.I.T. Press.

# About the Contributors

JAMES L. COLLINS, who received his Ed.D. from the University of Massachusetts, is associate professor of English Education at the State University of New York at Buffalo. He has authored articles, research reports, and book chapters dealing with language, writing, and the teaching of writing. He has also edited several books, including *Writing On-line: Using Computers in the Teaching of Writing*, co-edited with Elizabeth Sommers.

JANET M. ELDRED received her Ph.D. in English from the University of Illinois, Urbana-Champaign, and is currently assistant professor of English at the University of Kentucky. Her research interests include the work of M. M. Bakhtin, the female artist in literature, and the role of computers in composition studies.

RON FORTUNE, who received his Ph.D. from Purdue University, is an associate professor in the English Department at Illinois State University. His research and teaching focus on composition, rhetoric, and the connections between the study of writing and the study of literature. He has directed several funded projects examining students' writing processes and the teaching of writing. Currently, he directs a three-year National Endowment for the Humanities project concerned with connecting the teaching of writing and the teaching of literature in secondary English courses through the use of literary manuscripts. His published research includes articles on writing and problem solving, learning theory and English studies, and connections between instruction in writing and instruction in literature. In 1986, the Modern Language Association published *School-College Collaborative Programs in English,* a book he edited and contributed to.

LISA GERRARD, who received her Ph.D. from the University of California, Berkeley, is on the faculty of the UCLA Writing Programs, where, since 1980, she has used a mainframe and microcomputers in her teaching. She was one of the developers of *HBJ Writer* (formerly WANDAH). Her publications include the rhetoric *Writing with HBJ Writ-*

*er* and the anthology *Writing at Century's End: Essays on Computer-Assisted Composition.*

CHRISTINA HAAS received her Ph.D. in Rhetoric from Carnegie-Mellon University in 1987. She is currently a post-doctoral fellow in the English Department at Carnegie-Mellon and a consultant for interface design at the Information Technology Center there. She has published articles in *Research in the Teaching of English* and *College Composition and Communication,* and her research focuses on how technology and other factors shape the processes of reading and writing.

GAIL E. HAWISHER directs the program in English education at Illinois State University, where she is also an editor of *Computers & Composition,* a professional journal for writing teachers. Before receiving the Ph.D. from the University of Illinois, Urbana-Champaign, she was head of the English department at a large high school in Columbus, Ohio. Currently she is editing a collection of readings on the teaching of English to be published by SUNY Press. Her articles have appeared in the *English Journal, Research in the Teaching of English,* and *Computers & Composition.*

ANDREA W. HERRMANN is an assistant professor and the coordinator of graduate studies, Department of English, University of Arkansas at Little Rock. She teaches composition instruction, computers and writing, and sociolinguistics in the M.A. program in Technical and Expository Writing. An Ed.D. in applied linguistics from Teachers College, Columbia University, with more than 25 years secondary- and college-level teaching experience, she has conducted workshops and published articles on ethnographic research, composition, and computers.

DEBORAH H. HOLDSTEIN, who received her Ph.D. in comparative literature from the University of Illinois at Urbana-Champaign, directs the writing program at Governors State University, near Chicago. Her book, *On Composition and Computers,* was published by the Modern Language Association in 1987, and she has published widely on issues related to computers and composition. She is a member of the executive committee of the Conference on College Composition and Communication and has just completed another book, *Issues in Computers and Writing.* Holdstein is presently preparing a text and software to be published by Holt, Rinehart and Winston.

CYNTHIA L. SELFE, who received her Ph.D. from the University of Texas, Austin, lives in Houghton, a small town in Michigan's remote Upper

Peninsula. There, Selfe serves as associate professor and director of the Scientific and Technical Communication program at Michigan Technological University. Selfe studies the effects of computers on writers, writing processes, texts, and the communities that form among working communicators. In addition to being an editor of *Computers & Composition,* she has published extensively in many journals, among them *Research in the Teaching of English, College Composition and Communication,* and the *English Journal.* She is author of *Computer-Assisted Instruction in Composition: Create Your Own,* a book published by the National Council of Teachers of English (NCTE) in 1986.

MICHAEL SPITZER, who received his Ph.D. from New York University, is professor and chair of English at New York Institute of Technology. He created a computer conference for college English teachers funded by the Exxon Education Foundation, and he is project director for a New York State Education Department–sponsored computer conference. He chairs the NCTE's Assembly on Computers in English. As a member of the NCTE's Committee on Instructional Technology, he is working to establish an electronic network for council members.

JOHN THIESMEYER is associate professor of English at Hobart and William Smith Colleges in Geneva, New York, and received his Ph.D. from Cornell University. He was an assistant editor of an early computer concordance in the Cornell series and began studying other educational uses of computers in 1981. He is co-developer of *Editor,* a software system for text analysis. Subjects of his publications and papers include nineteenth- and twentieth-century literature, linguistics and prosodic theory, and computer-assisted writing.

BILLIE J. WAHLSTROM, who received a Ph.D. from the University of Michigan, works in the field of communication. During the last 11 years, she has written extensively for numerous publications, including the *Journal of Popular Culture, Writing Instructor, Collegiate Microcomputers, Computers & Composition,* and *Computers in the Humanities.* She directs the graduate program in Rhetoric and Technical Communication at Michigan Technological University, and her major research interests include the impact of gender on communication, technical video, and computers and communication processes. She has served as a communication consultant to state agencies, educational institutions, government, and business, including Paramount Pictures.

# Index